IN THE SHADOW OF THE GREAT REBELLION: THE LIFE OF ANDREW JOHNSON, SEVENTEENTH PRESIDENT OF THE UNITED STATES (1808-1875)

(A VOLUME IN FIRST MEN, AMERICA'S PRESIDENTS SERIES)

OTHER BOOKS IN THE
FIRST MEN, AMERICA'S PRESIDENTS SERIES
Barbara Bennett Peterson, Editor

Theodore Roosevelt: A Political Life
Tom Lansford
2004. ISBN 1-59033-990-8

Citizen Lincoln
Ward M. McAfee
2004. ISBN 1-59454-112-4

George Washington, America's Moral Exemplar
Barbara Bennet Peterson
2005. ISBN 1-59454-230-9

President James K. Polk: The Dark Horse President
Louise Mayo
2006. ISBN 1-59454-718-1

Franklin Delano Roosevelt, Preserver of Spirit and Hope
Barbara Bennett Peterson
2006. ISBN 1-60021-117-8

John Quincy Adams: Yankee Nationalist
Paul E. Teed
2006. ISBN 1-59454-797-1

President Herbert Hoover
Don W. Whisenhunt
2007. ISBN 978-1-60021-476-9

IN THE SHADOW OF THE GREAT REBELLION: THE LIFE OF ANDREW JOHNSON, SEVENTEENTH PRESIDENT OF THE UNITED STATES (1808-1875)

(A VOLUME IN FIRST MEN, AMERICA'S PRESIDENTS SERIES)

G.L. DONHARDT

Nova Science Publishers, Inc.
New York

For permission to use material from this book please contact us:
Telephone 631-231-7269; Fax 631-231-8175
Web Site: http://www.novapublishers.com

NOTICE TO THE READER

The Publisher has taken reasonable care in the preparation of this book, but makes no expressed or implied warranty of any kind and assumes no responsibility for any errors or omissions. No liability is assumed for incidental or consequential damages in connection with or arising out of information contained in this book. The Publisher shall not be liable for any special, consequential, or exemplary damages resulting, in whole or in part, from the readers' use of, or reliance upon, this material.

Independent verification should be sought for any data, advice or recommendations contained in this book. In addition, no responsibility is assumed by the publisher for any injury and/or damage to persons or property arising from any methods, products, instructions, ideas or otherwise contained in this publication.

This publication is designed to provide accurate and authoritative information with regard to the subject matter covered herein. It is sold with the clear understanding that the Publisher is not engaged in rendering legal or any other professional services. If legal or any other expert assistance is required, the services of a competent person should be sought. FROM A DECLARATION OF PARTICIPANTS JOINTLY ADOPTED BY A COMMITTEE OF THE AMERICAN BAR ASSOCIATION AND A COMMITTEE OF PUBLISHERS.

LIBRARY OF CONGRESS CATALOGING-IN-PUBLICATION DATA
Donhardt, Gary L.
In the shadow of the great rebellion : the life of Andrew Johnson, seventeenth president of the United States (1808-1875) / G.L. Donhardt.
    p. cm.
Includes bibliographical references and index.
ISBN 13 978-1-60021-086-0
ISBN 10 1-60021-086-4
1. Johnson, Andrew, 1808-1875. 2. Presidents--United States--Biography. 3. United States--Politics and government--1849-1877. 4. Governors--Tennessee--Biography. 5. Tennessee--Politics and government--To 1865. I. Title.
E667.D66   2006
973.09'9--dc22   2006006162

Published by Nova Science Publishers, Inc. ✦ New York

To Pat

CONTENTS

FOREWORD

President of the United States of America is an official title sought by many and won by only a few individuals. Most American Presidents are of high merit and political acumen and reflected wisdom, leadership, and integrity. This series titled *First Men, America's Presidents* published by NOVA Science Publishers contains a book length biography of each President of the United States of America. Every book contains information on the President's early education, professional career, military service or political service prior to the presidency, interpretative discussion of both domestic and foreign policies during each presidency, and the conclusion of their political lives in public service. Every presidential biography in the NOVA series has been written by a professional historian or political scientist well versed in the field of presidential scholarship. The two major themes of this series are the character traits marking success in the presidency, and the changes in the office of the presidency through America's history. Character matters in all walks of life, but perhaps matters most within the character of the President of the United States.

The duties of the President of the United States are delegated through Article II of the Constitution of the United States of America, and from the successive laws passed by Congress over time. Each president takes the Oath of Affirmation:--"I do solemnly swear (or affirm) that I will faithfully execute the Office of the President of the United States, and will to the best of my Ability, preserve, protect and defend the Constitution of the United States." The president's duties and responsibilities under the Constitution are to serve as "Commander in Chief of the Army and Navy of the United States, and the Militia of the several States, when called into actual Service of the United States." The president may invite the counsel and opinions of his various department heads upon any subject related to the execution of the duties of their offices, either in writing or orally as has become the custom within the president's Cabinet. The president "shall have the power to grant Reprieves and Pardons for Offenses against the United States, except in Cases of Impeachment." Every president has realized that each must administer through constitutional principles, as each was elected by the voting majority of the people to be their chief executive through the Electoral College. Each president of the United States "shall have Power, by and with the Advice and Consent of the Senate, to make Treaties, provided two thirds of the Senators present concur." As the president directs both the domestic and foreign activities of the government, he has the power to "nominate and by and with the Advice and Consent of the Senate....appoint Ambassadors, other public Ministers and Consuls, Judges of the Supreme Court, and all other Officers of the United States, whose Appointments are not herein otherwise provided for, and which shall be established by law." The president also receives foreign ambassadors and officials on behalf of the American people. The president "shall have the Power to fill up all Vacancies that may happen during the Recess of the Senate, by granting Commissions which shall expire at the End of their next Session." The president under the Constitution shall give Congress a State of the Union address every year to acquaint them with his policy agenda and plans for the future. Usually in this address to Congress he recommends "to their Consideration such Measures as he shall judge necessary and expedient." Above all, the president of the United States "shall take Care that the Laws be faithfully executed, and shall Commission all the Officers of the United States." A strong role for the President had been envisioned by the Founding Fathers who rejected the obsolete Articles of Confederation and replaced the framework of government with the Constitution of the United States. Article II of the Constitution outlining the powers of the presidency provided that the office of the President would be held by one individual. It provided the President with enumerated powers including the power of the veto. And stipulated that the president's election would be above the control of the Congress to ensure the separation of powers and the system of checks and balances. It stipulated that the president, vice president, and all civil officers of the United States *must govern in the name of the American people* lest they "be removed from Office on Impeachment for, and Conviction of Treason, Bribery, or other high Crimes and Misdemeanors."

From Presidents George Washington through John Quincy Adams candidates for the presidency were selected in caucuses of senators and congressmen and then the state legislatures indirectly chose the president through the selection of Electors to the Electoral College. This system had worked for Washington, Adams, Jefferson, Madison and Monroe—they were statesmen who held wide appeal within Congress and the state legislatures and claimed to represent the people. But as demands for greater democracy in the election process were heard, the process was changed. In the outcome of the election of 1824, John Quincy Adams was chosen president by the Congressional House of Representatives under constitutional law after no candidate had received a majority of the electoral ballots in the Electoral College. Jackson, the candidate who had received the most popular votes was not chosen president and his supporters called for more direct popular participation and worked to introduce changes. Hence, the voting process was altered in the name of democracy. In the election of 1828 President Andrew Jackson triumphed after voting had been given directly to the people and removed from the state legislatures. Democracy further triumphed by the elimination of the congressional caucuses in naming presidential candidates and the holding of national political party conventions to name them instead, allowing greater voice and participation of the people. The institution of the party convention to nominate presidential candidates remains, although winners in various state primaries command party delegates to vote the choice of the people. The Presidency, molded by the character and designs of each president, oversees command, administration, diplomacy, ceremony, legislation, and public opinion. The modern strength of the Presidency is a reflection of the mighty power of the United States within a global world.

The majority of America's presidents have served for one four-year term or less as some died in office. Four presidents served out part of their predecessor's term and won subsequent re-election in their own right: Theodore Roosevelt, Calvin Coolidge, Harry S. Truman, and Lyndon Baines Johnson. Only one president, Grover Cleveland, was elected to two discontinuous terms of office and thus was both the twenty-second and the twenty-fourth president of the United States. Several outstanding presidents have been elected to two four-year terms or more. They were: George Washington, Thomas Jefferson, James Madison, James Monroe, Andrew Jackson, Abraham Lincoln, Ulysses S. Grant, Grover Cleveland, William McKinley, Woodrow Wilson, Franklin D. Roosevelt, Dwight D. Eisenhower, Richard Nixon, Ronald Reagan, William Jefferson ("Bill") Clinton, and George W. Bush. Only one president, Franklin D. Roosevelt, was elected for a third and fourth term. Eight presidents have achieved their office as a result of being the vice-president of a preceding president who died in office or resigned: John Tyler, Millard Fillmore, Andrew Johnson, Chester Arthur, Theodore Roosevelt, Calvin Coolidge, Harry S. Truman, Lyndon Baines Johnson, and Gerald R. Ford. Additionally, John Adams, Thomas Jefferson, Martin Van Buren, Richard M. Nixon and George H.W. Bush also rose from the office of vice-president to president. Besides the vice-presidency as a stepping stone to the presidency, two thirds of the presidents elected had held congressional office earlier in their political careers. Twenty presidents had served as Governors of states or territories before being elected. They were: Thomas Jefferson (Virginia), James Monroe (Virginia), Andrew Jackson (Florida), Martin Van Buren (New York), William Henry Harrison (Indiana), John Tyler (Virginia), James K. Polk (Tennessee), Andrew Johnson (Tennessee), Rutherford B. Hayes (Ohio), Grover Cleveland (New York), William McKinley (Ohio), Theodore Roosevelt (New York), William Howard Taft (The Philippines), Woodrow Wilson (New Jersey), Calvin Coolidge (Massachusetts), Franklin D. Roosevelt (New York), Jimmy Carter (Georgia), Ronald Reagan (California), William Jefferson Clinton (Arkansas), and George W. Bush (Texas). Some states with larger voting populations and hence more electoral votes have seen their native sons rise to the presidency of the United States. The American Presidents have come from both coasts, east and west, and from both the upper tier and the lower tier of states geographically, north and south. When elected, the president becomes the president of 'all the people', not just those of his political party. Since the president acts as America's commander in chief, the majority of the presidents of the United States have served in the U.S. military. George Washington, Andrew Jackson, William Henry Harrison, Zachary Taylor, Franklin Pierce, Ulysses S. Grant, Rutherford B. Hayes, James Garfield, Chester Arthur, Benjamin Harrison, and Dwight David Eisenhower served in the capacity of generals. James Monroe, John Tyler, Abraham Lincoln, William McKinley, Theodore Roosevelt, Harry Truman, John F. Kennedy, Lyndon Baines Johnson, Richard Nixon, Gerald R. Ford, Jimmy Carter, Ronald Reagan, George Herbert Walker Bush, and George W. Bush also served their country in military service at various ranks, and always with dedication. The youngest elected president was John F. Kennedy (1960) at forty-three. The youngest man to ever serve as president was Theodore Roosevelt who at forty-two assumed the office following William McKinley's assassination. The average age for an elected president was fifty-four. The oldest elected president was Ronald Reagan at sixty-nine (1980) and seventy-three (1984).[1]

One of the major features of American constitutional development has been the growth of the presidency both in power and prestige as well as in new Cabinet positions, departments and agencies under the control of the president. The Federal government has grown mightily in comparison with the States' governments since the inception of the Constitution. Increases in presidential powers have been occasioned by wars, depressions, foreign relations, and the

---

[1] David C. Whitney and Robin Vaughn Whitney, *The American Presidents,* Garden City, New York: Doubleday, 1993, pp. v-ix.

agenda of the presidents themselves. Henry F. Graff, Emeritus Professor at Columbia University, described the office of the president as "the most powerful office in the world" in *The Presidents*. The Executive Office of the President (EOP) was created during the administration of President Franklin D. Roosevelt upon passage by Congress of the Reorganization Act of 1939. The EOP originally included the White House Office (WHO), the Bureau of the Budget, the Office of Government Reports, the National Resources Planning Board, and the Liaison Office for Personnel Management. In addition, wrote Henry F. Graff, the 1939 Act provided that an "office for emergency management" may be formed "in the event of a national emergency, or threat of a national emergency." [2] Today the White House Office has become "the political as well as policy arm of the chief executive." The larger, all encompassing Executive Office of the President has expanded through time to include a myriad number of departments in addition to the first five listed above and the president is advised by nearly 60 active boards, committees and commissions. During and immediately after World War II the following additional departments within the purview of the EOP were organized: Committee for Congested Production Areas, 1943-1944, War Refugee Board, 1944-1945, Council of Economic Advisers, 1946-, National Security Council, 1947-, and National Security Resources Board, 1947-1953. During the Cold War, additions to the EOP were made adding the following departments: Telecommunications Adviser to the President, 1951-1953, Office of the Director for Mutual Security, 1951-1954, Office of Defense Mobilization, 1952-1958, President's Advisory Committee on Government Organization, 1953-1961, Operations Coordinating Board, 1953-1961, President's Board of Consultants on Foreign Intelligence Activities, 1956-1961, Office of Civil and Defense Mobilization, 1958-1962, and National Aeronautics and Space Council, 1958-1993. By the Sixties, some of the earlier departments organized in the 1939 to 1960 decades were allowed to close, with newer agencies with a new focus and expanded technology taking their place. These newer agencies included: President's Foreign Intelligence Advisory Board, 1961-1977, Office of Emergency Planning, 1962-1969, Office of Science and Technology, 1962-1973, Office of Economic Opportunity, 1964-1975, Office of Emergency Preparedness, 1965-1973, National Council on Marine Resources and Engineering Development, 1966-1971, Council on Environmental Quality, 1969-, Council for Urban Affairs, 1969-1970, and Office of Intergovernmental Relations, 1969-1973. By the mid-Seventies, once again there was a general reorganization with some of

---

[2] Henry F. Graff, Editor, *The Presidents,* New York: Charles Scribner's Sons, Simon & Schuster Macmillan, 2nd edition, 1996, Appendix C pp. 743-745.

the earlier departments and offices being swept away and replaced by newer agencies reflecting new presidential agendas. Many of the new agencies reflected the urgencies in domestic policies and included: the Domestic Council, 1970-1978, Office of Management and Budget, 1970-, Office of Telecommunications Policy, 1970-1977, Council on International Economic Policy, 1971-1977, Office of Consumer Affairs, 1971-1973, Special Action Office for Drug Abuse Prevention, 1971-1975, Federal Property Council, 1973-1977, Council on Economic Policy, 1973-1974, Energy Policy Office, 1973-1974, Council on Wage and Price Stability, 1974-1981, Energy Resource Council, 1974-1977, Office of Special Representative for Trade Negotiations, 1974-, Presidential Clemency Board, 1974-1975, Office of Science and Technology Policy, 1976-, Office of Administration, 1977-, and Domestic Policy Staff, 1978-1981. Many of the departments, councils and agencies organized as part of the Executive Office of the President by the late Seventies and early Eighties included: Office of Policy Development, 1981-, Office of the U.S. Trade Representative, 1981-, National Critical Materials Council, 1984-, Office of National Drug Control Policy, 1988-, National Economic Council, 1993-. By the 21st Century the EOP continued several effective agencies started earlier: Council of Economic Advisers 1946-, National Security Council 1947-, Council on Environmental Quality 1964-, Office of Management and Budget 1970-, Office of Science and Technology Policy 1976-, Office of Administration 1977-, Office of the U.S. Trade Representative 1981-, Office of Policy Development 1981-, and the Office of National Drug Control Policy 1988-. In addition to the White House Office of the president, the Office of the Vice President functions and is administered as part of the EOP.[3] At the turn of the millennium the department of Homeland Security 2001- was established by presidential Executive Order and administered by the Executive Office of the President that continues to be evolutionary in response to new issues, demands, and events.

Capable presidents have responded to America's changing needs and responsibilities by retooling their administrations to meet new crises, opportunities, and challenges. This series *First Men, America's Presidents* published by NOVA explains the personal and public life of each President of the United States. Their qualities of character and leadership are aptly interpreted and offer strong role models for all citizens. Presidential successes are recorded for posterity, as are the pitfalls that should be guarded against in the future. This series also explains the domestic reasons and world backdrop for the expansion of

[3] Henry F. Graff, Editor, *The Presidents,* New York: Charles Scribner's Sons, Simon & Schuster Macmillan, 3rd edition, 2002, Appendix C pp. 743-747.

the Executive Office of the President. The President of the United States is perhaps the most coveted position in the world and this series reveals the lives of all those successfully elected, how each performed as president, and how each is to be measured in history. The collective life stories of the presidents reveal the greatness that America represents in the world.

Dr. Barbara Bennett Peterson
First Men, America's Presidents NOVA Series Editor
Professor of History, Oregon State University (retired)
Emeritus Professor University of Hawaii
Former Adjunct Fellow East-West Center
Professor of History, California State University San Bernardino, Palm Desert

PREFACE

With the death of Abraham Lincoln on April 15, 1865, Andrew Johnson was plunged into a national political morass. Johnson, a Southern Democrat and advocate of states' rights, had been chosen as Lincoln's second-term running mate. Now as Lincoln's successor, he faced a most difficult trial – a divisiveness that threatened to undo the fabric of a nation desperately trying to mend itself after a great civil strife. For this self-educated tailor from the hills of Tennessee it would prove to be a formidable task.

Albeit no stranger to national politics, Johnson was ill-prepared for this sudden change of fortune. Absent from Washington since 1862, he had limited political allies and little ability to foster new ones.[1] Adding to his difficulties, he was a Democrat serving in a Republican administration and a Southerner in the midst of a victorious North. It would have been a daunting task for the ablest of politicians – nearly impossible for one lacking political acumen.

Taking the helm as the 17th President of the United States, Johnson continued Lincoln's effort to reconstruct the Union following the Civil War. While Congress was in recess, he began his restoration process by pardoning many ex-Confederates who were willing to take the oath of allegiance, and by allowing the Southern states to re-establish their governments. But there were radical elements in Congress who bitterly opposed Johnson's approach to Reconstruction. They objected to his rapidity in bringing the former Confederate states back into the Union and his reluctance to support suffrage for the freed slaves. Likely, even Lincoln would have butted up against the same obstacles, but Johnson lacked his predecessor's finesse and soon found himself on a collision course with Congress.

Andrew Johnson learned his craft as a politician as he rose from alderman in an Eastern Tennessee village to president of the United States. The Constitution

---

[1] LeRoy P. Graf, Ralph W. Haskins, and Paul H. Bergeron, *The Papers of Andrew Johnson*. Vol. I., (Knoxville: University of Tennessee Press, 1972), p. xx.

was his fundamental authority and ultimate resource on all questions of state. He was an ardent stump speaker and was quite adept at power politics in the halls of Congress. Yet as the Chief Executive he showed such little political skill in assessing opposition and conquering obstacles during Reconstruction, that the party that put him in the White House ultimately turned from him and he was forced to defend his actions before the bar of the Senate in the country's first presidential impeachment trial.

Throughout the journey the Tennessee Tailor, born in abject poverty, fashioned himself as a man of the people. He always held a strong empathy for the common man and equally strong antipathy for members of the aristocracy. Having come from the lower class, *mudsill* as he referred to himself, he carried a deep compassion for the laborer in the workshop as well as the farmer the field.[2]

---

[2]George Fort Milton, *The Age of Hate; Andrew Johnson and the Radicals*, (New York: Coward-McCann, Inc., 1930), p. 60.

Chapter 1

A FRESH START IN TENNESSEE

Andrew Johnson was born in Raleigh, North Carolina on December 29, 1808 into a poor family. He was Jacob and Mary McDonough Johnson's third child.[1] Mary Johnson, known in the community as Aunt Polly, worked as a laundress and seamstress.[2] Jacob was a handyman and porter. At one time he served as a constable and captain of the town watch.[3]

In the spring of 1811, Jacob Johnson was part of a fishing outing on Hunters Mill Pond where he pulled three inebriated frolickers from the chilly waters after their boat capsized.[4] It was claimed that the effort so weakened his health that it took his life less than a year later.[5] With the loss of Jacob, life for the family became even more difficult. Andrew's mother continued to take in laundry and sewing to support her family as she had before her husband's death. But now hers was the sole source of income.

Mary had apprenticed her eldest son, William, to James J. Selby, a Raleigh tailor, and after a while Andy joined him. Tom Lomsden, journeyman at Selby's, recalled,

> One fall business was brisk and the boss wanted a 'prentice. He took in Andy, and the boy was right glad to get something to do to help along his old mother.... But, Andy couldn't leave his mother, and the boss agreed to give him what it would cost to feed and clothe him in money.[6]

---

[1]William was the oldest child followed by Elizabeth who died in childhood (Hans L. Trefousse, *Andrew Johnson, a Biography*, (New York: W.W. Norton and Company, 1989), p. 18).
[2]Milton, p. 60.
[3]Andrew was born in a two-and-a-half-story log cabin on Carrabus Street (Trefousse, pp. 18-19).
[4]Trefousse, p. 19.
[5]Milton, pp. 60-61.
[6]*The Daily American*, November 4, 1880, Vol. 6, # 1629.

This was an unusual arrangement, for most apprentices were required to reside in the home of the master. Sometime after Mary's second marriage, formal papers were drawn up to make Andy an apprentice.

APPRENTICE AGREEMENT[7]

This is to certify that it is my desire that my son Andrew Johnson is bound an apprentice to James J Selby, to learn the tailors [sic] trade, and that he is to serve him faithfully until he is twenty one years old.

Andrew Johnson was born in 1808 December 29th.
Novr. 8th 1818
Signed Mary Daughtry
by Turner Daughtry

The brothers were to serve as apprentices until they were of age and Selby was to provide food, clothing, lodging, and instruction on how to become a tailor. It was bound servitude – labor for room, board, and training. Selby had a great deal of control over his charges and by law could even flog them if he deemed it necessary.

Andy had a hunger for learning, even at this early age. Lomsden remembered, "Although Andy didn't know one letter from another he was always pestering me out of work hours to read to him."[8] At this time it was the custom for tailor shops to hire people to read to the workers. A variety of sources were used – newspapers, books, and even Congressional debates. With no formal education available to him, this was little Andy's exposure to education. A wealthy man named Hill used to come to the shop to read. Johnson asked to borrow a book from Hill who told him if he could demonstrate his ability to read he would give Andy the book. Johnson read from the book and became its owner.[9] He claimed it was the first thing he ever owned. That book in particular, the *American Speaker* which contained speeches of influential men, deeply influenced Johnson's life.[10]

---

[7]Graf *et al.*, Vol. XV., p. 583. Andy's mother had married Turner Daughtry whose signature appears on the agreement.

[8]*The Daily American*, November 4, 1880, Vol. 6, # 1629.

[9]Oliver Perry Temple & Mary B. Temple, *Notable Men of Tennessee, from 1833 to 1875, Their Times and Their Contemporaries*, (New York: The Cosmopolitan press, 1912), pp. 360-361.

[10]Graf *et al.*, Vol. XV., p. 542. John Savage, *The Life and Public Services of Andrew Johnson, Seventeenth President of the United States; Including His State Papers, Speeches and Addresses*, (New York: Derby & Miller, 1866), p. 23. *American Speaker; a Selection of Popular Parliamentary and Forensic Eloquence, Particularly Calculated for the Seminaries in the United States,* (Philadelphia: Birch & Small, 1811).

Andrew was a spirited child upon occasion caught running naked through the neighborhood.[11] Mr. Litchford, the foreman in Selby's shop, recalled that Andy was a harum-scarum boy – a restless youngster who was always climbing trees and fences and tearing his clothing much to the chagrin of Mrs. Selby, whose job it was to repair his clothes. In frustration, the mistress made him a heavy homespun shirt.[12]

In June of 1824, Andrew Johnson and an apprentice from another shop threw rocks at an old woman's house. When she threatened to make life difficult for the culprits, the boys ran off along with Andy's brother William and another apprentice.[13] Andy was but 15 years of age. Selby published several notices in the newspaper offering a $10 reward for the return of his boys.

TEN DOLLARS REWARD[14]

RAN AWAY from the Subscriber, on the night of the 15th instant, two apprentice boys, legally bound, named WILLIAM and ANDREW JOHNSON. The former is of a dark complexion, black hair, eyes, and habits. They are much of a height, about 5 feet 4 or 5 inches. The latter is very fleshy, freckled faced, light hair, and fair complexion. They went off with two other apprentices, advertised by Messrs Wm. and Chas. Fowler. When they went away, they were well clad – blue cloth coats, light colored homespun coats, and new hats, the maker's name in the crown of the hats, is Theodore Clark. I will pay the above Reward to any person who will deliver said apprentices to me in Raleigh, or I will give the above Reward for Andrew Johnson alone.

All persons are cautioned against harboring or employing said apprentices, on pain of being prosecuted[.]

James J. Selby, Tailor.

Fleeing Raleigh, the Johnson brothers first took refuge in Carthage, North Carolina, where they opened a tailor shop briefly before moving on to Laurens, South Carolina in the fall of 1824. They ran a shop in the town for about a year. A Mr. Simons, who boarded in the same house with the Johnson brothers, recalled

---

[11]"Did my old Grandfather when he sent his Coachman to whip him & his cousins, altogether known as 'Jesse Johnson's boys,' back to their cabin because they had a fancy to run naked on the road." (Beth G. Crabtree & James Welch Patton (eds.), *Journal of a Secesh Lady: The Diary of Catherine Ann Devereux Edmondston, 1860-1866*, (Raleigh: North Carolina Department of Cultural Resources, Division of Archives and History), p. 140).

[12]Savage, p. 16.

[13]Savage, p. 16.

[14]*The Star and North Carolina Gazettee*, June 25, 1824, Vol. 15, #26. The same ad ran on July 9 vol 15, #28, July 16, #29, and July 23, # 30. No ads were found for Fowler in these sections.

that Andrew was always reading.[15] It was in Laurens where Andrew fell in love with Sarah Word.[16] When the girl's mother learned that Andy wanted to marry her daughter, she immediately broke up the romance and unleashed a tirade of verbal abuse on the young man, accusing him of being a worthless vagabond out to get her property. Andrew was devastated and shortly thereafter returned to Raleigh.[17]

By now Selby had moved 20 miles outside of town. Andy went out to see him seeking employment or release, but he found neither. The two could not come to terms. Because Johnson had skipped out on his master, he knew he would have difficulty ever finding employment in North Carolina so he decided to leave the state.[18]

Andy's friend, Tom Lomsden, walked along with him as he headed out of town on a moonlit night with all of his earthly goods bundled over his shoulder.[19] Johnson went to Chapel Hill, where he joined a man named Brown on his way west. Reaching Knoxville, Johnson floated down to Decatur, Alabama, and took a job at a tailor shop in the town of Mooresville working for Joseph Sloss.[20] After a while he hiked up to Columbia, Tennessee where he found employment with James Shelton. He lived with the Sheltons for six months.[21]

When Andy learned that his mother was having financial problems, he returned to Raleigh to get her. In 1826, Andrew gathered his mother and stepfather and journeyed westward to Tennessee in a primitive wagon pulled by a blind horse.[22]

When Andrew Johnson was working his way to Tennessee from North Carolina, Millington Lytle befriended him and gave him 25 cents. It made a lasting impression on the young man. "It was more than any man ever done for me in the State, and should not go unrewarded," he later recalled.[23] In October of

---

[15]Trefousse, pp. 23-24. While in Laurens Court House, South Carolina, Johnson worked with a Mr. Denton. There he met W.H. Griffin the school master (Graf *et al.*, Vol. VIII., pp. 620-621).

[16]Sarah Word was born July 21, 1807. She married William Hance in 1824. Her father James Word died in 1819 in Laurens Co., South Carolina (http://www.northernfern.com/Genealogy/f_56.htm). Milton, p. 64. William Watts Ball, *The State That Forgot*, (Indianapolis: Bobbs-Merrill Company, 1932), p. 25.

[17]*New York Herald*, April 16, 1865, no Vol., #10,457.

[18]Trefousse, p. 24.

[19]*The Daily American*, November 4, 1880, Vol. 6, # 1629.

[20]Trefousse, pp. 25-26.

[21]Milton, p. 65.

[22]Temple, p. 357. Alexander D. Febuary, also a tailor from Raleigh, accompanied the family. Years later Febuary recalled their experiences as they crossed the mountains together. "Do you remember the Panther that came and knocked the skillet off the fire where we camped one night? And do you remember on the top of the Blue Ridge when you snapped your Shot-gun so often at a *bear*?" (Graf *et al.*, Vol. XV., p. 120).

[23]Graf *et al.*, Vol. XV., p. 173.

1868, when Johnson learned that his old friend was going blind, he attempted to repay the debt by appointing Millington's son to the post of Deputy Collector of Revenue in Burke County, North Carolina.

THE TENNESSEE TAILOR

The party arrived in Greeneville, Tennessee in May of 1826.[24] Following a tailoring job in the village that lasted six weeks, Andy moved on to Rutledge where he worked for six months. When he learned that the only tailor in Greeneville had departed, he returned to the village.

On May 17, 1827, eighteen-year-old Andy married Eliza McCardle, the 16-year-old daughter of a shoemaker.[25] Although he had no formal education, Johnson managed to learn to read and spell a little. His wife is credited with helping him improve his skills. The Johnsons rented a house on Main Street with a shop in the front which he ran with his partner, Hentle W. Adkinson. The living quarters were in the rear. Andy would charge $3.50 for a coat, a pair of paints went for $1.50, and an entire suit for $10.00.[26]

Johnson was always very proud of his profession as a tailor and his skill at the craft. Years later while serving as governor of Tennessee, he recalled his days as a tailor.

> I have the proud and conscientious satisfaction of knowing that I had the reputation of being a good mechanic, always making good, not to say better, fits than any of my competitors in business. My work never ripped or gave way, until the material out of which the garment was made was worn out. I never failed to have the work done according to promise; and carried punctuality and promptness into all transactions connected with the business of the shop, which are the main elements of success with any mechanic who expects to prosper by following his profession.[27]

Johnson developed an interest in politics, and his tailor shop became a gathering place for political discussion. John A. Parks, a young mechanic in Greeneville, would occasionally stop by to discuss topics of the day. One day the two got into a discussion about the origin of the American Indian and, finding

[24]Temple, p. 357.
[25]The Johnsons were married by Mordecai Lincoln, the first cousin of Abraham Lincoln's father (Graf *et al.*, Vol. I., pp. 4-5).
[26]Trefousse, pp. 29-30.

themselves on opposite sides of the issue, decided to hold a public debate. Andy lost the first round and asked for a rematch the next night. The second time around Johnson was better prepared and won.[28] Andy found he had a gift for making speeches and engaging in discourse. He loved debate and joined a debating club at Greeneville College.[29] There Andy met a teacher, Sam Milligan, who loaned him books and became his political advisor. The relationship would last a lifetime. It was understood that Milligan either authored or redacted all of the major papers and pronouncements coming from Johnson throughout his public career.[30]

In 1828, Eliza gave birth to the couple's first daughter Martha. In 1830, Martha was followed by Charles; in 1832, Mary; and in 1834, Robert. It would be 18 years before Andrew and Eliza had their last child Andrew Jr. known as Frank.[31]

EARLY POLITICAL AMBITIONS

In 1829, Johnson ran for alderman in Greeneville and won on the Mechanics' ticket, receiving 18 votes.[32] He was re-elected alderman the following year. In 1834, he was chosen mayor by the Board of Aldermen and served in that capacity intermittently over the next four years.[33] He prided himself on being a champion of the common people and an opponent of the aristocracy.

Johnson's feisty nature, which carried over into young adulthood, sometimes got him into trouble with the law. An altercation erupting over small-town politics resulted in Johnson being charged with assault and battery and fined $100. When the complainant did not appear in court, the fine was suspended. When Johnson served as a member of the 90th Regiment of the Tennessee militia, he was given a court martial over an unknown offense.[34]

Andrew Johnson was elected to the state legislature on anti-aristocratic sentiment. He spent two sessions in the Tennessee House representing Greene and Washington Counties. Johnson's tenure was unremarkable, distinguished only by his propensity to oppose legislation. He quickly developed a reputation that would shadow him his whole career: a distinction for being vehemently adverse to

---

[27]Graf *et al.*, Vol. II., p. 237.
[28]*Bristol News*, August 10, 1875, Vol. 10, # 50.
[29]Trefousse, p. 31.
[30]Temple, p. 156.
[31]Trefousse, p. 30.
[32]Trefousse, p. 32.
[33]Trefousse, p. 33.
[34]Trefousse, p. 34.

programs that spent the taxpayer's money. He opposed funding for the printing of a school bill, support for the lunatic asylum, and funds to cover the expenses of the legislative session.[35] He even opposed ministers opening legislative sessions with prayer.[36]

It was his opposition to improvements in transportation in East Tennessee that knocked him out of his congressional seat. He tried to block the charter of the Hiawassee Railroad in Eastern Tennessee because it would put innkeepers and teamsters out of business.[37] He also opposed the construction of macadamized roads. His constituents did not share his obstructionism, and brought about his defeat in the next election.[38]

In 1837, Johnson was back in Greeneville serving as mayor.[39] Two years later he was running for his old seat in the Tennessee House. In 1839, he ran against Brookins Campbell, who had defeated him in 1837. Johnson was on the Whig ticket with the understanding that no other Whig candidate would enter the contest. When another Whig jumped into the race, Johnson switched sides and became a Democrat.[40] Within a short time, the young legislator adopted Andrew Jackson as his political role model.[41]

Johnson was encouraged by Governor James K. Polk to run for the State Senate in 1841.[42] Andrew served one term during the 24th General Assembly representing Hawkins and Greene Counties. On December 7, 1841, Johnson submitted a resolution before the State Senate to create a committee to consider ceding counties in Eastern Tennessee to the federal government for the establishment of a sovereign, independent state to be named Frankland.[43] Furthermore, he requested that the governor contact his counterparts in Georgia, North Carolina, and Virginia to see if their states would be willing to relinquish counties for the cause. Johnson's resolution passed the Senate but the House deleted the instructions to the other governors.[44]

---

[35]Trefousse, pp. 38-39.
[36]Temple, p. 364.
[37]Temple, p. 364.
[38]Temple, p. 366. The macadamized roads consisted of three layers of stones on a sloped base. The top layer contained rocks of smaller diameter than those on the bottom. All layers were compacted with a roller.
[39]Trefousse, p. 40.
[40]Temple, p. 368.
[41]Milton, p. 76.
[42]Graf et al., Vol. I., p. 31.
[43]Johnson got the idea from John Wheeler's *Historical Sketches of North Carolina* (John H. Wheeler, *Historical Sketches of North Carolina from 1584 to 1851*, Vol. 2. (Philadelphia: Lippincott, Grambo and Co., 1851), p. 90).
[44]Graf et al., Vol. I., p. 61. *Journal of the Senate of Tennessee, at the Twenty-fourth General Assembly, Held at Nashville,* (Knoxville: James Williams, 1841), p. 495.

Johnson was no stranger to power politics. At this time, state legislatures appointed individuals to the United States Senate. In the 24th General Assembly, the Tennessee legislature had to fill two senatorial positions. The Democrats were in the majority in the Tennessee Senate and the Whigs the House. If the two houses were to meet in a joint session to pick the senators, as was the custom, the Whigs holding the majority over all would select two men of their own choosing. To block this effort and pressure the Whigs into giving up one of the seats, the Democrats refused to meet in joint session. Thirteen Democrats, known as the Immortal Thirteen, colluded to stall the process. Andy Johnson was one of their leaders. When the House clerk would make a request of the Senate for a joint session, a Whig senator would move for a vote which was met with a 13-to-12 defeat. With the political stalemate, the state of Tennessee went without senatorial representation. The Whigs made political fodder out of this obstruction and turned it against the Democrats in the next election.[45]

---

[45]Trefousse, pp. 46-47.

Chapter 2

U.S. CONGRESSMAN

In 1842, the politically-ambitious Johnson ran for a United States Congressional seat. Gerrymandering in Tennessee's First District created a favorable situation for the Democratic candidate who had a hand in redrawing the districts. The First District had been Whig territory as far back as 1836. While Johnson was in the state senate, he helped re-apportion the Congressional District to include Sullivan County, a Democratic area. The Democratic Congressman there had served in Washington several terms and desired to return but redistricting denied him that opportunity and provided Johnson with a ten-year run from December 1843 to March 1853 that would only end when his political opponents redistricted him out of the job.[1]

Who was this new congressman from Tennessee? Foremost, Johnson was a strong supporter of the United States Constitution which he saw as the bulwark of freedom. His speeches often contained variations of the admonishment:

> Stand by the Constitution of the country and all its compromises, as our only ark of safety, as the palladium of our civil and religious liberty, that we will cling to it as the mariner clings to the last plank, when night and the tempest close around him.[2]

Johnson firmly believed the burdens of the government should be upon the rich and not the poor.[3] He was against tariffs and taxes that pillaged the less fortunate, and looked with disfavor upon the undue burden placed upon the common man to fight the wars of the country.[4] Johnson's philosophy would bode well with his advocacy for free land for the landless. The Congressman believed

---

[1]Temple, pp. 216-217.
[2]Graf *et al.*, Vol. I., p. 507.
[3]Graf *et al.*, Vol. I., pp. 319-320.

the best way to promote prosperity was by supporting the settlement of the western territories. He became a strong supporter of providing un-appropriated quarter sections to those of little means, and pushed his Homestead Bill throughout his days in Congress.

To say that Johnson was a fiscal conservative would be an understatement. He was aggressive in his quest to keep governmental cost to a minimum. He not only opposed needless spending, he opposed just about all spending. Some of his fiscal battles would border on the ridiculous.[5]

Early on, Johnson expressed favor in setting term limits for elected offices.[6] He believed many of these professional politicians had stayed in office until they became imbecilic. They had lived in Washington so long they knew not how to live anywhere else and worst of all, some changed their politics to favor whoever was in power.[7] Johnson was also for the direct election of the president, vice president, and senators.

While Johnson's public pronouncements on slavery ameliorated over the years, his stance at this juncture in his career was that of an unyielding defender of the institution. He firmly believed Congress had no right to interfere with this states' rights issue.[8] Johnson often deflected attention from the Southern slavery question by pointing to the degrading servitude that flourished up North. He accused the abolitionists of callousness regarding the plight of laborers working in Northern factories. His attack on such hypocrisy was insistent.[9]

> They have great sympathy for suffering humanity abroad, but forget the wretchedness and oppression that exist at their own doors. One overlooks the white slavery that exists from necessity from poverty, resulting from the manufacturing establishments in the New England States.[10]

Northerners would say that if a worker did not like the working conditions, he could voluntarily walk away. Johnson would counter that the northern worker was bound and could not extricate himself.

> When we go to the North, don't we find the white man and white woman performing the same menial service the blacks perform at the South? ... The only

[4]Graf *et al.*, Vol. I., pp. 260 & 373.
[5]Graf *et al.*, Vol. I., pp. 207 & 442.
[6]Graf *et al.*, Vol. I., p. 280.
[7]Graf *et al.*, Vol. I., p. 435.
[8]Graf *et al.*, Vol. I., p. 500.
[9]Graf *et al.*, Vol. I., p. 419.
[10]Graf *et al.*, Vol. I., p. 252.

question is, as to the kind of slavery, white or black, voluntary or involuntary....
Let us now look at the men of the North -- so much opposed to our peculiar
institution. They are opposed to black slavery. They have found out that white
slavery is cheaper.[11]

Johnson was cognizant of the enormity of the slavery issue and warned that if
the North encroached upon this Southern institution, "the whole body politic
[would] wax so hot, that this mighty Union [would] melt in twain."[12]

THE 28TH CONGRESS

Johnson went to Washington as a member of the 28th Congress representing
the First District of Tennessee. He rented a room on North Capitol Street while his
wife remained in Tennessee. Johnson's first term was relatively uneventful as
might be expected of a freshman congressman. He was appointed to the
Committee of Claims and Committee on Expenditures in the War Department.[13]
He presented a number of petitions from his constituents in Tennessee, such as the
establishment of a postal route from Rogersville to Russellville and an
amendment to an appropriations bill to improve the Holston River and declare
Knoxville a port of entry.[14]

Always casting a critical eye on any expenditure, Johnson opposed legislation
that he believed resulted in needless expense. He was not above attempting to
micro manage budget cuts either, as demonstrated by his effort to reduce the
number of clerical employees in the House. Johnson requested the House clerk to
provide the number of authorized clerical positions in the House, the number
actually appointed, the salaries, each employee's state of origin, their job duties,
the fund from which they were paid, the hours they worked each day, the
employment obligation after adjournment, and an examination of how the duties
could be performed by a smaller staff. Johnson also opposed improvements on the
Ohio River.[15] He even balked at legitimate financial arrangements that benefited
him personally. As a member of the House he was due *per diem*, but thinking the
remuneration unjustified, he returned the money.[16]

---

[11]Graf *et al.*, Vol. II., p. 354.
[12]Graf *et al.*, Vol. I., p. 506.
[13]*Congressional Globe,* 28th Congress, 1st Session, December 12, 1843, p. 29.
[14]Graf *et al.*, Vol. I., p. 652.
[15]*Congressional Globe,* 28th Congress, 1st Session, March 11, 1844, pp. 368 & April 6, 1844, p. 489.
        Graf *et al.*, Vol. I., pp. 651-652.
[16]Milton, p. 79.

Johnson's first speech in Congress was in support of his political hero Andrew Jackson. During the War of 1812, Jackson was fined for having sanctioned martial law in New Orleans. In January of 1844, members of the House sought to redress this wrong and pushed to refund the ex-president the $1,000 fine imposed upon him in 1815. The resolution passed, and Jackson received his money plus six percent interest.[17]

Johnson was chosen as an alternative delegate to the 1844 Democratic Convention in Baltimore where he failed to support James Polk. Polk won his party's nomination and in the presidential election narrowly defeated the Whig candidate Henry Clay. Johnson's opposition to his fellow Tennessean's candidacy was a decision that would cause him serious problems in the future.

THE 1845 ELECTION

In the spring of 1845, Johnson returned to Greeneville to run for a second term against Rev. William G. Brownlow, the "Fighting Parson." It was a contentious campaign, and neither candidate hesitated in hurling scurrilous attacks upon his opponent.

Brownlow was a Methodist preacher and editor of the *Jonesborough Whig*, a publication he used to disseminate his political invectiveness. In a July 16th article he blasted Johnson as a vile slanderer, a black-hearted demagogue, and an unprincipled renegade. This was after Johnson had called him a devil and a hyena.[18] Brownlow's most damning attack came in a publication entitled *Ten Reasons for Believing Andrew Johnson to be an Atheist.* He lambasted Andrew's father and accused Andrew of being a bastard.[19] He charged Johnson with being an infidel who denied the authority of the Bible.[20] Brownlow even asserted that his opponent hired Brownlow's own brother to kill him.[21]

Johnson's remonstrance to Brownlow's attack appeared long after his victory in the fall election. The rebuttal was in the form of a 29-page, open letter to the working class of his congressional district entitled, *To the Freemen of the First Congressional District of Tennessee.*[22] Johnson expressed his frustration with the difficulty of defending himself against Brownlow's charges.

---

[17]*Congressional Globe,* 28th Congress, 1st Session, January 8, 1844, p. 119.
[18]*Jonesborough Whig,* July 16, 1845, Vol. 7, # 12.
[19]Graf *et al.,* Vol. I., p. 271. Trefousse, p. 58.
[20]Graf *et al.,* Vol. I., p. 221.
[21]Milton, p. 80.
[22]*Jonesborough Whig,* January 21, 1846, Vol. 7, #38. Graf *et al.,* Vol. I., pp. 220-273.

There is no means of inserting a glass window in the human bosom, thereby enabling the curious to pry into the recesses of the human heart, and ascertain what the inner man believes in relation to his future condition.... How is an individual, when a charge of this kind is alleged against him, to clear himself of it? If he merely says no, the charge is false, it will scarcely satisfy any one.[23]

Johnson laid down a challenge to all future antagonists.

I am resolved, henceforth, to defend my person and my character with all my means, my pen, my tongue, and with my last dollar, and with the last drop of blood that courses through my veins. I do not say this in the vain spirit of boasting, but if there are any, who are honorable and entitled to my notice, who doubt my sincerity in this declaration, let them make the experiment, and they will see.[24]

Johnson responded to Brownlow's charges against his parentage.[25] As to being an infidel, the Congressman affirmed his religious beliefs and in turn attacked Brownlow's hypocrisy.[26]

Men like these, pretending to be christians and disciples of Christ, have kept more souls that hungered and thirsted after righteousness out of the church of God, and have driven them headlong into an awful and dismal hell.[27]

On January 21, following Johnson's publication, Brownlow informed East Tennesseans that the Congressman frequented grog shops and card tables, as well as the village brothel. With one of Johnson's cousins hanged for murder and two others in prison, Brownlow claimed that Andrew Johnson was just, "one of a family of thieves and murderers, with *office*, the only pasport [sic] to respectability – a villain who deserves to be incarcerated, in irons, adjudged for life to the Penitentiary, or to the gallows, rather than passing to and fro as a member of Congress."[28] The enmity between these two would continue intermittently over the course of their careers.

---

[23]Graf *et al.*, Vol. I., p. 239.
[24]Graf *et al.*, Vol. I., p. 272.
[25]Graf *et al.*, Vol. I., p. 271.
[26]Graf *et al.*, Vol. I., p. 240.
[27]Graf *et al.*, Vol. I., p. 246.
[28]*Jonesborough Whig*, January 21, 1846, Vol. 7, # 38.

THE 29TH CONGRESS

Johnson returned to Washington as a member of the 29th Congress and focused his efforts on the passage of his Homestead Bill. On March 27, 1846, Johnson presented his legislation for the first time.[29] The bill offered 160 acres of public land free to every poor man who was the head of a household. This would be but the beginning of a long and arduous process.[30] Over the course of his entire career in the United States Congress, Johnson would repeatedly introduce this measure without success. It would be 16 years before a similar bill would pass.[31]

Johnson's bill was not the first of its kind. The idea of dispensing un-appropriated land had been considered by Congress before. Thomas H. Benton, senator from Missouri, had advocated similar legislation during the Seminole War in 1842. The United States, bent on territorial expansionism, was trying to unseat the Seminoles in Florida and meeting with little success. The Senator's plan was to entice farmers to occupy the land and hence pressure the Indians to leave. His bill offered free land in the interior of Florida to white citizens for permanent settlement.[32]

Johnson's Homestead Bill proved to be unpopular in a number of circles. With new non-slave western states coming into the Union, Southerners feared the bill would lead to a power imbalance in Congress. The Know-Nothing Party feared that homestead legislation would encourage Catholics to populate the western territories. And the railroads wanted unappropriated public land for themselves. The opposition made strange bedfellows. Thaddeus Stevens and Jefferson Davis found themselves on the same side of the issue.[33]

DAMNED CONTENTIOUSNESS

Andrew Johnson had his share of heated interchanges with his fellow members of Congress. He enjoyed exposing hypocrisy and taking on those he

---

[29]*Congressional Globe*, 29th Congress, 1st Session, H.R. 319, March 7, 1846.

[30]Graf *et al.*, Vol. I., pp. 300-301.

[31]Temple, p. 377.

[32]In May of 1842, President Tyler declared the War to be at an end and in August of that year Benton's bill was enacted. Just over a thousand settlers claimed quarter sections of land (Michael E. Welsh, "Legislating a Homestead Bill: Thomas Hart Benton and the Second Seminole War," *The Florida Historical Quarterly* 57:2 (October 1978): 158-159 & 168-171.)

[33]Milton, p. 82.

considered to be aristocrats. Upon occasion he was contentious beyond the point of being a mere annoyance.

In an exchange on the House floor with John Gorham Palfrey of Massachusetts in April of 1848, Johnson attempted to expose the pretentiousness of the Northern abolitionist. Referring to a particular black youngster in his argument, Palfrey expounded upon the advances being made by blacks. He stated they were getting closer to equality with the white man. Johnson tested Palfrey's sincerity. "Would the gentleman from Massachusetts be willing to see that interesting, talented, 'charming' negro boy, become the married companion of his own daughter?" Palfrey responded with a mouthful of political gobbledygook referring to "various conventional circumstances having relation to the habits of social life" and never truly answered the attack.[34] Johnson had made his point.

Johnson saw in Jefferson Davis an aristocrat who was fair game to assail. In May of 1846, when Representative Davis from Mississippi eulogized Zachary Taylor on the floor of the House, he inadvertently demeaned blacksmiths and tailors. The next day, Johnson was on the attack, expressing his disdain of the Congressman.

> [I] knew we had an illegitimate, swaggering, bastard, scrub aristocracy, who assumed to know a good deal, but who, when the flimsy veil of pretension was torn off from it, was shown to possess neither talents, information, nor a foundation.[35]

The Davis remarks had been made off-hand and not intended to offend, but Johnson blew them out of proportion. Davis tried to explain that he intended no insult, but Johnson would not be placated.[36]

Johnson's most damaging conflict was with President James K. Polk. Polk took office in 1845, while Johnson was in his second term in Congress. Although Johnson supported Polk's war with Mexico and Mrs. Polk had befriended the Congressman's daughter, the relationship was severely strained because Johnson had opposed the President's nomination at the Baltimore Convention in 1844.[37] The political wound was deep.

---

[34] *Congressional Globe*, 30th Congress 1st Session, April 11, 1848, p. 610.
[35] *Congressional Globe*, 29th Congress 1st Session, May 29, 1846, p. 885.
[36] *Congressional Globe*, 29th Congress 1st Session, May 28, 1846, pp. 877-878, 884-885, & 887.
[37] On April 11, 1846, Johnson's daughter, likely Martha, dined with President Polk and many of the representatives from Tennessee. Her father was not present due to some indisposition (Milo Milton Quaife, *The Diary of James K. Polk*, Vol. I., (Chicago: A.C. McClurg & Co., 1910), pp. 327-329. Graf *et al.*, Vol. I. p. 384.

The two had a candid conversation on July 21, 1846, when Johnson called upon Polk at the White House. He was there for a frank discussion and the President responded in kind. Johnson was clearly agitated having learned that Polk was displeased with him. The Congressman believed himself to have been loyal and supportive and was offended that his politics should be distrusted and his loyalty called into question. Polk said he had heard that Johnson and George W. Jones also of Tennessee were dissatisfied with his administration, and that when members of the House had urged them to support certain measures, the two had exerted their independence stating they were not under the control of anyone.[38] Polk recorded the confrontation in his diary.

> I told him that though I had reason to be dissatisfied with his course, I had never mentioned it to any of his constituents.... I told him that I had been the friend of Jones and of himself and that I had expected to receive from them that support which all preceding administrations had received from the members of Congress of their own party from their own State, but that instead of that not a word had been said in my vindication by either of them at times when I had been violently assailed by the Whigs in the [House of Representatives].... I sought to control no man's course, that he had a perfect right to differ with me if he chose to do so, and that if he did so the people and especially his democratic constituents, who were my friends, would judge between us.[39]

The meeting lasted for more than an hour. By the end of the session a much subdued Johnson was recalling the services he had given the President over the course of his administration. Johnson left professing that he had not opposed the President, but Polk did not believe him.

> The truth is that neither Johnson or Jones have been my personal friends since 1839. They were in the Baltimore Convention in 1844, and were not my friends then. I doubt whether any two members of that convention were at heart more dissatisfied with my nomination for the Presidency than they were.... Mr. Johnson, I was informed, said at Baltimore when my nomination was suggested that it was a "humbug." There are no two districts in Tennessee more democratic or in which I have more devoted friends than those represented by Johnson and Jones, and though I have it in my power, as I believe, by communicating the truth to their constituents to destroy them politically, I have not done so.... I would almost prefer to have two Whigs here in their stead.[40]

---

[38]Quaife, Vol. II., pp. 35-37.
[39]Quaife, Vol. II., pp. 39-40.

Johnson wrote that same day to his friend Blackston McDannel that Polk was not a man to be respected. He has about him those "who flatter him till he does not know him self [sic] – He seems to be acting upon the principle of hanging an old friend for the purpose of making two new ones.... I never betrayed a *friend*... I fear Mr Polk cannot say as much."[41]

While Polk promised there would be no political repercussions from his disagreement with Johnson, apparently word got back to some of Johnson's constituents that he was having problems with the President. In January of 1847, Johnson wrote again to Blackston McDannel in despair at the way the people back in Tennessee were viewing his fight with Polk. He began his letter, "My dear friend. *If there is one lefte [sic] that I dare call my friend.*"[42] Johnson even expressed doubts about Sam Milligan who was associating with some of the Congressman's old political adversaries in Greeneville. And Johnson was fed up with the village of Greeneville as well where some real estate deals had been unsuccessful.[43]

> I never want to own another foot of dirt in the *damned* town while I live.... If I should hapen (sic) to die among the damned Spirits that infest Greeneville, my last request before death would be for some friend (if I had no friend which is highly probable) I would bequeath the last dollar to Some negro as pay to take my dirty, Stinking carcas [sic] after death, out on some mountain peak and there leave it to be devoured by the vultures and wolves or make a fire Sufficien[t]ly large to consume the Smallest particle that it might pass in off Smoke and ride upon the wind in triumph over the *god for* saken [sic] and hell deserving mony [sic] loving, hypocritical, back bighting, sundy [sic] praying scoundrels of the town of Greeneville.[44]

Johnson's displeasure with Polk eventually got the best of him in February of 1847. His anger bubbled up to a public denunciation of the Administration on the floor of the House in his Wish-to-God Speech. Initially speaking on the tea and coffee tax, he blundered into an attack on the Democratic leadership for oppressing the poor. He wished to Almighty God that every American could see the abuse that was taking place in Washington. His desire, metaphorically speaking, was that all citizens of the United States could be collected in a huge

---

[40]Quaife, Vol. II., pp. 40-41.
[41]Graf *et al.*, Vol. I., p. 332.
[42]Graf *et al.*, Vol. I., p. 368.
[43]Graf *et al.*, Vol. I., p. 369.
[44]Graf *et al.*, Vol. I., pp. 369-370.

amphitheater and that the veil be pulled away to reveal all the governmental intrigues going on behind the scenes.[45]

The estrangement with Polk continued throughout the President's term. When Johnson attended Polk's New Year's Day open house at the White House in 1849, the Chief Executive noted the event in his diary.

> Professing to be a Democrat, he has been politically if not personally hostile to me during my whole term. He is very vindictive and perverse in his temper and conduct. If he had the manliness or independence to manifest his opposition openly, he knows he could not be again elected by his constituents. I am not aware that I have ever given him cause of offense.[46]

Johnson's utter disdain for the Southern upper class was at the heart of his contentious nature, likely a carryover from his impoverished childhood. He seemed to take exceptional delight in humiliating those he perceived as pretenders to aristocracy as evidenced in his speech on the admission of Texas in January of 1845. On the floor of the House he took a public jab at a bloodless duel between William Lowndes Yancey, Democratic Representative from Alabama, and Thomas Lanier Clingman, Whig Representative from North Carolina.[47] Later Johnson elaborated on the story in a letter to his Greeneville friend Blackston McDannel.

> The duel between Clingman and Yancy [sic] came off without either being injured... [Yancey] fired his pistol in the ground, the ball Striking a few feet from Clingman... throwing Some little dirt upon him, that he wheeled about half round [sic], with his mouth open, the muscles of his face completely let down, with a ghastly look. Streching [sic] his arams [sic] out like a pair of winding blades that were very loos [sic] at the crossing.... He not only made a copeous [sic] discharge of water, but that his Short bread come [sic] from him in grat [sic] profusion.[48]

THE 30TH CONGRESS

Oliver Temple, a 27-year-old Greeneville lawyer, ran against Johnson, who was seeking a third Congressional term. For a while it appeared that Johnson

[45]Graf *et al.*, Vol. I., p. 385.
[46]Quaife, Vol. IV., p. 265.
[47]Graf *et al.*, Vol. I., p. 191.
[48]Graf *et al.*, Vol. I., p. 185.

would lose the race. Temple found there was resentment among Democratic voters against the incumbent. Furthermore, the Democratic leadership was angry at Johnson as well. They wanted him to win but only by one vote. The interchange between the two candidates was hot, but Johnson prevailed.[49]

Andrew Johnson returned to Washington in the fall of 1847 as a member of the 30th Congress. Johnson busied himself with a number of issues. By now his views on railroads had changed, for railroads had become so important for his constituency that he dare not oppose them any longer.[50] Johnson made an address in defense of Polk's right as president to exercise the veto, a power that he himself would not be shy about using later in his own administration. As usual, Johnson was still pushing his Homestead Bill. Holding consistently to fiscal conservatism, he opposed such measures as the construction of a monument for the grave of John Quincy Adams, funding for presidential portraits in the White House, and the purchase of James Madison's papers.[51] Johnson continued his running battle with fellow congressmen over financing the Smithsonian Institution, established in 1846.[52] He argued that Congress had no authority to take money out of the "pockets of the people" to fund this project.[53]

There was a bill before Congress to purchase the remaining papers of James Madison from his wife Dolley. Mrs. Madison was having financial difficulties due to mismanagement and by this time had sold off her estate. In 1844, she offered her husband's remaining papers to Congress. The proposal before the legislature was to pay Mrs. Madison $5,000 a year and to invest an additional $20,000, the interest of which would be paid to her during her lifetime. The $20,000 principal would be bequeathed by her to whomever she pleased.[54] The peculiarities of this financial offer in May of 1848 were likely an attempt to help regulate her income and keep the money out of the hands of her alcoholic son from her first marriage.

Johnson saw the proposal as an excuse to give Dolley Madison a pension. He found it offensive that while Mrs. Madison was living in comfort, many widows of veterans were living on eight dollars a month. Johnson argued that the papers had already been purchased.[55] He was in error. While it is true that Dolley

---

[49]Temple, pp. 222-223.

[50]Trefousse, p. 73.

[51]Trefousse, p. 72. Graf et al., Vol. I., p. xxix.

[52]Graf et al., Vol. I., p. 349.

[53]Graf et al., Vol. I., p. 303. The original bequest of $515,169 was set up by the estate of James Smithson and donated to the United States in 1838. The funds were invested in Arkansas state bonds. When the state failed to cover the commitment, Congress considered funding the project out of the United States Treasury at a cost of $200,000 for the building alone (Graf et al., Vol. I., pp. 304, 349-350, & 472).

[54]Graf et al., Vol. I., p. 427.

[55]Graf et al., Vol. I., p. 427.

Madison had sold some papers to the government in 1837, additional manuscripts were being offered to Congress in 1844.[56] Congress eventually passed the bill.

THE 31ST CONGRESS

In his fourth term in Congress, Johnson, true to character, continued his penchant for fighting spending. He opposed the purchase of George Washington's Farewell Address, appropriations for the Patent Office, and funds to search for a lost expedition in the Arctic – all in the name of economy.[57]

Johnson's Homestead Bill was proving problematic. In the 30th Congress, his friend George W. Jones attempted to re-introduce the bill for Johnson who was ill. He did not meet with success. Now in the 31st Congress, Johnson introduced the Homestead Bill again and moved that it be referred to the Committee on Agriculture. The motion was denied. A plethora of speeches and motions met with disappointing results.

In February of 1851, Johnson introduced an amendment to the Constitution which put presidential, senatorial, and judicial elections more directly in the hands of voters. He proposed that every state be divided into regions with popular elections held, resulting in one vote being registered from each district.[58] The idea of electing a president by popular vote had been advocated years earlier by Andrew Jackson and Thomas H. Benton.[59]

THE 32ND CONGRESS

Johnson's fifth and final term was in the 32nd Congress. While he did propose a 20 percent increase in pay for all governmental employees working as mechanics and common laborers, he continued his trend of opposing spending.[60] Riding his financial-exigency hobbyhorse, he opposed appropriations for the Army and Navy.[61]

---

[56]Graf *et al.*, Vol. I., p. 428.
[57]Trefousse, p. 77.
[58]Graf *et al.*, Vol. I., p. 605.
[59]Graf *et al.*, Vol. I., p. 607. James D. Richardson, *A Compilation of the Messages and Papers of the Presidents, 1789-1897*, Vol. II., (Washington: Government Printing Office, 1896-1899), p. 448.
[60]Graf *et al.*, Vol. II., p. 76.
[61]Trefousse, p. 81.

Johnson amended his Homestead Bill on March 30, 1852. The bill passed the House but, to Johnson's disappointment, it died in the Senate. While the bill's defeat was disheartening, the publicity helped build political clout for him in the North. Johnson received numerous invitations to speak before land-reform groups such as one organized by land reformer George Henry Evans.[62] Johnson did not fare as well among his fellow Southerners. As a slave owner, the Congressman likely experienced dissonance over the free-land issue. His Homestead Bill offering free land would work to undo the institution of slavery.

Andrew Johnson was gerrymandered out of the House seat by Gustavus A. Henry in 1852.[63] His days in the United States House of Representatives were over.

---

[62]Trefousse, p. 80.
[63]Graf *et al.*, Vol. II., p. xv. Trefousse, pp. 79 & 82.

Chapter 3

GOVERNOR OF TENNESSEE

Having lost his seat in the House through political redistricting, Johnson sought consolation for his ill-fated political career through messianic imagery. "My political garments have been divided and upon my vesture do they intend to cast lots."[1] Albeit far from crucifixion, the termination of his ten-year stint in the House of Representatives was at an end. The redistricting brought on by the Tennessee Whig legislature and Gustavus A. Henry, its architect, so changed the First District as to make any re-election bid by a Democrat highly improbable. But Johnson was not ready to abandon political life. He confessed to Sam Milligan that given the right circumstances he might be persuaded to run for governor of Tennessee.[2]

ELECTION OF 1853

Johnson sought the nomination of his party for the gubernatorial election of 1853. When the state Democratic convention met in Nashville in April, Andrew Ewing was the favorite throughout most of the state. But a careless remark made early on would lead to his undoing. Ewing had concurred with the opinion expressed by another that Johnson should get the nomination because he had been gerrymandered out of his seat in Congress. While Ewing did not recall ever making such a statement, he honored it and, when he was nominated, he withdrew

---

[1]Graf *et al.*, Vol. II., p. xv. Matthew 27.35.
[2]Graf *et al.*, Vol. II., p. xvi.

his name throwing his support behind Johnson. Johnson later rewarded his loyalty by supporting Ewing's opponent in the 1857 senatorial election.[3]

The Whig gubernatorial candidate was Gustavus A. Henry. It was Johnson's fashion to push a competitor as far as he could. Before debating Henry for the post, Johnson inquired if his opponent was a fighter. When he learned that Henry was a peaceable and courteous gentleman, Johnson said, "Then, I will give him hell."[4]

During the campaign, Johnson debated Henry throughout the state. Henry was hoping to ingratiate himself with the Irish population in Memphis by pointing out that Johnson had voted against a bill in Congress to send relief to the people of Ireland suffering through the potato famine of 1847. Johnson, in anticipation of the ploy, displayed a receipt for his contribution to the cause – money he personally donated. Then he asked his opponent how much money he had contributed.[5]

In October of 1853, Johnson was back in Nashville – this time as the governor of the state of Tennessee. Johnson's first inaugural address, known as the Jacob's Ladder Speech, related progressive democracy to Jacob's visionary ladder leading to heaven. While one elevated man religiously, the other raised man politically.[6] In the speech, Johnson recommended changes in the state judiciary, improvements in the educational system, the elimination of double taxation on commercial transactions, the establishment of broader funding for road improvements, and modifications of the penal system. Johnson went on to discuss the merits of his Homestead proposal and the preservation of public lands for posterity. He concluded with a line that would close many of his speeches, the people "never deserted me, and *God* being willing, I will never desert them."[7]

As governor, Johnson's successes were few, but this was not entirely his fault. At this time the office of governor in Tennessee held little power. He had no veto and held little authority to enforce the laws of the state. Furthermore, his ability to dispense patronage and make appointments was limited. About all he could do was try to persuade lawmakers to pass his legislation. His primary vehicle was the biennial message.[8]

In Johnson's first message to the Tennessee legislature, he addressed the indebtedness of the state, noted that the entire public road system was defective,

---

[3]Temple, p. 379.
[4]Temple, p. 461.
[5]Graf *et al.*, Vol. II., p. 163-164.
[6]Graf *et al.*, Vol. II., p. 176-177.
[7]Graf *et al.*, Vol. II., p. 183.
[8]Trefousse, p. 90-91.

pointed out that the common school fund was totally inadequate, and condemned the prison system. He advocated court reform – the reorganization of the court system such that the chancery and the court of law become one court.[9] He sought to abolish the Bank of Tennessee, and establish the statewide adoption of regulated weights and measures.[10] According to Johnson, Tennessee was at the bottom of the list on education save one other state.[11] He paraphrased Aristotle and Diogenes saying, "Education is a companion which no misfortune can suppress – no clime destroy – no enemy alienate – no despotism enslave."[12] The Governor proposed collecting a statewide tax to support education.[13] The state penitentiary system was also a failure, according to Johnson, who saw no hope in attempting to reform inmates. "There is not one in every thousand convicts whose moral condition is improved by such imprisonment; but, on the contrary, most of them if not all, are made worse than they were before."[14] The penitentiary system was being operated like a mechanics institute, supported by the state treasury. It stood in competition with law-abiding craftsmen in the state.[15] And, despite his absence from the national scene, Johnson continued to promote the passage of his federal Homestead Bill and his constitutional amendments providing for the direct election of the president and senators and a 12-year term limit for Supreme Court Justices.[16]

The legislature did not act upon Johnson's priorities.[17] His effort to liquidate the Bank of Tennessee failed, and his constitutional amendments were considered but not sanctioned.

In February of 1854, a Tennessee bill authorized freed blacks to be transported to the Western Coast of Africa.[18] The act assigned the governor to make all necessary arrangements to send these former slaves to a United States

---

[9]Graf *et al.*, Vol. II., p. 203.

[10]Graf *et al.*, Vol. II., p. 197 & 204.

[11]Actually, Tennessee was lowest in literacy save North Carolina and Arkansas according to the federal census figures from 1850 (J.D.B. DeBow, *Statistical View of the United States: Embracing Its Territory, Population--White, Free Colored, and Slave--Moral and Social Condition, Industry, Property, and Revenue, the Detailed Statistics of Cities, Towns and Counties: Being a Compendium of the Seventh Census to Which are Added the Results of Every Previous Census, Beginning with 1790, in Comparative Tables, with Explanatory and Illustrative Notes, Based Upon the Schedules and Other Official Sources of Information,* (Washington: Beverley Tucker, Senate Printer, 1854), pp. 145, 151, & 152).

[12]Graf *et al.*, Vol. II., pp. 195 & 207.

[13]Graf *et al.*, Vol. II., p. 194.

[14]Graf *et al.*, Vol. II., p. 198.

[15]Graf *et al.*, Vol. II., p. 199.

[16]Graf *et al.*, Vol. II., pp. 205-206 & 208.

[17]Trefousse, p. 93.

[18]*Acts of the State of Tennessee, passed at the first session of the thirteenth general assembly for the years 1853-4,* (Nashville: M'Kennie & Brown, 1854), Chapter L., p. 121.

seaport for deportation to Africa. Johnson appointed his son Robert to escort the blacks to their port of departure at Baltimore from where they would be transported to Liberia.[19]

ELECTION OF 1855

In 1855, Johnson ran for a second term as governor with his party re-nominating him by acclamation.[20] His opponent was Meredith P. Gentry nominated by the Whig and the American (Know Nothing) parties.[21] The two candidates scheduled a series of state-wide debates beginning in May. Johnson went out of his way to provoke the opposition. It is not surprising numerous threats of violence were made against him during the campaign. His enmity for the Know Nothings and his intemperate tongue almost led to bloodshed on more than one occasion.

In his very first speech in Murfreesboro, Johnson tore into the Know Nothings. "Show me a Know-Nothing, and I will show you a loathsome reptile on whose neck every honest man should put his feet."[22] Voices from the audience cried out, "Lie. Lie." Then the sound of pistols being cocked was heard throughout the hall. Johnson paused for a moment then continued. Gentry responded in a gentlemanly manner but failed to adequately defend the fledgling party, much to the disappointment of his supporters.[23] On another occasion Johnson appeared before a crowd with a revolver in hand. Laying his pistol on a table he addressed the crowd,

> Fellow-citizens, I have been informed that part of the business to be transacted on the present occasion is the assassination of the individual who now has the honor of addressing you. I respectfully propose that this be the first business in order.

---

[19]Graf *et al.*, Vol. II., p. 447.
[20]Milton, p. 88.
[21]Temple, p. 383. The Know Nothing party grew out of the anti-immigrant resentment of the 1840s. The large number of immigrants coming into the country posed a threat to native-born Americans. The party started out as a secret society. When members were asked about their organization they were to reply that they knew nothing. As the party grew it became less secretive and took on the name American Party. The organization advocated limits on immigration, residency requirements for citizenship, and the prohibition of voting rights and the holding of public office for foreign-born individuals.
[22]Temple, p. 385.
[23]Temple, p. 386.

Therefore, if any man has come here to-night for the purpose indicated, I do not say to him, let him speak, but let him shoot.[24]

After a moment of silence Johnson said, "It appears that I have been misinformed."[25] He continued his speech.

Toward the end of the canvas, Gentry became very ill, and the two candidates decided to cancel the rest of the debates. Word spread of Johnson's magnanimity in agreeing to terminate the speaking tour. The next scheduled stop was Knoxville where it was agreed that Johnson and a spokesperson for Gentry would address the crowd and tell them there would be no further speeches. Gentry's spokesman gave a three-minute explanation of the situation followed by Johnson who gave his full speech. Johnson continued onto the rest of the appointments saying, "I am not allowed by agreement with my competitor to make a speech. If I were allowed to do so, I would say..." then he would go into his address.[26]

Although Johnson lost in Eastern and Western Tennessee, Middle Tennessee again gave him a victory. He won the election to the second term. William G. Brownlow published a prayer in the *Knoxville Whig* asking God's forgiveness for the citizens of Tennessee for electing Johnson governor.[27]

Johnson's second inaugural was brief. At 11:00 a.m. on October 22, he was taken to the House of Representatives. A prayer preceded the delivery of his speech. His address was a brief affirmation of his proposals from his first term. "They were my views and sentiments then, they are mine now," he said.[28] Again he closed with, "The people have never deserted me, and *God being willing*, I will never desert them."[29] The entire ceremony was over in 15 minutes.[30]

Johnson's legislative address was also a rehashing of his agenda from the first term. He pointed out the need for internal improvements, changes in the banking industry, a tax revision, judicial reform, stopping the use of convict labor, and a push for the Homestead Bill and constitutional amendments.

Johnson's second term as governor was as unremarkable as the first. He did not have an effective relationship with the legislature. Again, the House and Senate failed to act on his proposals. During his second term, they did pass the uniform weights and measures proposal and authorized the acquisition of Andrew

---

[24]*Harper's Weekly*, October 16, 1875, Vol. XIX., #981, p. 839.

[25]*Harper's Weekly*, October 16, 1875, Vol. XIX., #981, p. 839.

[26]Temple, p. 389.

[27]E. Merton Coulter, *William G. Brownlow; Fighting Parson of the Southern Highlands*, (Chapel Hill: The University of North Carolina Press, 1937), p. 121.

[28]Graf *et al.*, Vol. II., p. 342.

[29]Graf *et al.*, Vol. II., p. 343.

[30]Trefousse, p. 100.

Jackson's Hermitage.[31] The state of Tennessee purchased Jackson's Mansion and 500 acres for $48,000. The property was offered to the federal government for the expressed purpose of establishing a southern branch of West Point. The offer was accepted in 1857 by the U.S. Senate Committee on Military Affairs, but Northern opposition to a southern military academy was so strong that the Senate failed to take additional action and the offer was rescinded. The state sold all but 50 acres.[32]

In a speech in Huntsville, Alabama, Johnson remarked that although he was no disunionist, it was time that those in the South took a firm stand for their rights. Southerners had conceded their rights until there were few left. Johnson said he had stricken the word *compromise* from his vocabulary. "Vice... would not hesitate to enter into a controversy with virtue, if it thought there was any prospect of settling the difficulty by compromise."[33]

In early 1857 on a return trip from Washington, Johnson was in a railroad accident that left him disabled for the rest of his life. The train ran off the tracks and Johnson sustained a crushed right arm which never did heal properly.[34] The accident, however, did not slow Johnson down. His political ambition continued unabated, and by the end of 1856, he had decided not to seek a third term as governor. Johnson wanted more than his adopted state could provide and sought national office again.[35]

---

[31]Trefousse, p. 100.
[32]Graf *et al.*, Vol. II., pp. 464-465.
[33]Graf *et al.*, Vol. II., p. 444.
[34]Graf *et al.*, Vol. VII., p. 307.
[35]Graf *et al.*, Vol. II., p. xxviii.

Chapter 4

U.S. SENATE

In 1857, a sweeping Democratic victory in Tennessee assured that the legislature would appoint a Democrat to the United States Senate. Johnson sought the honor. He had actively campaigned for those in his party during the election even going so far as to pay some of their expenses out of his own funds.[1] The effort paid off. The Tennessee legislature sent him to the United States Senate at the end of his second term as Governor. Johnson served from December 1857 to March 1862, during which time he would only see his wife once and that was in 1860.[2]

Johnson returned to Washington with his usual vigor, making the St. Charles Hotel his residence. He found the environs in the District more to his liking than that of Nashville.[3] Little had changed in Johnson's political philosophy since he was in the House. He still prided himself as being a man of the people, dedicated to the homestead movement and bent on bringing economy to government. He continued to oppose governmental spending on such things as the transcontinental railroad, franking privileges for Congressmen, and expenditures for the construction of the U.S. Capitol.[4]

HOMESTEAD BILL

Johnson introduced his homestead legislation on December 22, 1857. It was referred to the Committee on Public Lands. On February 1 of the following year,

---

[1]Trefousse, p. 107.
[2]Trefousse, p. 111.
[3] Trefousse, p. 111.
[4]Trefousse, p. 117.

the bill passed the House but was stopped in the Senate.[5] Johnson reintroduced his homestead legislation again on May 20, 1858 in a discursive appeal. It stalled. Undaunted, he introduced his bill again on December 20, 1859. Amendments were made to it on April 11, 1860 to placate Southern objections. On April 17 a different set of amendments were suggested. The Senate finally passed the bill on May 10. The House passed a similar measure and the two bills went into conference. After three conference sessions, the bill made it through the House, and on June 19, the Senate accepted the compromise.[6] At long last, Johnson had his Homestead Bill before President Buchanan. The Senator, who thought he had the President's word on its passage, was surprised when "Old Buck" vetoed it. Johnson surmised that Southern legislators had garnered the President's support to kill the legislation, for a number of them later changed their vote prohibiting the override of the veto.[7] Johnson's beloved legislation would come to fruition later at the hands of the Republicans.[8]

EXPENDITURES FOR PUBLIC WORKS IN WASHINGTON

Johnson was always trying to bring economy to government by reducing and eliminating unnecessary expenses. In June of 1858, there were appropriations under consideration for improvements in Washington. Among them, one million dollars to complete an aqueduct bringing water into the city, grading the mall and planting trees budgeted for $10,000, and putting an extension on the Capitol costing another $750,000.[9] The Senator opposed these expenditures.

Johnson favored returning the District to Maryland.[10] Failing that, he thought the citizens of Washington should cover half of the costs of running the city. While some in Congress argued that government projects provided employment opportunities, Johnson was adamant.

The most dangerous doctrine that ever was sustained in any government... that the Government must be the giver out of jobs for the sake of giving employment to the great mass of people! The theory is wrong.... In proportion as you make

---

[5]Trefousse, p. 116.
[6]Trefousse, pp. 119-121.
[7]Milton, p. 92-93.
[8]Robert W. Winston, *Andrew Johnson, Plebeian and Patriot*, (New York: H. Holt and Company, 1928), p. 126.
[9]Graf *et al.*, Vol. III., pp. 170 & 172-173.
[10]Trefousse, p. 114.

the people dependent on the Government, the Government controls the people, instead of the people controlling the Government.[11]

CAMPAIGN FOR THE PRESIDENCY, 1860

Johnson sought his party's nomination for the presidency in 1860, but he had little backing.[12] In August of 1859, he wrote a letter to the editor of the *Chattanooga Advertiser* saying that he never was an aspirant to the presidential office, but should political office seek him, he would respond favorably.[13]

The Tennessee Democratic Convention met in January of 1860 in Nashville and endorsed Johnson as its candidate. At the National Convention in Charleston that year, there was a split between Southern and Northern Democrats, and the convention, unable to make a decision, adjourned to meet again in Baltimore in June.[14] Johnson, unable to garner the support needed, had his name withdrawn.[15] The moderates nominated Stephen Douglas and the other faction nominated John Breckinridge.[16] Lincoln's victory in the presidential election triggered major events all too familiar in the annals of the nation.

PROPOSED CONSTITUTIONAL AMENDMENTS

When the 36th Congress convened, John Brown's raid on Harpers Ferry and his failed attempt to free slaves was the consuming topic of conversation. The issues of slavery and secession would divide this Congress and the nation. Andrew Johnson would be right in the center of the debate.

On December 13, 1860, Johnson introduced Constitutional amendments to help keep the South in the Union. His attempt was but one of many such efforts in Congress at the time. 1) The first amendment sought to change the mode of electing the president and vice president. The legislation put the election of the president and vice president directly into the hands of the people. Furthermore, it alternated the eligibility of candidates between Northerners and Southerners. 2)

---

[11]*Congressional Globe,* 35 Congress, 1st Session, June 1, 1858, p. 2589.
[12]Graf *et al.,* Vol. III., p. xxiii.
[13]Graf *et al.,* Vol. III., pp. 290 & 292.
[14]While in Charleston, Andrew's son Charles went on a drinking spree. Robert managed with some difficulty to get him home (Graf *et al.,* Vol. III., p. 589).
[15]Graf *et al.,* Vol. III., pp. xxv-xxvi.
[16]Trefousse, p. 125.

Likewise, senators would be elected by popular vote. 3) The Supreme Court justices would be appointed for twelve-year terms with vacancies filled alternatively by men from the North and South.[17] Also on December 13, Johnson introduced an un-amendable amendment on slavery. He proposed dividing the country into slave and non-slave states and forcing the return of all runaways to their owners.[18]

SPEECHES ON SECESSION

But the desire for secession could not be deterred, and on December 17, 1860, South Carolina adopted a secession ordinance. The next day, Andrew Johnson spoke on the floor of the Senate, delivering a speech that began late in the day and concluded on the 19th. The speech initially addressed the Constitutional Amendments before Congress, but soon devolved to the topic of secessionism.[19] While Johnson admitted that redress was necessary on many issues, secession was not the answer. Secession would only bring the government to an end. He advocated that the push for states' rights was best fought in the legislature with its basis being the Constitution. He denied that a state had the right to secede from the Union. Quoting Andrew Jackson, Johnson said, "A state could not secede, since 'such secession does not break a league but destroys the unity of a nation.'"[20] If states were able to secede from the Union then the government was no stronger than "a rope of sand."[21] The Senator stated that the dissolution of the Union would in effect spell the death knell for slavery.[22]

Johnson made the compelling argument that no one state had the right to withdraw without the consent of the others. Territories were not acquired without a price. Texas entered the Union with war debts which were covered by the other states and was given an additional $10,000,000 which came from taxpayers all over the country. Was Texas admitted just for her benefit or for the benefit of the states as a whole? Louisiana cost the government $15,000,000 in the purchase from France.[23] In 1815, when the British threatened invasion, Andrew Jackson along with men from Tennessee, Kentucky, and other states drove the invaders

---

[17]Graf et al., Vol. III., pp. 692-696.
[18]Graf et al., Vol. III., p. 696.
[19]Graf et al., Vol. IV., pp. 3-4.
[20]Graf et al., Vol. IV., p. 17.
[21]Graf et al., Vol. IV., p. 9.
[22]Graf et al., Vol. IV., p. 33.
[23]Graf et al., Vol. IV., pp. 24-28.

away. With the admission of Louisiana all of the states had free access to the navigable waters of the Mississippi.[24] In 1811, the United States paid Spain $6,000,000 for the Florida territory and authorized $25,000,000 to remove the Seminoles from the swamps. Florida was anxious to be admitted into statehood then, but no longer wanted to be part of the United States.[25]

Johnson chided South Carolina, asking what her grievance was. Was it the propagation of slavery into the new territories? No, for in the last session of Congress senators from South Carolina voted to make that unnecessary.[26] The way to handle grievances was to bring them forth and if after a reasonable time they were not reconciled and all other means exhausted then consider removal from the Union.[27] The real reason for secession was that Lincoln was elected. "It is because we have not got our man."[28] But, why should Lincoln's election be an issue? He was a minority president by nearly a million votes.[29] There were more votes cast against Lincoln in the North than votes against him in the South. The Congress had the ability to thwart anything Lincoln would want to do. If the secessionist senators had not vacated their posts, the Lincoln opposition would have had a majority of six. Lincoln could not have made his cabinet without Senate approval. He could not have sent a foreign minister abroad. He could not have even appointed a postmaster making over $1,000 without Senate approval.[30]

> We have it in our power – yes, this Congress here to-day has it in its power to save this Union, even after South Carolina has gone out.... You can do it. Who is willing to take the dreadful alternative without making an honorable effort to save this Government? ... Let us stand by the Constitution; and in preserving the Constitution we shall save the Union; and in saving the Union, we save this, the greatest Government on earth.[31]

Johnson said he voted against Lincoln, spoke in opposition to him, and expended funds to defeat him, but was not ready to leave the Union because Lincoln was elected President. On the contrary, he was willing to wait four years to help turn him out of office in the next election.[32] Secession had long been a cherished idea among Southern leaders who only needed to find an issue that

---

[24]Graf et al., Vol. IV., p. 25.
[25]Graf et al., Vol. IV., p. 27.
[26]Graf et al., Vol. IV., p. 39.
[27]Graf et al., Vol. IV., p. 41.
[28]Graf et al., Vol. IV., p. 42.
[29]Graf et al., Vol. IV., p. 42.
[30]Graf et al., Vol. IV., pp. 43 & 51.
[31]Graf et al., Vol. IV., pp. 45-46.
[32]Graf et al., Vol. IV., p. 43.

would galvanize the masses in favor of leaving the Union. Slavery was that issue and the election of Lincoln the spark that ignited the effort.[33]

There was an exuberant eruption of applause in the galleries as people cheered for the Senator. Grinnell of Iowa gave him three cheers. Southern lawmakers, on the other land, demanded the galleries be cleared.[34]

Johnson's December 18-19 address was powerful and apropos. Northerners were looking for a message of optimism and the Senator from Tennessee provided it. His speech was a beacon of light to the North – the first word of hope from a Southern lawmaker since the conflict began. In an instant, Johnson became very popular in the Northern states. Down South was another matter. The speech added to Johnson's abhorrence in the South where he was considered a traitor. He was burned in effigy in Western and Middle Tennessee. There were some Southerners, however, who supported his position. Hurley, the editor of the *Nashville Democrat* and even Brownlow, Johnson's one-time archrival in Eastern Tennessee, backed him.[35]

The news of the speech enjoyed a wide circulation about the country. More than 36,000 copies were printed and circulated. Letters of both support and disapproval poured in, and Johnson was sought out as a speaker. The *New York Tribune* praised him.

> The speech of Gov. Johnson of Tenn. in the Senate, to-day, was a most happy and powerful effort, and is spoken of very highly by all parties. Republican and Democratic Senators listened with marked attention, and, at one time, quite a number of members of the House were on the floor. He utterly denied the constitutional right of secession, and desired that the President should firmly carry out the laws, regardless of consequences.... All Conservative men agree that it is the best speech which the Governor ever has made.[36]

On February 5 and 6, 1861, Johnson delivered another attack on the Senate floor against secession. In this speech, he employed imagery used 14 years earlier on the floor of the House in his Wish-To-God Speech where he talked of assembling all of the American people in a huge amphitheater to consider the question of preserving the Union.[37] What protection can South Carolina provide

---

[33]Graf *et al.*, Vol. IV., p. 153.
[34]Milton, p. 104.
[35]Graf *et al.*, Vol. IV., p. 148.
[36]*New York Tribune*, 12-20-1860, Vol. 20, # 6133.
[37]Graf *et al.*, Vol. IV., p. 237.

those states that follow her in secession, he asked. By going out of the Union the tax burden has drastically increased for its residents four fold.[38]

He concluded with a convoluted imagery that twisted the demise of the Union with his own. "When this Union is interred, I want no more honorable winding sheet than that brave old flag, and no more glorious grave than to be interred in the tomb of the Union."[39] Likely he got so wound up he did know who or what was being buried, but by the end of the speech it really did not matter. He could have said anything and been applauded by the Unionists.

Johnson's second address received an equally positive reaction. Accolades came from *The New York Tribune* where Johnson's speech was noted as "the most scathing review of the Secessionists and their schemes yet heard in Congress, and will exert a powerful influence on the Tennessee election."[40] The paper conjectured that the speech would be a powerful influence in Tennessee.

Johnson received a letter from J. Warren Bell of Springfield, Illinois stating that several people had raised Johnson's name for a cabinet post in the Lincoln administration and even talked about him as Lincoln's successor. Consideration of a cabinet post found its way into the *Washington Evening Star* of February 28.[41]

Johnson had joined the side of the Unionists. While he did not abandon his state or Southern issues, he was solidly for the preservation of the Union above all else. He was thoroughly convinced that the Southern states could be most effective if they did not secede.

Why was Johnson so public in his support? Senator Thomas Bragg of North Carolina advanced a theory in his diary entry of February 5, 1861. "Johnson has all along entertained the opinion that he was one day to be President.... He knows that in a Southern Confederacy he would be nowhere – Hence he rather sides with the North."[42]

In the turmoil of secessionism, Andrew Johnson stood firm in his support for the Union. While one can argue his motives, one cannot question his adherence to his principles of upholding the Constitution. His position in 1861 was in line with his earlier stands. He was an unabashed supporter of the Union.

There is little evidence that Johnson's stand in support of the Administration was a ploy to gain favor with Lincoln. There was little hope of any immediate reward for his stance. If he were trying to ingratiate himself with the President,

---

[38]Graf *et al.*, Vol. IV., pp. 234-235.
[39]Graf *et al.*, Vol. IV., p. 254.
[40]*New York Tribune,* 02-07-1861, Vol. 20, #6,174.
[41]Graf *et al.*, Vol. IV., pp. 291-292.
[42]Clyde Edward Pitts (ed), *Thomas Bragg Diary, 1861-1862*, (Chapel Hill: Southern Historical Collection, University of North Carolina Library, 1966) pp. 43-44.

admonishing the South to remain in Congress to fight the President was not the way to do it. Furthermore, in the future he demonstrated his loyalty to the Union by putting his life on the line to back his position.

Secessionists saw Johnson's pro-Union stance as treasonable. Again he was burned in effigy, and had some Southerners gotten a hold of him he might have been incinerated for real. Meanwhile in the North he was the spokesman for Unionism – a light in the all-too-dark gloom of a foreboding sea of discontent. Lincoln was very impressed with the Senator and gave him discretion over patronage in Tennessee.[43]

For the first time in his political career, Andrew Johnson enjoyed the adulation and approval of national political leaders that he so deeply craved.[44]

While Johnson maintained that Tennessee would remain solidly in the Union, she did not, eventually choosing to favor the Confederate cause. But when Governor Harris attempted to pull Tennessee out in February of 1861, he failed.[45] Johnson's speech was credited with turning voters away from thoughts of secession, at least for awhile.

On March 3, 1861, the last day of the 36th Congress, Johnson spoke on the floor of the Senate. The topic was treason. "Show me the man… who has fired on our flag… and I will show you a traitor." The Senator was interrupted with applause and a warning to the galleries from the President *pro tempore*. Johnson continued, "I would have them arrested, and if convicted… I would execute them!" A spectator waved his hat and yelled to the presiding officer, "Arrest and be damned!"[46] Johnson continued and after a while motioned with his hand that he was through. The galleries erupted. Spectators stood on their seats waving their hats in the air and cheering for Andy.[47]

ACCOSTED ON A TRAIN AT LYNCHBURG

Johnson stayed in Washington to handle patronage issues after the adjournment of the session. In April, he returned to Tennessee to participate in the election. On his way home, his train passed through Virginia where trouble awaited him. The train reached Lynchburg after dark, where a large crowd had gathered with cries to hang the traitor. Johnson's car was surrounded and he had a

[43]Trefousse, p. 138.
[44]Graf *et al.*, Vol. IV., p. xxxiv.
[45]Temple, p. 399.
[46]Temple, pp. 397-398.
[47]*Congressional Globe,* 36th Congress, 2 Session, March 2, 1861, p. 1356.

scuffle with a couple of men who entered the car. When one interloper tried to pull his nose, Johnson pulled his gun.[48] Things could have easily escalated into real trouble. Fortunately for Johnson, Louis T. Wigfall of Texas was on the same train. Wigfall calmed the mob and asked them to give Johnson a hearing. Johnson likely failed to persuade any in the crowd. He told them forthright that he was a Union man and as the train pulled out, the crowd was yelling, "Hang him!" The scene was about to be repeated in Bristol, but as the train approached the scheduled stop, a Confederate officer, acting under orders from Jefferson Davis, ordered the engineer to move on to Jonesboro without stopping.[49]

In April, Johnson canvassed the state of Tennessee in support of the Union. Thomas A.R. Nelson, a Whig Congressman and Unionist, joined him. They spoke all over Eastern Tennessee.[50] With great danger to personal safety, the two preached their anti-secessionist message urging people to remain steadfast in support of the Union. They met a great deal of open hostility. When Brownlow heard that Johnson's life was in danger, he sent his son to escort the Senator over the back roads to Greeneville.[51]

The June 8th election confirmed that Tennessee was in support of secession and Johnson could no longer safely remain in his state. Leaving his family in Greeneville, Johnson returned to Washington by way of the Cumberland Gap on June 12. Shortly thereafter, the Gap became occupied with secessionist troops. After Johnson got into Kentucky, he started giving speeches and was hailed a hero. He reached Washington on June 21. On July 4 when the Senate met in special session, Johnson was present – the only Southerner from a secession state in attendance.[52]

Secessionists intercepted a letter to Johnson from northern industrialist Amos Lawrence offering financial assistance. William G. Swan, a Knoxville lawyer, forged a letter in return to Lawrence using Andrew Johnson's name in an attempt to swindle $10,000.[53]

---

[48]Temple, p. 467. William Hardwick tried to pull Johnson's nose (Graf *et al.*, Vol. VII., pp. 206-207, Vol. VIII., p. 367, Vol. XIV., pp. 18-19, & 21.)

[49]Milton, pp. 105-106.

[50]Temple, p. 399.

[51]Trefousse, p. 142.

[52]Graf *et al.*, Vol. IV., pp. 491-492. Trefousse, pp. 142-143.

[53]William G. Brownlow, Stephen V. Ash (ed.), *Secessionists and Other Scoundrels: Selections from Parson Brownlow's Book*, (Baton Rouge: Louisiana State University Press, 1999), p. 128. Trefousse, pp. 142 & 406.

BILL APPROPRIATING ARMS TO EAST TENNESSEE

By late July, Union supporters in East Tennessee were in peril. Unionist were relating stories of the atrocities that had befallen them with the invasion of Rebel forces and begging for weapons to defend themselves. Some people had been harassed, jailed, and even executed.[54]

On July 20, 1861, Johnson sponsored a bill in the Senate to supply $2,000,000 in arms to the Unionists in East Tennessee. Although the Senator acted unilaterally, he received widespread support in both houses of Congress. Three days later the bill was recommended by the Military Affairs Committee and passed the Senate the same day. The House passed it on July 27, and it was signed into law July 31. Even though the legislation became law in eleven days, it would still be months before arms would reach their intended destination.

The conditions in Eastern Tennessee were deplorable. Rebels were pillaging the countryside taking everything of value and all the prisoners they could. As pressure mounted, many Union sympathizers living in East Tennessee had to flee for their lives leaving their families behind. Some escaped to the mountains; others attempted to make their way north across the border into Kentucky.[55] Commissioners from the Confederacy gave the citizens of Knoxville until August 16, 1861, to demonstrate their obedience to the new Confederate government or be forced to serve in the Confederate army.[56]

Early in the second session, Johnson approached General George McClellan asking for relief in East Tennessee.[57] In December of 1861, McClellan sent 10,000 rifles and 10,000 uniforms/equipment to General Don Carlos Buell for relief in the region.[58]

SLAVERY AS A PRETEXT

On July 27, Johnson, speaking on the floor of the Senate, elaborated more on slavery as a pretext for secession. Secessionists, he said, were looking for an excuse to break off from the federal government for a long time and they seized upon the election as a justification. Conciliation was what Southern legislators

---

[54]Trefousse, p. 145.
[55]Graf et al., Vol. IV., p. 681.
[56]Graf et al., Vol. IV., p. 670 & Vol. V., pp. 104-105.
[57]Trefousse, p. 148.
[58]Graf et al., Vol. V., pp. 68-69.

feared most. Their goal was to leave Congress before any compromise could materialize.[59]

There was a proposal in the Senate, in the form of an un-amendable amendment that would have placed the institution of slavery beyond the reach of any future actions of Congress.[60] If all the secessionist senators had stayed, the Senate would have been able to render Lincoln ineffective.

Johnson reminded his listeners of the hubris of the South. In April the Secretary of War for the Confederacy had bragged that his flag "would float over the dome of the old Capitol, at Washington, before the 1st of May."[61]

---

[59]Graf *et al.*, Vol. IV., p. 634.
[60]Graf *et al.*, Vol. IV., pp. 614-615.
[61]Graf *et al.*, Vol. IV., p. 627.

Chapter 5

MILITARY GOVERNOR OF TENNESSEE

In 1862, Forts Henry and Donelson fell to the federals on February 6th and 16th. Nashville, Tennessee (with no real defense) was soon abandoned by Confederate troops. Governor Harris looted the state treasury and archives before leaving the Capital.[1]

With the Union victory at Donelson, Lincoln asked Johnson to resign his senatorial seat to take the military governorship of Tennessee and serve at the rank of brigadier general. The appointment of governor was by executive order under the War Powers Act. The Senate unanimously affirmed his military commission. While the Northern press approved of the selection, many in the military establishment had reservations.[2] As to the choice of governor, General William Nelson believed that the people of Tennessee should make the decision and not the President of the United States. General Don Carlos Buell also thought such an appointment ill advised. But, Lincoln saw Johnson's consistent stance for the Union, his support for the Administration, and his unwavering devotion to the Constitution as patriotic. For the politically-ambitious Johnson, he had but few options. His term in the Senate would soon expire and without a state legislature to reappoint him, he would be out of a job.[3]

Johnson, the first of the military governors to administer a secessionist state, was appointed on March 3 with a wide breadth of power which included the authority to establish tribunals, suspend the writ of *habeas corpus*, take possession of all public buildings, and seize all vacant property owned by secessionists. He was to care for all abandoned slaves and to provide for the sick and destitute. Johnson would serve at the pleasure of the President or until the loyal inhabitants

---

[1]Graf *et al.*, Vol. V., p. xxxvi.
[2]Graf *et al.*, Vol. V., pp. 177-178.
[3]Trefousse, pp. 153-154.

of the state organized a civil government in compliance with the United States Constitution.[4]

Governor Johnson arrived in Nashville on March 11. His entry into the state of Tennessee was unpretentious. The last leg of the trip from Washington was especially humbling. A dilapidated train, comprised of remnants from other locomotives, was hastily assembled at Bowling Green, Kentucky.

> The result was an engine patched up from odds and ends, without head-light, cow-catcher or cab. It looked a snorting wreck on wheels. There were a few cars attached; one was a box car, in which sat the Hon. Andrew Johnson, Military Governor of Tennessee, *en route* for its capital…. On a level track the engine was a success, but whenever an up grade was struck, every body but the Honorable Andrew got out and footed it, while the engine made running jumps to reach the top. Finally, late at night, the passengers reached Edgefield, and crossed the river to Nashville.[5]

Tennessee citizens held divided loyalties. There was determined support for the Union in the east and strong backing for the Confederacy throughout the rest of the state. Johnson's task was a daunting one. The people of Tennessee were living in a war zone. Continual threats of Confederate raiding parties and guerrillas harassing Union sympathizers created an environment of intimidation.

Under federal occupation, Nashville became a staging area for supplying Union operations. Refugees and freed slaves relocated there. But many secessionists still lived in the Capital. The City was a focal point for conspiracy and intrigue with spies and smugglers continually passing back and forth through the lines.[6]

Johnson moved into the St. Cloud Hotel[7] and occupied a small, plain room, "half filled by a bed." It would be four months before he commandeered Lizinka Campbell Brown's house near the Capitol for his residence.[8]

---

[4]Graf *et al.*, Vol. V., p. 177 & Vol. VI., pp. 212-213.

[5]William R. Plum, *The Military Telegraph During the Civil War in the United States: with an exposition of ancient and modern means of communication, and of the federal and Confederate cipher systems; also a running account of the war between the states.* Vol. I. (Chicago: Jansen, McClurg & Company, 1882), p. 204.

[6]Graf *et al.*, Vol. V., p. xlv. Mary E. Clements, an operative for General William T. Sherman, requested a house in Nashville for her five little boys and two servants. As soon as her family was settled she was ready to get back to work (Graf *et al.*, Vol. VI., p. 712). Martha E. Mitchell was looking for a house for her children and herself in Nashville. It has been surmised that Mitchell was involved in espionage for General John M. Corse (Graf *et al.*, Vol. VII., pp. 310-311).

[7]Twenty year old Laura Carter, the attractive daughter of Johnson's hotelier at the St. Cloud Hotel, was arrested for spitting on Union officers from the porch of her father's establishment. When

On March 13, 1862, a large crowd gathered in front of Johnson's residence. As an army band serenaded, the Governor appeared on the balcony and spoke for an hour. Noting that slavery was but a pretext for the South to leave the Union, he pointed to the real cause of the war – disappointed ambition among the Southern aristocrats who feared the loss of power in Washington.[9]

Two days later, William G. Brownlow made his way through the lines into Nashville. On the 20th, he was greeted by the new military governor who had been his political opponent for a number of years.[10] When the two met they "rushed into each other's arms, and wept like children."[11] Their previous mutual animosities had been put aside as they tried to save the Union, which they both loved.

While Johnson's speeches demanded that traitors be punished, in practice he showed a great deal of leniency.[12] The Governor had a great empathy for the common man whom he thought had been seduced by the upper class into supporting the rebellion. For the longest while he believed that most Tennesseans were really Unionists who had been coerced into joining the Confederate cause.

When Johnson first arrived in Nashville things were chaotic. He immediately set out to re-establish order. He seized the Bank of Tennessee and what court records were left behind by the fleeing Confederate Administration.[13] He required the city council and Mayor of Nashville, Richard B. Cheatham, to take an oath of allegiance to the Union. When they refused he had them replaced or, in the case of the Mayor, had him incarcerated until he took the pledge. He also made an effort to bring relief to families broken by the war by assessing the inhabitants of Nashville for the support of the impoverished wives and children of Confederate soldiers.[14]

The secessionist clergy were an exceptionally bothersome lot for the Governor. The flames of discontent, being fanned by pro-secessionist sermons, were quickly brought under control with the arrest of the most loathsome of the preachers. Some, Johnson sent to northern prison camps and others he banished

---

interrogated, Laura swore she would dance on Johnson's grave. "You must n't (sic) mind these little rebels. There is no harm in Laura. Dance on my grave, will she? She will plant flowers instead." After Johnson died, Laura who had married a Union officer, put flowers on the grave of her old friend, Andrew Johnson (Truman, p. 436).
[8]Graf *et al.*, Vol. V., p. liv.
[9]Graf *et al.*, Vol. V., p. 202.
[10]Brownlow, pp. 144-145.
[11]Coulter, p. 211.
[12]Graf *et al.*, Vol. V., p. 203.
[13]Graf *et al.*, Vol. V., pp. 208-209.
[14]Trefousse, pp. 155-156.

south. "These assumed Ministers of Christ have done more to poison and corrupt the female mind in this community than all others," he wrote.[15]

Johnson made arrangements for a number of pro-Union meetings to be held in and around Nashville. On May 12, 1862, a Union rally was held in the Tennessee House of Representatives. There Johnson warned, "If the Union goes down, we go down with it. There is no other fate for us. Our salvation is the Union, and nothing but the Union."[16] The Governor once again espoused that treason must be trampled, traitors punished, and slavery was but a pretext for breaking up the federal government.

With all the guerilla activity in the area, any foray into the countryside was at great peril. On the 24th, Johnson took an un-escorted train south of Nashville to a Union meeting held in Murfreesboro. There, he urged those supporting the Rebel Cause to return to the Union. That night Johnson stayed at the William Spence mansion outside of town. Late in the evening it was discovered that 600 of Morgan's men had been dangerously close by, with the intent of capturing the Governor. The next day while Johnson was waiting for his train to return to Nashville, he gave an energetic speech to the Minnesota and Michigan regiments from atop of a freight car.[17]

In early June a Union meeting was held in Columbia where Neil S. Brown, former governor of Tennessee, joined Johnson on the stump. By the 7th of the month, the last of the rallies was held in Shelbyville because the guerillas had become too threatening.[18]

RELIEF TO SOLDIERS IN PRISONS

Johnson was besieged with appeals from Tennesseans who had been forced into Confederate service and were now confined in Northern prison camps where conditions were far from salubrious. Even Sarah C. Polk, the wife of the former President of the United States, wrote to Johnson asking him to release a prisoner. Letters from these prisoners led to Johnson commissioning an emissary to secure their release.[19]

In March of 1862, Johnson sent Connally F. Trigg to Camp Chase near Columbus, Ohio to check on the condition of Confederate prisoners from

[15]Graf *et al.*, Vol. V., pp. 595-596.
[16]*New York Herald*, April 25, 1865, no vol., #10,465.
[17]*New York Herald*, April 24, 1865, no vol., #10,465.
[18]*New York Herald*, April 24, 1865, no vol., #10,465.
[19]Graf *et al.*, Vol. V., p. 401.

Tennessee. The Governor instructed him to take copious notes of all interviews noting those who expressed a desire to swear the oath of allegiance.[20] Trigg called upon the governor of Ohio and secured interviews with prisoners. He found a number who were ready to take the oath.[21] By the time Trigg left Camp Chase he had 500 to 600 letters from Tennesseans and about 200 letters written by soldiers from other states.[22] Many of the letters were signed by more than one man.

In June of 1862, Lincoln asked Johnson if he wanted control over all Confederate prisoners from Tennessee.[23] The Governor jumped at the opportunity and was given authority in August to exchange or discharge Tennessee captives from Union prisons.[24] Johnson appointed ex-governor William B. Campbell as a commissioner to visit the various Union prisons to lay out terms of release to the Tennessee inmates who were willing to take the oath.[25]

Johnson also received letters from Eastern Tennesseans languishing in Southern prisons where conditions were horrible beyond description.[26] These men too desperately wanted to be exchanged.[27] Among their number was the Governor's nephew who was being held in an attic room with 50 others.[28]

PROBLEMS WITH MILITARY SUPPORT

Johnson was continually soliciting help from the military and beseeching the President and the Secretary of War for support for loyal Unionists. One can easily understand why Johnson meddled in military affairs. He had the responsibility of protecting a civilian population in great danger – a population that was not always the major concern of the military establishment. The situation was untenable and destined to cause conflict.

Johnson especially had a strong dislike for General Don Carlos Buell, whom he surmised was a Southern sympathizer. It was no secret that Johnson wanted the General removed from the theatre. In April of 1862, when Buell left Nashville for Shiloh he took many troops from the area, much to the consternation of the

---

[20]Graf *et al.*, Vol. V., p. 219.
[21]Graf *et al.*, Vol. V., p. 264.
[22]Graf *et al.*, Vol. V., p. 276.
[23]Graf *et al.*, Vol. V., p. 439.
[24]Graf *et al.*, Vol. V., p. 446.
[25]Graf *et al.*, Vol. V., pp. 308 & 603.
[26]Graf *et al.*, Vol. VI., p. 592.
[27]At first the Lincoln Administration withheld exchange of prisoners because the act would have acknowledged the sovereignty of the Confederacy (Graf *et al.*, Vol. VI., p. 258).
[28]Graf *et al.*, Vol. VI., pp. 328, 386, 405, & 486.

Governor. Johnson wrote to Buell on April 24 asking that the General not remove a Minnesota Regiment from Nashville and other corps from Lebanon and Murfreesboro.[29] "The effect of removing the troops," he argued, "is visible in the face of every secessionist. Secession was cooling down and great reaction in favor of the Union was taking place."[30] The Governor's request was ignored. The next day, Johnson communicated with Stanton that the 69th Ohio no sooner arrived than Buell redeployed them. Johnson complained that this regiment was ordered to report to him.[31] The Governor also shared with the President his exasperation.[32] Lincoln suggested that Johnson talk to General Henry W. Halleck who controlled the region.[33] Johnson wasted no time in drafting a message to Halleck protesting the removal of the 69th.[34]

Not the least of Johnson's concerns was the welfare of Eastern Tennessee where conditions were growing more and more serious. Appeals came to the Governor. One citizen wrote:

> They are driving the Union families out of the country by scores, and are murdering and shooting them down on all occasions. They arrested 400 Union men before my family left – drove them through the street, starving for water and something to eat, and sent them to Atlanta to work on fortifications. – my son John says that they shot down fifty of these before they started them to Georgia.[35]

In May of 1862, Johnson issued a warning to guerrilla raiders in his state: In every case where a Union man was arrested by prowling bands, five or more secessionist sympathizers in the neighborhood would be imprisoned. And, when Union families had property destroyed, Rebel supporters would be made to provide restitution.[36]

In June, Johnson appealed again to Henry Halleck to liberate East Tennessee, but the General's priorities were not those of the Governor. Halleck curtly put things into military perspective.

---

[29]Graf *et al.*, Vol. V., pp. 301 & 330.
[30]Graf *et al.*, Vol. V., p. 331.
[31]Graf *et al.*, Vol. V., p. 334.
[32]Graf *et al.*, Vol. V., p. 336.
[33]Graf *et al.*, Vol. V., p. 338.
[34]Graf *et al.*, Vol. V., p. 340.
[35]Graf *et al.*, Vol. V., p. 357.
[36]Graf *et al.*, Vol. V., p. 374.

East Tennessee will very soon be attended to[.] we drive off the main body of the enemy before we can attack his other Corps[.] the head must be attended to first and the toe nails afterwards[.][37]

That same month, Johnson communicated with Stanton that there was a need for two cavalry regiments in Eastern Tennessee to stop the atrocities being perpetrated on the people of that region.[38] Confederate troops were riding through the countryside looking for Union sympathizers, thousands of which were forced to hide in the mountains or make their way across the border into Kentucky. Confederates were repairing the railroad into East Tennessee with the idea of hauling off the wheat and oat crop to Virginia. They were taking horses, cattle, and sheep and were murdering inhabitants.[39]

Stanton responded immediately giving authorization to form two regiments.[40] The next day, the Governor asked his son Robert to convert his infantry unit into a cavalry corps.[41] This was welcomed news for Robert who wanted to head such a component. Robert's 4th Tennessee infantry was officially transformed into a cavalry unit on June 26.[42] Andrew Johnson authorized his son to purchase horses. If he could not find them he was to take mounts from secessionists and provide certifications for governmental reimbursement.[43] But Robert procrastinated. By the end of July, he still had not procured horses or equipment for his corps, and the Governor had to make arrangements himself with the quartermaster in Louisville to obtain horses.[44]

On July 10, Johnson wrote to Lincoln complaining about the lack of cooperation from the military and strongly suggested changes in personnel to bring relief to Eastern Tennessee.[45] The President responded the next day in frustration.

Do you not my good friend perceive that what you ask is simply to put you in Command in the west. I do not suppose you desire this. You only wish to Control in your own localities, but this you must know may derange all other parts [.][46]

---

[37]Graf *et al.*, Vol. V., p. 442.
[38]Graf *et al.*, Vol. V., p. 495.
[39]Graf *et al.*, Vol. VII., p. 52.
[40]Graf *et al.*, Vol. V., p. 496.
[41]Graf *et al.*, Vol. V., p. 498.
[42]Graf *et al.*, Vol. V., p. 499.
[43]Graf *et al.*, Vol. V., p. 527.
[44]Graf *et al.*, Vol. V., pp. 581, 586, & Vol. VI., p. 231.
[45]Graf *et al.*, Vol. V., pp. 549-550.
[46]Graf *et al.*, Vol. V., pp. 551-553.

Although Lincoln chastised Johnson, he remained empathetic with his plight and told Halleck to confer with the Governor.[47]

Johnson's struggle over Eastern Tennessee would last his whole term as governor. He would continue to push Washington to bring relief to the region.[48] Although General Ambrose E. Burnside liberated East Tennessee in September of 1863, the respite would only last until early November when Confederate General James Longstreet returned.[49] Throughout the summer of 1864, marauding bands of Confederates could still be found scattered from just north of Knoxville to the Virginia border.[50] Letters of distress continued to plead for help lest loyal Union supporters should give up.[51] One letter accusing Johnson of never making an effort to relieve Eastern Tennessee had to be exceedingly painful to the Governor.[52]

When Union soldiers, hearing of the distress their families were suffering in the eastern part of the state, deserted their units to return home, Johnson appealed to General George H. Thomas and secured amnesty for them.[53] Many of these men served under Alvan Gillen who eventually lead Union troops on an expedition into Eastern Tennessee in September of 1864, to hunt down and kill the Confederate raider John H. Morgan.[54]

SIEGE OF NASHVILLE

The Battle of Shiloh and the Union pursuit of the Rebels into Corinth, Mississippi left the defenses at Nashville exposed. Raids by Nathan Bedford Forrest and John Hunt Morgan kept the city in a stir.[55] Johnson was very determined to stand by Nashville and not let it fall back into the hands of the Rebels. He was equally resolved not to be taken alive by the enemy. On July 13, when a Rebel force of 6,000 under Forrest captured Murfreesboro, Johnson began an effort to fortify the Capital. Forrest advanced closer to Nashville burning the homes of Northern sympathizers along the way. Johnson declared that the first shot fired on the Capital would signal the destruction of the home of every

---

[47]Graf *et al.*, Vol. V., p. 553.
[48]Graf *et al.*, Vol. VI., p. 323.
[49]Graf *et al.*, Vol. VI., pp. xlv, 363, & 359.
[50]Graf *et al.*, Vol. VI., pp. 707 & 720.
[51]Graf *et al.*, Vol. VII., pp. 26-27.
[52]Graf *et al.*, Vol. VI., p. 734.
[53]Graf *et al.*, Vol. VII., p. 98.
[54]Graf *et al.*, Vol. VII., pp. 137 & 157.
[55]Trefousse, p. 158.

prominent secessionist in town. Apparently, secessionists took him at his word for they held a meeting with Forrest to implore the General not to attack the city.

Johnson likely felt encouraged when in August General Don Carlos Buell sought out his help in developing an information network in Eastern Tennessee comprised of a series of couriers and informants to supply military intelligence. Johnson agreed to take immediate action.[56] But any appreciation for Buell soon vanished when in September of 1862, Confederate General Braxton Bragg crossed the Tennessee River at Chattanooga and headed north toward Nashville. Johnson protested to the President that instead of confronting the enemy, General Buell took a defensive posture leaving all the country open to the Rebels. The Governor said if Buell had purposely set out to surrender the state, he could not have done a better job. This letter made its way into Northern papers, possibly leaked by Johnson himself to garner support for Eastern Tennessee. [57]

On September 5, Bragg occupied Murfreesboro, and Nashville was overflowing with refugees and apprehension. The next day Buell was in Nashville with plans to abandon the city. Johnson believed that every Union supporter would be shot if the Union army vacated.

Granville Moody, a Methodist evangelist, went to the Capitol to talk to the Governor. "Moody, We are sold," Johnson said. "Buell has resolved to evacuate the city."[58] He asked the preacher to pray. The two were soon on their knees in prayer with Moody asking for Divine intercession and Johnson amening him along the way. At the end of the session, Johnson said, "Moody, I don't want you to think that I have become religious because I asked you to pray, but, Moody, there is one thing that I do believe: I believe in Almighty God; and I also believe the Bible; and I say, *I'll be damned if Nashville shall be surrendered!*"[59]

On September 11, General Thomas took command of the Capital after receiving word from his superordinates in Washington to hold the city at all costs. Nashville fortifications were being constructed at a rapid pace. Meanwhile refugees were arriving daily, telling tales of devastation at the hands of the guerillas.

By September 30, outside communication was cut off and Nashville was under a state of siege. People attempting to leave were quickly captured by guerillas before they got very far. Food was scarce and there was a great uneasiness among the residents. Some of their anger was taken out on Rebel

---

[56]Graf *et al.*, Vol. V., pp. 604-605.
[57]Graf *et al.*, Vol. VI., p. 5.
[58]Milton, p. 111.
[59]Milton, p. 112.

sympathizers within the confines of the city. Nightly assassinations were frequent.[60] Threats against Johnson were almost endemic.[61]

For two months Nashville was cut off from Northern support. But the Governor was steadfast. During the siege he threatened to shoot anyone who talked of surrender.[62] The *Nashville Dispatch* reported that Johnson would burn the city before he would let it fall into the hands of Rebels again. The reporter said, "If the rebels retake Nashville, they will find his remains under the ruin[s] of the Capitol."[63]

For some time the Confederates in Eastern Tennessee had put pressure on Johnson's family to leave Greeneville. On April 21, 1862, the family was ordered to pass through Confederate lines, but given her state of health, Mrs. Johnson asked for an extension. It was not until the later part of September when she informed Confederate authorities that she was in good enough health to travel and asked for the appropriate papers to cross the lines.[64] The Johnson home would be converted into a Confederate hospital.

On October 10, Charles Johnson moved his mother Eliza, sister Mary Stover, her husband, and three children through the lines to arrive in Murfreesboro at 9:00 p.m. in a cold rain. They had a difficult time finding a place to stay, but after a couple of hours they managed to beg a spot on someone's floor. The next day at 6:00 in the morning General Nathan Bedford Forrest told them Jesus Christ could not pass through his lines and they should return home to Greeneville on the 7:00 train.[65] When word got around that the Johnsons were in town little hospitality was extended. That night the family found an abandoned house where the women stayed while the men slept in a baggage car courtesy of a railway employee.

The following day, Confederate Governor Harris and Andrew Ewing, one-time representative from Tennessee and judge on General Braxton Bragg's military court, telegraphed Richmond for permission to let the Johnson family pass. The family was soon informed that General Forrest had made arrangements for them to move through to Nashville under a flag of truce.[66] But for the intervention of the Davis Administration it is unlikely the family could have proceeded further.

On October 12, Johnson's family arrived in Nashville. It was Mrs. Johnson's intention to continue on immediately to Cincinnati to visit her son Robert whom

---

[60]*New York Herald*, April 24, 1865, no vol., #10,465.
[61]Graf *et al.*, Vol. V., p. 269.
[62]Graf *et al.*, Vol. VI., p. xxxii.
[63]Trefousse, p. 160.
[64]Graf *et al.*, Vol. V., pp. 352-353.
[65]Trefousse, p. 161.
[66]Graf *et al.*, Vol. VI., p. 23.

she feared she would never see again, but the siege forced Eliza to stay in Nashville for the duration.[67] In December, family members took her north to Vevay, Indiana for her health.[68]

Two attacks on Nashville were repulsed on November 5. Johnson watching the events from the cupola of the Capitol and to the very end promised he would shoot anyone who talked of surrender. On November 14, General William S. Rosecrans arrived bringing relief to the troubled city.[69]

The General complained to Johnson that his troop movements had been compromised in the Louisville press. He stated that the person responsible for publishing the information said he did so with Andrew Johnson's approval. Such leaks had to stop.[70]

SLAVERY[71]

When slaves in Tennessee realized that freedmen were working for wages, many slipped away from their masters. The protests from slaveholders did not go unnoticed by the Governor.[72] On September 22, 1862, Lincoln issued an announcement that on New Years Day he would emancipate the slaves held in areas under rebellion. Johnson told the President that such a proclamation would be problematic for Tennessee slave owners who were Union supporters. Petitioning the President on December 4, the Governor asked to have his state excluded from the areas affected.[73] Lincoln removed Tennessee from the list.[74]

SWING AROUND THE CIRCLE

Following his pro-Union Senate speech in December of 1860, Johnson received numerous invitations for speaking engagements in the North. He passed up most due to pressing governmental business. But in February of 1863, Johnson began a protracted speaking tour of the Northern States -- his *Swing Around the*

---

[67]Graf *et al.*, Vol. VI., p. 52.
[68]Trefousse, p. 168.
[69]*New York Herald*, April 24, 1865, no vol., #10,465.
[70]Graf *et al.*, Vol. VI., p. 62.
[71]Johnson's own slaves stayed on with the family and worked as hired servants (Graf *et al.*, Vol. VII., p. 399).
[72]Graf *et al.*, Vol. VI., p. xlvii.
[73]Trefousse, pp. 165-166. Graf *et al.*, Vol. VI., p. 85.

Circle, the name he used for such extended expeditions. The tour started in Indianapolis and ended in Washington with stops in Columbus, Harrisburg, Philadelphia, New York, and Baltimore.[75] The purpose of the tour was to rally support for the Lincoln Administration. Large enthusiastic crowds turned out everywhere. The final speech was in the House Chamber with Lincoln and his Cabinet present.[76]

In his Indianapolis speech, Johnson decried that slavery was only a pretext for the South to leave the Union. He read from an old manuscript written by Andrew Jackson. Jackson pointed out that the South was merely looking for an excuse to secede from the Union in his day, and he predicted the next situation that would be used for disabling the Union would be the slavery question.[77] The Governor also read from the *Montgomery Daily Advertiser*, "It has not been a precipitate revolution, but with coolness and deliberation has been thought of for forty years. For ten years this has been the all-absorbing question."[78] Johnson said Southern aristocracy wanted to secede for a number of years and Lincoln's election provided the excuse.[79] The real goal was to establish a Southern Confederacy.[80] When Lincoln became president, the opposition held the majority in the House and Senate. Lincoln would have been stymied had the South remained in the Union. After Davis and other Southerners left Congress, Thomas Corwin, Republican from Ohio, sponsored an amendment that would have exempted slavery from interference by future amendments. The issue passed Congress with a two-thirds vote and was awaiting passage by three-fourths of the states at that time.[81] Johnson's speech was a powerful message coming from a Southerner.

---

[74]Graf *et al.*, Vol. VI., p. 114.
[75]Graf *et al.*, Vol. VI., p. lii.
[76]Graf *et al.*, Vol. VI., p. liv.
[77]Graf *et al.*, Vol. VII., p. 224. John S. Bassett (ed.), *Correspondence of Andrew Jackson*, Vol. 5.,
        1931, p. 72.
[78]Graf *et al.*, Vol. VI., p. 151.
[79]Graf *et al.*, Vol. VI., p. 150.
[80]Graf *et al.*, Vol. VI., p. 152.
[81]Graf *et al.*, Vol. VI., p. 155.

HUMAN SUFFERING[82]

By the summer of 1864, the refugee problem in Nashville was acute.[83] Displaced persons were pouring in from Georgia and Alabama -- brought in on the trains and left in a pitiful condition. Among their numbers were the old and infirm as well as little children, sick and in want. Seeking shelter, searching for lost relatives, trying to recover property, and attempting to provide for the essentials of life became very difficult for these people. Johnson was inundated with inquiries and was empathetic to their plight. The Ladies Aid Society made an effort to alleviate their suffering with private funds.[84]

MILITIA ENROLLMENT

With Sherman's Atlanta Campaign drawing off many troops in September of 1864, there was an increase in Confederate cavalry raids into Tennessee.[85] It was determined a state militia was needed to fill the void. The Tennessee Militia Enrollment Proclamation was issued on September 13.[86] The order requested the registration of all able-bodied male residents of all races between the ages of 18 and 50. Local magistrates in districts throughout the state were to act as enrollment commissioners in their areas.[87]

The enactment was to take place in the fall of 1864 and spring of 1865, but the effort did not go according to plan.[88] There were major problems with the implementation of the enrollment. Justices of the Peace, who were designated to enlist men in the militia, were threatened by Confederate marauders.[89] Citizens who saw enrollment in the militia as tantamount to enlisting in the Union Army joined Rebel guerrillas and went south. Some Union sympathizers went north into Canada to escape conscription. Many of those who stayed requested exemptions.[90]

---

[82]During the summer of 1863 there was a growing problem with venereal disease in Nashville. Military officials controlled prostitution in the city by licensing prostitutes. Weekly examinations helped get those who were infected hospital treatment and certified the rest to continue in the business (Graf *et al.*, Vol. VI., pp. 717-718.).

[83]Graf *et al.*, Vol. VII., p. 206.

[84]*New York Times*, October 16, 1864, Vol. XIII, #4075.

[85]Graf *et al.*, Vol. VII., p. 161.

[86]Graf *et al.*, Vol. VI., p. 326.

[87]Graf *et al.*, Vol. VII., pp. 159-161.

[88]Graf *et al.*, Vol. VII., p. 119.

[89]Graf *et al.*, Vol. VII., p. 201.

[90]Graf *et al.*, Vol. VII., p. xxix.

MOSES OF THE COLORED MAN

On October 24, a torchlight parade of blacks in Nashville called upon the Governor who favored them with a speech. Without approbation from Lincoln, Johnson offered emancipation to the slaves of Tennessee. The state had been exempt from Lincoln's Emancipation Proclamation at Johnson's request. Now in a complete reversal, Johnson became emancipator. In his address he adroitly hid his earlier request for exemption. Referring to Lincoln's Emancipation Proclamation, he told the crowd, "For certain reasons, which seemed wise to the President, the benefits of that Proclamation did not extend to you or to your native state."[91] He then made his own decree giving freedom to every black in Tennessee. But Johnson did not stop there. He dangled the possibility of subdividing secessionist plantations and landholdings into small farms for ex-slaves. He talked about breaking up large estates like Harding's 3,500 acre Belle Meade plantation. It was this kind of reckless talk that created false hopes that would fuel unmet expectations in the future.[92]

Johnson said he wished a Moses would rise up to lead the blacks to freedom. "You are our Moses," shouted several people in the crowd. "We want no Moses but you!" Johnson was quick to accept the call. "Well, then," replied the Governor, "humble and unworthy as I am, if no other better shall be found, I will indeed be your Moses, and lead you though the Red Sea of war and bondage, to a fairer future of liberty and peace."[93]

This supposedly impromptu rally and Johnson's extemporaneous address were likely contrived. It is not difficult to imagine that Johnson had several people in the audience to shout on cue, "You shall be our Moses."[94] But to what end? He had no reason to curry favor with the blacks of Nashville. His sole purpose was for political advantage. The speech would make its way into the press where it played well with Northern sympathies and supported Johnson's national political aspirations. That Johnson freed the slaves would be a political mantra that he would sing for years.

On November 12, another torchlight procession of 4,000 blacks arrived at the Governor's residence. In Johnson's speech he repeated several familiar themes, defining freedom as the opportunity to support oneself by engaging in honest labor, admonished blacks to educate and properly clothe their children, and honor

---

[91]Graf *et al.*, Vol. VII., p. 251.
[92]Graf *et al.*, Vol. VII., pp. 251-253.
[93]Graf *et al.*, Vol. VII., pp. 252-253.
[94]*Nashville Daily Times and True Union*, October 25, 1864, Vol. 1, #213.

the institution of marriage.[95] In February of 1865, the blacks of Nashville presented Johnson with a gold watch inscribed, "PRESENTED TO His Excellency THE HONORABLE ANDREW JOHNSON, MILITARY GOVERNOR OF TENNESSEE, by the COLORED PEOPLE OF NASHVILLE, for his *Untiring Energy in the Cause of Freedom.*"[96]

But where was Moses when it was discovered that the living conditions in the black refugee quarters in Nashville were in a deplorable condition? In December of 1864, six dead bodies covered with vermin were found in the crowded barracks. The stench was suffocating and it was obvious that the refugees had not been provided with a sanitary environment.[97] Reports of a twenty-five percent morality rate were made by the War Department the previous August. Where was their deliverer? Where was their Moses? Johnson likely felt no animosity toward ex-slaves; he just saw them as inferior beings. While the Governor investigated the situation in the refugee barracks, there is no evidence that the despicable conditions were ever corrected.

ELECTIONS

Lincoln had long hoped a referendum in Tennessee would show support for the Union and bring the state back into the fold. On July 3, 1862, the President wrote to Johnson imploring him for such a referendum. "If we could, somehow, get a vote of the people of Tennessee and have it result properly it would be worth more to us than a battle gained. How long before we can get such a vote?"[98] Whether this was wishful thinking on the President's part or pressure on Johnson to skew an election is unknown.

Lincoln did get a presidential election in the state. Governor Johnson ordered an election for November 8, 1864, open to voters who had taken an oath of allegiance. In addition to requiring fidelity to the Union, the oath cleverly eliminated voters who favored the Democratic platform, which promised to negotiate a peace with the Confederacy.[99] Voters were asked to affirm that they would "oppose all armistices or negotiations for peace with rebels in arms."[100]

---

[95]Graf *et al.*, Vol. VII., pp. 281-283.
[96]Graf *et al.*, Vol. VII., p. 481.
[97]Graf *et al.*, Vol. VII., pp. 344-345.
[98]Graf *et al.*, Vol. V., p. 532.
[99]Milton, pp. 135-136. Wounded Indiana soldiers, not allowed by their state to vote in the field, were given a 15-day furlough to go home to vote (*New York Times*, 10-16-1864, Vol. XIII, #4075).
[100]Milton, p. 135.

A statewide convention was held on January 9-14, 1865, authorizing an election to be held on February 22 for vacant state offices.[101] Again, the election was to be open to all Union men who had subscribed to the strict loyalty oath.[102] Why did Johnson wait so long to call a state constitutional convention? It seems obvious he did not want to vacate his post until he had another position.[103]

[101]Temple, p. 412.
[102]Graf *et al.*, Vol. VII., pp. 436 & 438.
[103]Temple, p. 412.

Chapter 6

ASCENSION TO THE EXECUTIVE BRANCH

In hopes of gaining a wider appeal in the 1864 elections, the Republicans changed their name to the Union Party. There would be another significant change as well. Lincoln was looking for a new vice president. His don't-change-horses-in-the-middle-of-the-stream policy only applied to the presidency.[1] The politics of Hannibal Hamlin, his first-term vice president, had turned radical, and Hamlin's reigns were cut as Lincoln sought a more suitable running mate.[2]

Benjamin C. Truman served as Johnson's secretary while Johnson was the military governor of Tennessee. In fulfilling his duties he carried dispatches directly to President Lincoln who always inquired of Johnson's abilities. In private conversations with the President, Truman spoke favorably of the Governor.[3]

In the spring of 1864, the President sent Major General Daniel Sickles on a fact-finding tour of Tennessee, Louisiana, and South Carolina to check on the conditions of blacks and to measure the impact of his Amnesty Proclamation.[4] Truman was an old friend of the *New York Herald* correspondent Tom Cook who was traveling with Sickles as a volunteer aid. The reporter confided that the General was asked by Lincoln to see if Johnson would be a suitable candidate for the Vice Presidential position in the next election.[5] Upon learning that Lincoln was considering Johnson on the ticket, Truman immediately notified his boss of

---

[1] Graf *et al.*, Vol. VI., p. lxvii.
[2] Graf *et al.*, Vol. VI., p. lxii.
[3] *New York Times*, July 13, 1891, Vol. XL., #12,442.
[4] Graf *et al.*, Vol. VI., p. 687.
[5] *New York Times*, July 13, 1891, Vol. XL., #12,442.

the news. The Governor sent his aide to Washington on the next train to find Colonel John W. Forney and have him support Johnson's interests.[6]

Rumors of Johnson's questionable habits were either never reported or overlooked. Likely no one really wanted to know. The party needed all the strength it could garner, and besides he was only filling the Vice Presidential slot then considered a nominal position. "A Union party must have a Union ticket."[7] And, Johnson suited the bill.

When asked at the Baltimore Convention who he desired to be his second-term running mate, Lincoln named Andrew Johnson.[8] Lincoln had several strategic reasons for his selection. The Confederacy was enjoying the support of England and France. Choosing a Southerner as a running mate might mitigate that backing. Furthermore, the election of Johnson would draw in the support of the War Democrats and widen the political base for the Union (Republican) Party in border states. The choice of a governor from a reconstructed state would show the advancement in restoration. Finally, Johnson's hard line that treason must be made odious quite likely appealed to Northerners who thought Lincoln too soft.

Johnson, with ambitions for the presidency, relished the opportunity to become Vice President. In writing to his son Robert over three years earlier concerning the vice presidential position on the 1860 presidential ticket, he remarked, "There Could be no Safer positin [sic] to Secure the first place four years hence than Second place on the ticket now." In that letter he was already cognizant of his place in history as one who held political office "from the lowest to highest... a very remarkable fact to record in history."[9]

At the convention on June 7, William G. Brownlow, Johnson's frequent adversary, gave him an endorsement that won over the delegation. "We have a man down there whom it has been my good luck and bad fortune to fight untiringly for the last twenty-five years."[10] The next day Lincoln was re-nominated and Johnson became his running mate.[11]

The Republican newspapers liked the choice, but not all were thrilled with the selection. Thaddeus Stevens asked, "Can't you get a candidate for vice president without going down into a damned rebel province for one."[12] The Lincoln-

[6]Benjamin C. Truman, "Anecdotes of Andrew Johnson," *The Century Magazine*, Vol. 81, # 1, January 1913, p. 437.
[7]*Harper's Weekly*, September 14, 1867, Vol. XI., #559, p. 578.
[8]Graf *et al.*, Vol. VI., p. 730.
[9]Graf *et al.*, Vol. III., p. 573.
[10]Graf *et al.*, Vol. VI., p. lxviii.
[11]Trefousse, p. 179. Graf *et al.*, Vol. VI., p. 721.
[12]Milton, p. 44.

Johnson ticket gathered a majority of popular and electoral votes in the fall of 1864.[13]

Johnson requested that Lincoln allow him to remain in Nashville during the presidential inauguration so that he could participate in William G. Brownlow's investiture as governor of Tennessee. But the President insisted that Johnson's presence in Washington was essential.[14] Johnson went to Washington for the March 4th inaugural.

THE INAUGURATION

On the eve of the 1865 inauguration, Johnson and his friends celebrated late into the evening. The Vice-President Elect awakened the next day hung over and possibly still inebriated. When he arrived at the Capitol he remarked to Hannibal Hamlin that he needed a drink. The out-going Vice President, likely still smarting from being passed over for a second term, obliged Johnson and sent for a bottle of whiskey.[15] When it came time for Johnson to deliver his speech, he was almost incoherent. It was clear to most that he was intoxicated. His intonation fluctuated from a loud "backwoods shout" that reverberated in the lobby of the Capitol to an almost inaudible whisper that could not be heard in the gallery just above him. He annoyed his audience by repeating over and over again the phrase, "I announce here to-day." One of his announcements was that "Tennessee was personified in Andrew Johnson."[16] In acknowledging a number of dignitaries, he inadvertently forgot the name of the Secretary of the Navy and had to ask someone on the platform.[17] Finally, after 20 incredulous minutes, Hamlin convinced his successor to bring his speech to closure.[18]

Johnson's rambling remarks were an embarrassment to the President and caused a great deal of consternation among Cabinet members. Lincoln told the marshal not to let Johnson speak again during the ceremony.[19]

Those who saw the humiliating spectacle were outraged to see the second most powerful man in the country drunk at his inaugural. The display was so

---

[13]Trefousse, p. 184.

[14]Graf *et al.*, Vol. VII., pp. xxiii-xxiv.

[15]Trefousse, p. 188.

[16]*Cincinnati Daily Enquirer*, March 9, 1865, Vol. 30, #111. There is early evidence of Johnson thinking of himself and Tennessee as one (Graf *et al.*, Vol. III., p. 573.).

[17]Graf *et al.*, Vol. VII., pp. 506-507.

[18]*Cincinnati Daily Enquirer*, March 9, 1865, Vol. 30, #111. Graf *et al.*, Vol. VII., p. 507.

[19]Milton, p. 147.

serious that a Senatorial caucus considered asking him to resign.[20] So appalled was Senator Henry Wilson that he introduced an order to remove all intoxicating liquors from the Capitol.[21]

All present were mortified including two men who would later serve on Johnson's Cabinet. Orville Browning said that it was a disreputable display, offensive to all decent people who heard him.[22] Gideon Welles, the Secretary of the Navy said, "The Vice-President elect made a rambling and strange harangue, which was listened to with pain and mortification."[23]

D.R. Locke, writing under the pseudonym Petroleum V. Nasby, lampooned the Vice President.

> His breath, so long disguised with aristocratic drinks, hed bin naturalized with whisky! He could barely git onto the stand – his eyes wuz uv a dead fish color, his nose wuz uv the ginrous hue prevalent at Dimokratic caucuses, and his tongue wuz thick.[24]

Suffering from post-inauguration regret, Johnson contacted the Senate reporter asking him to preserve the notes from the speech and to send him a copy of what had been said.[25] Some creative editing in the official record *The Globe* helped save face.[26] Lincoln also put a pleasant spin on the whole embarrassing affair telling the Secretary of the Treasury that he had known "Andy Johnson for many years [and]… Andy ain't a drunkard."[27]

The press had a field day. The *New York Herald* said the speech was "remarkable only for its incoherence."[28] The *Cincinnati Enquirer*, quoting the *New York Tribune*, called it "the most remarkable and utterly inappropriate harangue that ever fell from the lips of a Vice President."[29] The *Cincinnati Gazette* said, "He bellowed for half an hour the idiotic babble of a mind besotted

[20]Milton, p. 148.
[21]Graf *et al.*, Vol. VII., p. xxvi.
[22]Orville Hickman Browning, *The Diary of Orville Hickman Browning*, Vol. II. (Springfield, Ill: Trustees of the Illinois State Historical Library, 1925), p. 9.
[23]Gideon Welles, *Diary of Gideon Welles, Secretary of the Navy Under Lincoln and Johnson*, Vol. II. (Boston: Houghton Mifflin, 1909), p. 252.
[24]Petroleum V. Nasby, *Andy's Trip to the West, Together With a Life of Its Hero*, (New York: J.C. Haney & co., 1866), pp. 24-25.
[25]Graf *et al.*, Vol. VI., p. 514.
[26]Milton, p. 149.
[27]Hugh McCulloch, *Men and Measures of Half a Century; Sketches and Comments*, (New York: C. Scribner's Sons, 1888), p. 373.
[28]*New York Herald*, March 3, 1865, no vol., #10,415.
[29]*Cincinnati Daily Enquirer*, March 9, 1865, Vol. 30, #111.

by a fortnight's debauch."[30] The press too recommended that Johnson resign immediately. The nation "cannot afford to keep open the risk of such an alternative in case of the death or disability of the President."[31] His was an inauspicious beginning indeed.

Although he had no official duties to perform, Johnson remained in Washington after the inaugural. He could have easily slipped away to attend Brownlow's installation in Nashville as he initially intended, but he likely hung around to make amends with the President.[32] Johnson met with Lincoln on April 14. It would be their last encounter.[33] While there is no official record of what was discussed, a White House secretary gave an account that Johnson had said, "If he were President he would not make it too easy for the rebels."[34] But Lincoln's philosophy, which was more lenient, would prevail for the time being.

Lincoln proposed that upon surrender, Confederate troops would receive their rights as citizens of the United States and the governments in existence would remain in control until Congress could impart others. As long as the soldiers of the Rebellion put down their weapons, the President had little concern with how the armistice took place. Grant shared this sentiment as witnessed by the generous terms he offered Lee at his surrender on April 9. Confederate General Joseph E. Johnston's army was still in the field.

THE LINCOLN ASSASSINATION

On the evening of April 14, Johnson was in his room on the second floor of the Kirkwood House, recovering from typhoid fever which he had contracted before the inaugural. L.I. Farwell, the former governor of Wisconsin, was attending the play *Our American Cousin* at Ford's Theater that night. After witnessing Lincoln's assassination, he ran to the Kirkwood House to warn the Vice President. Arriving at the hotel, he ordered a guard placed at the front door, one on the stairway, and one at Johnson's room. He then banged on the Vice President's door. Johnson opened to the news that President Lincoln had been shot. At first he sent Farwell to check on the President's condition, and then about

---

[30] *Cincinnati Daily Gazette*, March 9, 1865, Vol. 76, #217.
[31] *Cincinnati Daily Gazette*, March 9, 1865, Vol. 76, #217.
[32] Graf *et al.*, Vol. VII., p. lxii.
[33] Shortly after arriving in Washington, Johnson claimed to have had a conversion with Lincoln in which he discussed the conditions in Tennessee. No evidence has been found to veryify this meeting (Graf *et al.*, Vol. X., pp. 153 & 157).
[34] Graf *et al.*, Vol. VI., p. lxiii.

2:00 a.m. he went himself accompanied by Farwell and the commander of the provost guard.[35] He stayed but briefly and was asked to leave when Mary Lincoln, who despised him anyway, made one of her emotional outbursts.[36]

Johnson soon learned that Secretary of State William H. Seward had been seriously injured in the plot to kill the President. Although Seward's wounds were severe, they would not prove fatal. Nine days before the attempt on his life, the Secretary had suffered a broken jaw in a carriage accident. Ironically, this would prove to be a fortuitous accident. Seward was bedridden in the care of his family and an invalid soldier recuperating from his own wounds. A wire harness had been fashioned to hold Seward's jaw in place while it healed. During the attempt on Seward's life, the jaw brace blocked the knife blows from his assailant and saved the Secretary's life.[37]

Johnson felt the burden of the office as he awaited what he believed would be the inevitable news of Lincoln's demise.

> I walked the floor all night long feeling a responsibility greater than I had ever felt before. More than one hundred times I said to myself ["]What course must I pursue, so that the calm and correct historian will say one hundred years from now 'He pursued the right course[.']" I knew that I would have to contend against the mad passions of some and self aggrandisement [sic] of others. Men who had never seen an armed enemy would now cry for blood.... Mr. Lincoln might have been able to compel obedience to the constitution and the law but I doubted my ability to do so.[38]

Lincoln died at 7:22 the morning of April 15, and Andrew Johnson was thrust into the position of finishing the job his predecessor had started. It would fall on him to bring the prodigal states back into the Union, transform society from one permitting slavery, and restore the economy of a nation that had been at war. Could Johnson, full of apprehension and self-doubt, serve as the architect of restoration? How would he help heal a nation in mourning? How would he handle the conflicting expectations of what to do with the South?

[35]Milton, p. 161.

[36]Philip B. Kunhardt, Jr., Philip B. Kunhardt III, & Peter W. Kunhardt, *Lincoln: An Illustrated Biography*, (New York: Knopf, 1992), p. 361.

[37]McCulloch, p. 223. Kunhardt *et al.*, pp. 358-359.

[38]W.E. McElwee, Tennessee State Library and Archives, Micro file #1203, Box 1 Item #13, p. 3.

SEVENTEENTH PRESIDENT OF THE UNITED STATES

In the early-morning hours of the 15th, Stanton encouraged Johnson to proceed with his inauguration as soon as possible and asked him what arrangements he preferred. Johnson chose to be sworn in at his rooms at the Kirkwood House. Chief Justice Salmon P. Chase administered the oath of office between 10 and 11 o'clock on the 15th.[39] Andrew Johnson became the seventeenth president of the United States. His speech was somber and to the point unlike his vice-presidential speech the previous month.

> The duties of the office are mine. I will perform them. The consequences are with God. Gentlemen, I shall lean upon you. I feel that I shall need your support. I am deeply impressed with the solemnity of the occasion and the responsibility of the duties of the office I am assuming.[40]

After the swearing-in ceremony, Johnson asked the Cabinet members to remain. He expressed his desire that each stand by him.[41]

Attorney General James Speed and Secretary of the Navy Gideon Welles arranged the first Cabinet meeting which was held at 12:00 noon that day. Johnson announced to his Cabinet that his platform would be essentially that of the former Chief Executive.[42] The next day the Cabinet met again and Johnson,

---

[39]Trefousse, p. 194. McCulloch, pp. 374-375.
[40]*New York Herald*, April 16, 1865, no vol., #10,457.
[41]McCulloch, p. 376.
[42]Welles, *Diary of Gideon Welles*, Vol. II., p. 289.
    Johnson's Cabinet
    Secretary of State – William H. Seward
    Secretary of the Treasury – Hugh McCulloch
    Secretary of War – Edwin M. Stanton
                    – Ulysses S. Grant (ad interim)
                    – John M. Schofield
    Attorney General – James Speed
                    – Henry Stanbery
                    – Orville H. Browning (ad interim)
                    – William M. Evarts
    Post Master General – William Dennison
                    – Alexander W. Randall
    Secretary of the Navy – Gideon Welles
    Secretary of Interior – John P. Usher
                    – James Harland
                    – Orville H. Browning (Graf *et al.*, Vol. X., Appendix I.).

likely feeling the anxiety of the tragic events, he said he would not "treat treason lightly, and the chief Rebels he would punish with exemplary severity."[43]

The nation's outlook was dismal. Years later, Johnson reflected on the circumstances of assuming the position of Chief Executive.

> The whole country was in a blazing political conflagration when it fell to my lot to administer the office of President. Ambitious polititions [sic] were seeking power and place by fanning sectional hate and waving the bloody shirt. Then too there were many in whose hearts vengence [sic] had assumed the robes of virtue. For them, the south must be made to suffer.[44]

A Radical caucus wasted little time in meeting with the new president. They suggested a list of cabinet replacements, but Johnson who remained uncommitted only assured them of his desire to punish treason. The committee was satisfied for the moment, thinking he was one of them.[45]

Robert T. Lincoln wrote to Johnson on April 25 that his mother could not leave the White House for another two and a half weeks, and begged the President's indulgence. The Lincolns would stay until late May. In the mean time Johnson roomed with Preston King in the home of Samuel Hooper, a representative from Massachusetts, and set up his presidential office in the Treasury Building.[46] Secretary Welles suggested Johnson occupy the State Department until Seward recovered from his wounds but Stanton intimated that he did not want Seward's papers to be disturbed.[47]

Johnson had hardly settled in when word came of Confederate General Joseph E. Johnston's surrender to General William T. Sherman. At 8:00 the night of April 21, the Cabinet convened to deal with a communication received from Sherman. The General had just accepted the surrender of Johnston's Army and provided generous terms similar to those given Lee.[48] Lincoln had won over

---

[43]Welles, *Diary of Gideon Welles*, Vol. II., p. 290-291.

[44]McElwee, p. 4.

[45]George W. Julian, "George W. Julian's Journal – The Assassination of Lincoln," *Indiana Magazine*, Vol. XI., #4, December 1915, p. 335. Gideon Welles was invited to the War Department on the evening of the April 16th, immediately following Lincoln's death. Several Radical congressmen were in attendance including Senator Sumner. To Welles astonishment, Stanton shared Cabinet papers with the group – papers not yet thoroughly discussed in Cabinet meetings (Welles, *Galaxy*, p. 528).

[46]Graf *et al.*, Vol. VII., p. 639. Preston King served as a Representative and a Senator from New York. In 1865, he was appointed as collector of the New York port. In November of that year he leaped to his death into the New York harbor.

[47]Welles, *Diary of Gideon Welles*, Vol. II., pp. 289-290.

[48]Confederate soldiers were granted total amnesty and allowed to keep their property (Michael L. Benedict, *A Compromise of Principle: Congressional Republicans and Reconstruction 1863-*

General Sherman with his idea of a merciful peace, and Sherman was merely carrying out the wishes of the former President.[49] But following Lincoln's assassination, the terms of this peace were repugnant to many in Washington, especially Stanton who branded Sherman a traitor. The sentiment in the country had shifted. There were few Northerners ready to extend forgiveness. The terms of the surrender were re-negotiated.[50]

Many messages from well-wishes arrived in Washington, including one from Johnson's grandson and namesake who was in awe of his grandfather's catapultion to fame. The youngster wrote to the President from Nashville on April 22. "I would like to see you dear Grandpa since you are Priesident [sic] and see if it is my Grandpa yet."[51]

Many other messages came to Johnson in support of his ascension to the Chief Executive position. Some went so far as to proclaim that God's hand was in Lincoln's assassination.[52] One supporter believed that God permitted the assassination to fill the hearts of loyal citizens against treason.[53] More than one feared that Lincoln would have been too soft on the Rebels.[54] An Iowan wrote of the former president, "We loved and trusted to his judgment but were fearing that he would exercise too much leniency."[55] A citizen from Indiana cautioned, "Our late Beloved President lost his life by presumeing [sic] to [sic] mutch [sic] upon the goodness of the people. Dont [sic] do that yourself."[56] Even former Vice President Hannibal Hamlin wrote on May 3, giving Johnson his support. "We have no true men with us who are not delighted with your course…. The accounts of traitors remain to be settled. That done as I am sure you will do it, and I trust then you will have a time of peace and quiet, and the whole country will advance most rapidly in its course of unequalled prosperity."[57] Things could not have been further from the truth.

1869, (New York: W.W. Norton, 1974), p. 101). Sherman believed he was totally authorized to negotiate terms with Johnston and those terms would be the same as offered to Lee by Grant (Edward Chase, *The Memorial Life of General William Techumseh Sherman,* (Chicago: R.S. Peale, 1891), p. 506).

[49]Welles, *Diary of Gideon Welles,* Vol. II., p. 297. Welles believed Lincoln had met with Grant and Sherman to impress upon them the need to offer liberal terms to Rebels willing to surrender (Gideon Welles, "Lincoln and Johnson," *The Galaxy,* Vol. XIII., April 1872, p. 523).

[50]Graf *et al.,* Vol. VIII., p. 241.

[51]Graf *et al.,* Vol. VII., p. 621.

[52]Graf *et al.,* Vol. VII., p. 555.

[53]Graf *et al.,* Vol. VII., p. 570.

[54]Graf *et al.,* Vol. VII., p. 580.

[55]Graf *et al.,* Vol. VII., p. 650.

[56]Graf *et al.,* Vol. VIII., p. 74.

[57]Graf *et al.,* Vol. VIII., pp. 20-21.

What kind of president was Johnson going to be? Before the election he had been very tough on punishing treason. At this point, he remained non-committal and various factions held the hope that he was on their side. The Radicals saw the new president as being tough on Rebels. Conservatives trusted that he would keep Lincoln's policies. Southerners believed that he was one of them. But Johnson would not be all things to all people and most would be disappointed. While Johnson did believe treason should be punished, he had empathy for those who had been coerced into following the rebellious leaders. For the misguided, there would be amnesty.

The Radical leadership within the Republican Party was pleased that Lincoln was no longer an obstacle. While they mourned him publicly, in private they saw his removal as a Godsend. Immediately the Radicals pushed the new president to abandon Lincoln's plan, have Lee tried for treason, and establish voting rights for blacks.[58] Johnson was visited by Charles Sumner who petitioned for suffrage for the freed slaves. The Northern Radicals had mixed motives in desiring the vote for freedmen. Some saw it as a fundamental freedom found in the Declaration of Independence. Others saw it as just punishment for Southern whites who rebelled. Many saw the potential black vote as a benefit to the Republican Party. There was some hypocrisy in their insistence for, at the time, only six states in the North allowed blacks to vote.

A number of state delegations called upon the new president in the early days of his administration. In his speeches to these various bodies is seen a softening of Johnson's earlier hard-line rhetoric that appeared just following the assassination. On April 18, he met with the Illinois Delegation. After blasting treason, he talked of applying mercy. With the Massachusetts Delegation, he espoused rigid justice to the guilty traitor and compassion and mercy to the misguided.[59] In the interview with the Pennsylvania Delegation on May 3, he called for uniting mercy with justice.[60] With the Ohio Delegation, he espoused mercy.[61]

In a rambling speech before the Indiana Delegation, Johnson presented his harshest stance against treason.

> The time has arrived when the American people should understand what crime is, and that it should be punished, and its penalties enforced and inflicted.... Treason must be made odious, that traitors must be punished and impoverished.[62]

---

[58]Upon hearing this, the Confederate General appealed to Grant for help. Grant interceded for Lee and Johnson was in support. Lee would not be tried.
[59]Graf *et al.*, Vol. VII., p. lx.
[60]Graf *et al.*, Vol. VIII., p. 22.
[61]Graf *et al.*, Vol. VII., p. 610.
[62]Graf *et al.*, Vol. VII., pp. 611-612.

He quoted Robert Toombs, "When traitors become numerous enough, treason becomes respectable."[63] Johnson's harsh rhetoric was softened with the extension of mercy for those who had been coerced and misled. Representative George W. Julian of Indiana reported that while the President's support of the Radical agenda was favorable, he was appalled at Johnson's bad grammar, poor pronunciation, and incoherent thought. The other members of the Indiana Delegation shared his mortification.[64]

When some of Johnson's friends from Tennessee went to Washington to seek clarification on his ideas for the restoration of the South, they were ushered in to see the President who was in the bathroom shaving. He told them to relax. "Boys... I am not going to hang anybody."[65]

Petroleum V. Nasby, writing on "Androo" Johnson's ascension to the position of Chief Executive, explained,

> He wuz by nachur and education, a Dimokrat, but he hed bin with the Ablishnists jist long enough to learn that they wuz a higher grade uv bein's. Ther wuz two conflictin' forces pullin' at him – the desire acquired, to be a respectable man, and the disposition natural, to be a Dimokrat.... His fust step wuz his thrownin' off the uncomfortable robe uv Moses. The garment had never fitted him no more than a soldier's overcote wood an organ grinder's monkey. He quit the Moses biznis, all to wunst, and the world saw this difference between him and the eminent Jew uv that name. Moses took his Hebrews clean through the Red Sea. Androo took his'n thro', but j'st ez they wuz climbin' up the bank, turned and shoved em back agin.[66]

Most of Johnson's family moved into the White House in June.[67] Robert delayed in Tennessee using the excuse that he needed to tend to his father's papers, but he tarried because of his excessive drinking.[68]

Because Johnson's wife Eliza was now an invalid, his daughter, Mrs. Martha Patterson, became the mistress of the White House. Martha was the wife of Senator David T. Patterson and a very unpretentious woman. She made the butter for the residence and could frequently be found working at her sewing machine. "We are plain people from Tennessee, temporarily in high place, and you must not expect too much of us in a social way," she said.[69]

---

[63]Graf et al., Vol. VII., p. 613.
[64]Julian, p. 337.
[65]Milton, p. 183.
[66]Nasby, Andy's Trip to the West, Together With a Life of Its Hero, pp. 25-26.
[67]Trefousse, p. 209.
[68]Graf et al., Vol. VIII., p. 386.
[69]Milton, p. 231.

It was very rare for Eliza Johnson to be seen in public. But claiming chronic debilitation might have been a convenient excuse for being a recluse. Oliver Temple, who lived near the Johnsons in Greeneville, Tennessee for 28 years, had no recollection of ever seeing her in the village.[70]

THE LINCOLN CONSPIRATORS

John Wilkes Booth, Lincoln's assassin, was killed on April 26 and eight conspirators faced a military tribunal for Lincoln's murder in early May. It was Stanton's desire that all be tried and executed before Lincoln's body was placed in the ground.[71] While that proved to be overly ambitious, the trial did move along very quickly.

There were fears that Johnson too would be assassinated. On the very day of Booth's death, word came that two men in St. Louis where overheard plotting against the President. One said the presidency would soon be vacated by the knife. "It also appears they are afraid if Booth is caught he will expose the whole thing. thare [sic] has been parties sent to Washington to arrange things thare [sic] [.]"[72]

SLAVERY

Johnson's opinion on slavery, at least his public pronouncements, changed over the course of the war. Initially he was pro-slavery and adamant that the only way for the institution to survive was with a strong Union. In time he moderated his views. By February of 1863, he affirmed that given a choice between owning slaves and having a healthy Union, he would take the Union.

> I am for the Government of my fathers with negroes. I am for it without negroes. Before I would see this Government destroyed I would see every negro back in Africa, disintegrated and blotted out of space.[73]

By September of 1863, Johnson's condemnation of slavery was drawing headlines in northern papers such as the *New York Times* and *Chicago Tribune*.[74]

---

[70]Temple, p. 360.
[71]Welles, *Diary of Gideon Welles,* Vol. II., p. 303.
[72]Graf *et al.*, Vol. VII., p. 644.
[73]Graf *et al.*, Vol. VI., p. 156.
[74]Graf *et al.*, Vol. VI., p. liv.

In his Heart-of-the-masses speech in Nashville on August 26, he said, "Slavery was a cancer on our society and the scalpel of the statesman should be used not simply to pare away the exterior... but to remove it altogether."[75] He said slavery was a curse that should be wiped out without delay. The Nashville speech likely gave Johnson great credibility with Northerners. His speaking tour through the northern states must have impressed him with the political advantages of changing his views.

In a speech delivered in January of 1864, Johnson responded to an argument that slaves were not suited for freedom because all they had ever known was servitude and therefore, their introduction into freedom must be gradual. Thus the argument went, they should remain as slaves for the present. Johnson exposed the faulty logic of the conundrum.

> It is said the negroes are not qualified to be free; because they have been slaves so long they are unfitted to be freem[e]n, and shall not be permitted to enjoy the privileges of freemen; but by way of making them competent, it is proposed to keep them in slavery nineteen or twenty years longer. In the first place it would not do to have them free, because they have been slaves, and in the second place they should be kept in slavery to qualify them for freemen.[76]

By April of 1864, Johnson sounded like a northern abolitionist. In two speeches in Knoxville he advocated the destruction of slavery for the sake of the white man.[77] He said emancipation did more to free the white man than the black. By the end of the war, Johnson was an advocate for the complete and immediate emancipation of the slaves. "What right have I, what right have you, to hold a fellow-man in bondage?" he asked.[78] "You say the Negro won't work if the stimulus of the lash and of force is removed. How do you know that? Have you tried the stimulus of wages and of kind treatment?"[79]

By war's end, the question was what to do with the freedmen. Johnson suggested the freed slave would be best off in Mexico or some other locale suited to his nature.[80] Johnson drew the line when it came to enfranchising blacks to positions of power in the government. Freedom was not the same thing as entitlement to vote or hold office. For Johnson, it was still a white man's world.

---

[75]Graf *et al.*, Vol. VI., p. 344.
[76]Graf *et al.*, Vol. VI., p. 581.
[77]Graf *et al.*, Vol. VI., p. 671.
[78]Graf *et al.*, Vol. VI., p. 672.
[79]Graf *et al.*, Vol. VI., p. 675.
[80]Graf *et al.*, Vol. VI., p. 582.

At the beginning of the war, Johnson said slavery was only an excuse for separation. By April of 1864, he was saying that slavery had caused the war.[81] He went from being a supporter of the institution to calling it a cancer that needed to be eradicated. Regardless of changes in his official position on the slavery issue, his relationship with black individuals remained consistently paternalistic. He could be generous as when he responded to a request from his former slave, Samuel, who asked him to sell a lot for a black school. Johnson conveyed the property without charge.[82] But, blacks would always remain an inferior race in his eyes.

[81]Graf et al., Vol. VI., p. 671.
[82]Graf et al., Vol. XII., pp. 183 & 237.

Chapter 7

PRESIDENTIAL RESTORATION

Although Johnson would not officially declare the War's end until April 2, 1866, the War of the Rebellion was in effect over with Joseph Johnston's surrender to William Sherman on April 21, 1865.[1] People both north and south eagerly anticipated the country's return to normalcy. But achieving normalcy would not be an easy task. While disorder is expected following any great tumult like war, a civil conflict is all the more difficult with lingering bitterness and resentment on both sides. In these early months following the surrender, the country was in great peril. The very principles upon which the Democracy was founded were threatened and the potential of usurpation was at the highest it had ever been since the founding of the Union.

Johnson set out to bring the Southern states back into the Union on his own. Although encouraged to call a special session of Congress, he refused. Instead he moved expeditiously to complete the restoration process by the time Congress convened in December of 1865.[2] His plan was to bring the former Confederate states back into the Union as painlessly as possibly and to do so while Congress was in recess.

Lincoln had formed his ten percent plan in December of 1863. When ten percent of the population of a former Confederate state had accepted his amnesty program and his policies on slavery, a government could be formed. Lincoln's amnesty offer was extended to all except Confederate military of high rank, civilian officials serving in the Confederate government, and those who had left Congress or the military in support of the Rebellion. In July of 1864, Congress responded to President Lincoln's leniency with the Wade-Davis bill, legislation that sought to re-establish the power of Congress and place a military governor

---

[1]Graf *et al.*, Vol. X., p. 352. Texas would not surrender until August 20, 1866.
[2]Trefousse, p. 216.

over each Confederate state. Under these constraints, only when the majority of white males in a state took the oath, could a constitutional convention be called. Wade-Davis set the expectation that the Confederate debt would be repudiated and slavery would be abolished.

Lincoln let the bill die with a pocket veto and went on with his own policy. By the time of his death, Virginia, Arkansas, Tennessee, and Louisiana had established governments.[3]

In his last Cabinet meeting, Lincoln urged a plan of restoration that Johnson would continue. Lincoln was pleased that the war was ending just as Congress was going out of session. Secretary of the Navy Gideon Welles recalled, "There were none of the disturbing elements of that body to hinder and embarrass us. If we were wise and discreet, we should reanimate the States and get their governments in successful operation, with order prevailing and the Union reëstablished, before Congress came together in December."[4]

After the surrender, most Southern leaders anticipated retribution and punishment. They were prepared for the worst and were ready to comply with nearly any terms, at least at first. While they had been disposed to reconciliation in the spring of 1865, by the fall of that year they had becoming obstinate. Attitudes changed when it was learned that Johnson was ready to give them concessions for which they had not even dared to ask.[5] When they realized that Johnson was not going to inflict punishment on them, they lost their willingness to acquiesce.[6] Leniency brought contempt. J.T. Trowbridge, writing in 1866, talked of the feeling in the South at this time.

> They expected no mercy from the government, for they deserved none. They were prepared to submit to everything, even to negro suffrage; for they supposed nothing less would be required of them. But the more lenient the government, the more arrogant they become.[7]

[3]Patrick W. Riddleberger, *1866 The Critical Year Revisited*, (Lanham, MD: University Press of America, 1984), p. 4.
[4]Welles, *Galaxy*, p. 526.
[5]Whitelaw Reid, *After the War: A tour of the Southern States, 1865-1866*, (New York: Harper & Row, 1965), p. 219.
[6]Trefousse, p. 232. Orville Browning, Johnson's Secretary of the Interior, met Robert E. Lee at a social gathering in September of 1868. Lee told him that immediately following the surrender, Southerners were ready to support the Union as before, but he added, "They were in a much better temper of mind for the accomplishment of this result at the close of the war than they were now" (Browning, Vol. II., p. 217).
[7]J.T. Trowbridge, *The South: A Tour of Its Battle-fields and Ruined Cities, A Journey Through the Desolated States, and Talks With the People,* (Hartford, CT: L. Stebbins, 1866), p. 189.

A Southerner from Huntsville, Alabama wrote,

> As a southern man I am truly sorry to have it to Confess to you, that there is a great want of sincerity on the part of our people towards the Government.... Make them do right before they get back into the Union.[8]

Johnson was not wise enough to sense the exigency of corrective measures for the South nor the necessity of dispensing justice to appease the North. Some evidence of contrition on the part of the conquered would have gone a long way in appeasing Northerners and preventing a worse fate for the South. Had Johnson been smart enough to measure out an appropriate means of punishment, Northerners might have been mollified and the tribulations of the Reconstruction that followed might have been avoided. Johnson had but a fleeting time to act -- sadly he missed the opportunity.[9] Instead his magnanimity brought contempt.

Johnson saw reconstruction, or restoration as he put it, as a presidential prerogative. His goal was to see that the former Confederate states re-established their governments as soon as possible. According to Johnson, these states had not gone out of the Union, only experienced temporary suspension of their governments.[10] Johnson's restoration would begin on May 29, 1865, with the creation of an amnesty program and the establishment of the first of the provisional state governments.

AMNESTY

The road to recovery began with the issuance of amnesty to many of those who fought for the Confederacy. Lincoln had held out this carrot on December 8, 1863 and again on March 26 the following year.[11] On May 29, 1865, Johnson offered his version, the first of his four amnesty programs. Pardons would be granted to those who took the pledge that they would defend the Constitution of the United States and abide by all laws regarding emancipation.[12] The oath could be administered by any qualified civil official or commissioned military officer.[13]

---

[8]Graf *et al.*, Vol. IX., p. 386.
[9]Trefousse, pp. 215 & 233.
[10]Graf *et al.*, Vol. VIII., p. 154.
[11]Graf *et al.*, Vol. VIII., p. 128.
[12]Graf *et al.*, Vol. VIII., p. 129.
[13]Graf *et al.*, Vol. VIII., p. 130.

There were exemptions to Johnson's first amnesty plan. These included agents of the Confederate government, members of the judiciary who supported the Southern Cause, officers in the Confederacy with the rank of colonel in the army and lieutenant in the navy, those who left Congress to join the Rebellion, those military officers who resigned their federal commissions to avoid resisting the Rebellion, those who mistreated Union prisoners of war, absentees who aided the Rebellion, members of the Confederacy who were educated at West Point or the Naval Academy, governors of the Confederate States, those who left their homes under the protection of the United States and passed through federal lines into the Confederacy to aid the Rebellion, those who engaged in the destruction of commerce in support of the Confederacy, Confederate prisoners of war, those persons voluntarily participating in the Rebellion with property estimated at $20,000 or more, and those who had previously taken Lincoln's oath and violated it.[14] Johnson had always believed that affluent Southerners had forced the poor into the fight, hence, the proscription against those with property.

Those not meeting the conditions for amnesty could apply directly to the President for a pardon. Consequently, Johnson received an enormous number of visitors daily; people seeking an audience in hopes of being granted a remission or making a claim. Over 50 percent of all the pardons granted in Alabama, North Carolina, and Virginia alone were processed in the months of June, July, and August of 1865.[15] The practice, which was to admit all who came in the order of arrival, quickly became unmanageable.[16] The anterooms and hallways of the White House were filled with petitioners seeking release.[17] Johnson likely enjoyed having aristocratic Southerners grovel for absolution. The process afforded him the opportunity to prod his former foes. At one point Johnson addressed the crowd of pardon seekers sardonically.

> It was a little singular that most of the non-combatants who had come here from the South for pardon assert that they did nothing, were opposed to the rebellion at the beginning, only acquiesced, and thought the rebel government ought to have surrendered earlier and stopped bloodshed; yet not one of them took advantage of the amnesty proclamation offered by Mr. LINCOLN, an act which would have shown sincerity on their part.[18]

---

[14]Graf *et al.*, Vol. VIII., pp. 129-130.
[15]Graf *et al.*, Vol. VIII., p. xxix.
[16]Graf *et al.*, Vol. XV., p. 494.
[17]Welles, *Diary of Gideon Welles,* Vol. II., p. 342.
[18]Graf *et al.*, Vol. VIII., p. 634.

Many prominent Confederates applied for pardons, including George E. Pickett,[19] Robert E. Lee,[20] Joseph E. Johnston,[21] and Nathan Bedford Forrest who said in his application letter that having been "fairly whipped," he was now seeking amnesty.[22] Lucy Holcombe Pickens, wife of Francis W. Pickens former governor of South Carolina, sought a pardon for her husband as did the wife of General James Longstreet.[23] Andrew Jackson, III, offspring of the adopted son of President Andrew Jackson, applied for a Presidential pardon. Because President Jackson was Johnson's political hero, it was not surprising the pardon was granted on the day the request was received.[24]

Pardons were critical to owning property, as Confederate General Braxton Bragg discovered when his plantation was seized and sold at auction by the federal government in January of 1866. He sued to recover his property after he had been pardoned on July 4, 1868, but his appeal was denied for he had not been pardoned when the land was confiscated.[25]

How did Southerners view Johnson's amnesty plan? Some saw it as merely a debasing hoop through which they had to jump.

> Who considers it binding? No one. Not one person whom I have heard speak of it but laughs at and repudiates every obligation it imposes. It binds one no more than a promise at the pistols point to a highwayman![26]

Johnson was very liberal in offering amnesty. He wanted to put the war behind him quickly with little thought to healing the wounds. Some were not ready to forgive and forget that quickly. Northerners who lost loved ones in the war wanted to see justice – not necessarily revenge but justice, and they did not find it in Johnson's amnesty program.[27]

A former Union soldier expressed the reason for punishing traitors,

> God forbid that half a million of our bravest and best men should be sent to untimely graves by a set of unhallowed traitors and that these despicable scoundrels should go unwhipped [sic] of justice…. I stood eight hours under fire

---

[19]Graf *et al.*, Vol. VIII., pp. 164-165.
[20]While Lee never received a personal pardon from the President he was pardoned under Johnson's later Christmas Day amnesty proclamation of 1868 (Graf *et al.*, Vol. VIII., pp. 232 & 234).
[21]Graf *et al.*, Vol. VIII., p. 335.
[22]Graf *et al.*, Vol. VIII., p. 331.
[23]Graf *et al.*, Vol. IX., pp. 21-22 & 302.
[24]Graf *et al.*, Vol. IX., p. 54.
[25]Graf *et al.*, Vol. IX., p. 207.
[26]Crabtree, p. 716.
[27]Trefousse, p. 228.

at Antietam and saw thousands of our brave men shot down. Therefore talk not to me of mercy or sympathy for Lee any more than for Jeff Davis.... I say let [Lee] hang and die.[28]

Various callers would continue into the summer to pay visits to the new president to probe him on his views. On the evening of June 11, Johnson spoke with a number of Conservatives who came by the White House. He told them his desire was to restore all of the states to the Union and to bring success to the country before he would leave office. Fifty Southerners from various states called upon the President to express their cooperation. He responded with a brief address in which he said,

> I am of the Southern people, and I love them and will do all in my power to restore them to that state of happiness and prosperity which they enjoyed before the madness of misguided men in whom they had reposed their confidence led them astray to their own undoing.[29]

The report of this meeting found its way into several newspapers in September of 1865.[30] An immediate reaction came from Joseph Medill, owner and editor of the *Chicago Tribune*, who gave Johnson some advice.

> You may affect to despise the Radicals: but their votes made you President.... They Control 20 states and both branches of Congress. Four fifths of the soldiers sympathise [sic] with them. Can you afford to quarrel with these two million voters? ... Don't show so much eagerness to rush into the embrace of the "$20,000 rebels." They will suck you like an orange and when done with you throw the peel away.[31]

PARDON BROKERAGE

A pardon-brokerage business soon developed in Washington with Mrs. Lucy Cobb and Mrs. Ella Washington as the chief operators. Lafayette C. Baker, special agent in the War Department, would be the one to expose the scandal.[32]

[28]Graf *et al.*, Vol. VII., p. 586.
[29]Graf *et al.*, Vol. IX., p. 66.
[30]*New York Herald*, September 12, 1865, no vol., #10,603.
[31]Graf *et al.*, Vol. IX., p. 82.
[32]Graf *et al.*, Vol. IX., p. 371.

When it was discovered that Isaac Surratt, son of Lincoln-conspirator Mary Surratt, was in Baltimore, General Lafayette C. Baker placed detectives outside of the White House to protect the President. While Surratt was never spotted at the President's residence, one of the guards reported that there were some strange things going on in the Executive Mansion. The agent got to know the staff quite well, and discovered a very conspicuous pardon brokerage business in operation. One of the key brokers was Mrs. Lucy Cobb who was at the White House all hours of the day and night, and boasted to the detective that she could obtain a pardon from the President at any time. When asked how she did it, Cobb said she had an understanding with Johnson who dared not refuse her. Rumors were circulating that Mrs. Cobb was having an affair with the President.[33]

A detective reported on the unladylike character of Mrs. Cobb. One day while she was sitting in the East Room of the White House, the detective remarked that she had a pretty foot. She responded, "You have never seen my legs," and immediately raised her skirt well above her knees. Cobb bragged that she could have any employee on the White House staff dismissed if she liked.[34] On another occasion when Baker's men stopped her from entering the front entrance of the White House she went around back through the kitchen and up to the President's private quarters.[35]

Baker set up a sting operation by having a former provost marshal general pose as a Rebel officer with a fictitious application for a pardon. The provost marshal was introduced to Cobb, who promised for $300 to deliver a full, unconditional pardon. The normal process took two to five weeks. Cobb promised a pardon within 12 hours. She even provided a written contract.[36]

When Cobb was detained by Baker, she threatened, "Arresting me will cost you your commission."[37] She was right. It did. When Baker took his evidence on Cobb to the President, he became furious with Baker for his probe. He became very indignant and asked Baker what business it was of his to interfere in this matter. Later, grand jury indictments were made against Baker who lost his commission over the ordeal.[38]

Ella B. Washington, the wife of a Confederate Colonel Lewis Washington, was a major pardon broker whom it was alleged did ten times the business that

---

[33]Trefousse, p. 228.
[34]La Fayette C. Baker, *History of the United States Secret Se*rvice, (Philadelphia: L.C. Baker, 1867), p. 602.
[35]Baker, p. 603.
[36]Baker, pp. 593-594.
[37]Baker, p. 596 marked 696 in error.
[38]Baker, p. 604.

Cobb did.[39] She too had access to the White House and enjoyed the friendship of the President.[40] Baker commented that she was, "a woman of more than ordinary attractions, her influence at the Departments had become very great."[41] Mrs. Washington threw lavish parties at her boarding house in Georgetown of which Secretary of the Treasury Hugh McCulloch and Orville Browning, then secretary to the President, were among the dignitaries in attendance. Upon occasion, McCulloch, while supposedly on governmental business in New York, went to Mrs. Washington's country house near Harper's Ferry instead.[42] Another sting operation was attempted to snare Ella Washington, but this ruse failed.

PROVISIONAL GOVERNMENTS

Provisional governors were appointed and state conventions were called in North Carolina, South Carolina, Florida, Mississippi, Georgia, and Alabama. Texas delayed holding its convention until early 1866. On May 29, North Carolina established a provisional government. William W. Holden was made governor. That summer, Johnson appointed William L. Sharkey as governor of Mississippi, James Johnson governor to Georgia, Andrew J. Hamilton to Texas, Lewis E. Parsons to Alabama, Benjamin F. Perry to South Carolina, and William Marvin to Florida.[43]

Johnson directed his governors as to what he expected. The state constitutional conventions had to repeal secession, repudiate all debts incurred by the former Confederacy, and do away with slavery by ratifying the Thirteenth Amendment which freed slaves in all the states, not just those covered by the Emancipation Proclamation.[44] But Johnson stopped short of demanding black suffrage. In doing so he missed an element that was very important to Radical Republicans.[45]

In the early months of his presidency, Johnson was unfettered and at liberty to construct his own approach to restoration without interference. Congress was out

---

[39]Lewis Washington had been taken hostage by John Brown during his raid at Harpers Ferry (*The Confederacy: Selections from the Four-volume Macmillan Encyclopedia of the Confederacy* (New York: Macmillan Library Reference USA, 1998), p. 265).

[40]Graf *et al.*, Vol. VIII., p. 547.

[41]Baker, p. 606.

[42]Baker, pp. 606-607.

[43]Graf *et al.*, Vol. IX., Appendix III.

[44]The Thirteenth Amendment was proposed to state legislatures on January 31, 1865, and ratified on December 6, 1865.

[45]Graf *et al.*, Vol. VIII., p. xxx.

of session and he was free to exercise executive privilege in bringing the Southern states back into the Union.

The Mississippi Constitutional Convention met in August of 1865 with the President suggesting to Governor Sharkey that voting rights be extended to blacks who could read the United States Constitution, write their names, owned real estate valued at least $250, and paid taxes on that property. The move would have involved so few ex-slaves as to make virtually no difference in election outcomes, but the Mississippi delegates would not comply. Such an act would have likely placated many Radicals. There were other irritants as well. The Convention elected Benjamin G. Humphrey, a former Confederate brigadier, as governor and delayed ratification of the Thirteenth Amendment prohibiting slavery.[46]

The Alabama Convention met in September and repudiated its war debt, abolished slavery, and passed an ordinance legalizing marriages between blacks.[47] That same month, South Carolina revoked its secession ordinance and asked the President to exonerate Jefferson Davis. The Florida Convention met in October abolishing slavery, voiding the Confederate debt, and renouncing secessionism.

During the North Carolina Constitutional Convention in October, there was resistance to expunging the Confederate debt incurred by the war.[48] Johnson contacted Governor Holden to insist that the entire Confederate debt be repudiated. This communication provided the impetuous needed to get the delegates to act.[49] Holden responded two days later that the Convention had disclaimed every dollar of Confederate debt.[50]

When the Georgia Convention assembled in October, the state's old secession ordinance was repealed and slavery abolished in short order. The obstacles for Georgia were the war debt and what was to happen to Jefferson Davis. The President wrote to James Johnson stressing that Georgia should repudiate the Confederate debt without hesitation.[51] The Convention nullified the debt.

By the time Congress came back into session, the Carolinas, Georgia, Alabama, Mississippi, and Florida had all amended their constitutions, abolished slavery, rescinded secessionism, and held elections for congressmen and senators who were ready to take their seats in Washington. These states were back in the fold with few demands placed upon them or any real punishment imposed.[52]

---

[46]Trefousse, pp. 223-224.
[47]Graf *et al.*, Vol. IX., p. 147.
[48]Milton, p. 254.
[49]Graf *et al.*, Vol. IX., pp. 255-256.
[50]Graf *et al.*, Vol. IX., p. 260.
[51]Graf *et al.*, Vol. IX., p. 299.
[52]Trefousse, p. 219.

RACIAL CONFLICTS

Given the history of enslavement in the United States, only the most naive of persons would expect racial harmony at emancipation. Problems between the races were severe and endemic throughout the South.

In the late summer of 1865 and well into the spring of 1866, whites in the South were fearful of a black uprising. A Northerner living in Florida wrote to the President, "There is really a danger of an insurrection that would surprise you if you were aware of it."[53]

In early September of 1865, a distraught Andrew Johnson wrote to General George H. Thomas concerning a rumor coming out of Greeneville that blacks had taken over his house and turned it into a brothel. "It was bad enough to be taken by traitors and converted into a rebel hospital, but a negro whore house is infinitely worse."[54] Thomas put the rumor to rest by assuring the President that his house was occupied by a white family, placed there by his son-in-law David Patterson.[55]

A few days later, Johnson again wrote to General George Thomas fearing that an uprising was imminent. Concerned that problems might arise within the military, Johnson suggested discharging a number of black soldiers.[56] Thomas tried to calm the President's fears.

> I believe in the majority of cases of collision between whites and negro Soldiers that the white man has attempted to bully the negro, for it is exceedingly repugnant to the Southerners to have negro Soldiers in their midst.[57]

If the President of the United States was jumping to conclusions it can be expected that citizens throughout the country were on edge, grasping onto rumor and expecting the worst.

There were numerous clashes between whites and blacks throughout the South. In Georgia a black soldier was shot after threatening to use his bayonet on a white citizen, and a white was shot at while walking peaceably along the street. A group of white men fired on unarmed black men, women, and children.[58] A

---

[53]Graf *et al.*, Vol. IX., p. 305.
[54]Graf *et al.*, Vol. IX., p. 26.
[55]Graf *et al.*, Vol. IX., p. 27.
[56]Graf *et al.*, Vol. IX., p. 48.
[57]Graf *et al.*, Vol. IX., p. 57.
[58]Graf *et al.*, Vol. IX., pp. 344-345.

party of black soldiers accompanied by black civilians invaded a private residence and three or four of the perpetrators were killed.[59]

A private from Indiana reported ongoing atrocities against blacks in Georgia where ex-slaves were being killed by their former masters. "The masters say they had rather kill them than see them free."[60] He encountered a black woman looking for her 14-year old daughter who had run off from her master because of ill-treatment. The mother had been sent to bring the daughter home with the warning that if she did not find the child by night fall, she would receive 100 lashes across her back. The soldier assessed, "I have no doubt [she] rec'd her promised 100 lashes for though I esteem the rebel portion of this county professional liars I think they keep all such promises."[61]

Those living in some country parishes in Louisiana were in fear of their personal safety because of armed blacks. Robberies were daily events and murders commonplace.[62] Blacks in Louisville, Kentucky complained that city guards carried bull whips to beat them on the streets after dark.[63] In Alabama blacks were threatening whites with annihilation.[64] From Oxford, Mississippi, came accusations that black troops on the streets would not yield to ladies. A black delegation from Richmond complained that authorities in their town would not let them walk the streets to pursue their business or go to church without a pass, and even with a pass there was no protection against arrest, violence, and abuse.[65]

In North Carolina there were daily conflicts with the black military.

> Ladies have been violently elbowed and shoved off the sidewalk, by the guard while officers looked on with approving smiles commending the gallant act. The soldiers armed with Bowie knives and revolvers thereby intimidating the defenceless [sic] citizens have committed robberies in open daylight and fired on the Police.[66]

There were remote areas in Texas where slaves were still being bought and sold. While some former slave owners were empathetic with the plight of the

---

[59]Graf *et al.*, Vol. IX., p. 557.
[60]Graf *et al.*, Vol. VIII., p. 148.
[61]Graf *et al.*, Vol. VIII., p. 149.
[62]Graf *et al.*, Vol. VIII., p. 503.
[63]Graf *et al.*, Vol. VIII., p. 204.
[64]Graf *et al.*, Vol. IX., p. 89.
[65]Graf *et al.*, Vol. VIII., p. 211.
[66]Graf *et al.*, Vol. VIII., p. 486.

blacks, others were vengeful against them because they could not revenge themselves against the federal government.[67]

Alarming reports from Tennessee told of anarchy, murder, and rape.[68] In Knoxville black soldiers forced white residents off the sidewalks at the point of the bayonet and arrested the Chief of Police.[69] Elsewhere in Eastern Tennessee black troops were shooting white citizens and discharged white soldiers were running off blacks.[70]

While most of the allegations held merit, some were unfounded. A Nashville resident claimed black soldiers entered her house, threatened her family, and shot her dog. Johnson had General Fisk look into the matter immediately. Fisk investigated to find that no black soldier had entered the house. No one had been threatened. A dog was shot only when it was set to attack a soldier.[71]

Given the insurmountable problems facing the nation at this time it is difficult to imagine how any president could have managed. Had Lincoln not been assassinated he too would have faced these huge difficulties. But with few exceptions, Johnson turned a deaf ear to most of these troubles.

ECONOMIC CONFLICTS

One of the major economic problems facing the South following the Civil War was the decline in the black workforce. Many blacks refused to return to life on the plantation. Many of the freedmen in Mississippi had left the state. Those who remained congregated in the towns refusing to work the fields.[72]

> We have about 1200 Negros [sic] in this Camp and not one in fifty will try to do any thing for themselves or when they get a home they will not stay but come back to Camp in two or three days to frolick [sic] and play.[73]

Accusations were made that officials at the Freedmen's Bureau had planted the idea that after the first of the year blacks would be given land owned by whites.[74] Consequently, many blacks sat by idly waiting for their 40 acres and a

---

[67]Graf *et al.*, Vol. IX., p. 263.
[68]Graf *et al.*, Vol. IX., p. 337.
[69]Graf *et al.*, Vol. IX., p. 418.
[70]Graf *et al.*, Vol. VIII., p. 686 & Vol. IX., p. 11.
[71]Graf *et al.*, Vol. IX., pp. 148 & 176.
[72]Graf *et al.*, Vol. IX., pp. 357 & 358.
[73]Graf *et al.*, Vol. VIII., p. 597.
[74]Graf *et al.*, Vol. VIII., p. 636 & Vol. IX., pp. 263 & 599.

mule. Many Southern whites thought something had to be done to compel blacks to return to the fields.

Soon Black Codes, designed to re-establish social and economic order, were enacted in the former Confederate states.[75] Their effect was to force former slaves to remain in subordinate roles. Mississippi passed a law requiring all blacks under the age of 18 to be apprenticed to a white person, preferably their former masters. The apprentice could be whipped and if he or she ran away could be put in jail upon capture. Vagrant blacks could be incarcerated and if unable to pay the fine, could be hired out to work off their fine. If a freedman stopped work he was in violation of his contract and could be auctioned off. If blacks were working for a white employer and left before the contracted period they would lose all wages earned.[76] If a black man failed to provide for his children he would be placed with employers. Blacks could not keep guns or bowie knives – the only exception was for those in the military. Blacks could not ride in first-class accommodations on trains unless accompanying their employers.[77] South Carolina also enforced apprenticeships. With the exception of farming, no black could engage in a trade as an artisan or shopkeeper without a license. Each would-be merchant had to pay $100 a year. Even a mechanic had to pay $10 a year.[78]

Some Northern states had vagrancy laws that were very similar to the Black Codes in the South. In Illinois, for instance, a man found loitering could be obligated to work for four months – his services going to the highest bidder.[79]

DISSATISFACTION AMONG CABINET MEMBERS

Reorganizing the Presidential Cabinet would have been expected with any new administration, but Johnson was hesitant to make changes and persevered with the Cabinet Lincoln had left him. This was an opportunity the Tennessee Tailor should have never allowed to slip through his fingers.

As early as March of 1865, Secretary of the Navy Gideon Welles shared his concerns with Johnson that Post Master General William Dennison, Secretary of Interior James Harlan, Attorney General James Speed, and Secretary of War Edwin M. Stanton seemed to advise strategies which played into the hands of the

---

[75]Milton, p. 280.
[76]Milton, pp. 281-282.
[77]Trefousse, p. 230.
[78]Milton, p. 283.
[79]Beale, p. 194.

radical element in Congress.[80] Some of Johnson's friends also saw certain Cabinet members as obstacles to Johnson's success and they suggested that Seward and Stanton be removed.[81] Senator Doolittle of Wisconsin encouraged Welles to persuade the President to act in all haste to change the membership of his Cabinet. Johnson did not wish to dismiss Seward and he was unable to decide on what action to take with the others.[82]

THE EXECUTION OF FOUR LINCOLN CONSPIRATORS

Mrs. Mary Surratt was charged with being one of the conspirators in the Lincoln assassination. After the first day of deliberations, five of the nine officers were unwilling to have Mrs. Surratt sent to the gallows. A two-thirds vote was required for the Commission to find someone guilty. Stanton was displeased with their verdict and suggested that the court formerly condemn her but then ask the President for leniency to put off her sentence. The argument was proposed that the possibility of her being hanged would force her son John Surratt from hiding. Stanton got his six-to-three vote and Mrs. Surratt was sentenced to death. Immediately the judges petitioned the President for leniency. Judge Joseph Holt was to lay the case and appeal before Johnson on July 5.

Verdicts on the eight Lincoln assassin conspirators were handed down on July 5, 1865. Judge Holt conferred with the President for about three hours after which Johnson told his assistant that a decision had been made and he did not want to hear any appeals. When further appeals came to the White House they were repulsed.[83] Surratt's daughter made a personal visit to the presidential mansion where she collapsed on the steps in the presence of the President's daughter. Secretary of the Treasury Hugh McCulloch also witnessed this sad event. According to the Secretary, Johnson also dismissed the writ of *habeas corpus* issued on Mrs. Surratt's behalf the morning of her execution.[84]

How could the President have been so callous as not to even entertain an appeal? What was the compelling rush to execution? A few days more to consider

---

[80]Milton, p. 320. Beale, pp. 100-101.
[81]Milton, p. 336.
[82]Every time there was trouble, Seward would leave town (Welles, *Diary of Gideon Welles,* Vol. II., pp. 392 & 575).
[83]Graf *et al.*, Vol. VIII., pp. 357 & 362.
[84]Milton, p. 210 & McCulloch, pp. 225-226.

appeals would not have cheated the hangman for long. Justice indeed was strained and compassion numbed at the tumult of this national tragedy.[85]

On July 7, Mrs. Surratt met her end at the end of a rope along with three others.[86] Both accolades and death threats followed the executions.[87] A great deal of controversy would later surface for Johnson over the Surratt affair. The four remaining conspirators were to be confined to hard labor in an Albany, New York prison, but within ten days Stanton sent them to an island in the Dry Tortugas, 70 miles west of Key West, to remove them far from any meddling judge with a writ of *habeas corpus*.[88]

---

[85]McCulloch, p. 226.

[86]Browning, Vol. II., pp. 37 & 155.

[87]Graf *et al.*, Vol. VIII., pp. 368-369 & 375-376.

[88]Graf *et al.*, Vol. VIII., p. 357. Welles, *Diary of Gideon Welles,* Vol. II., p. 334. At the end of his life, Johnson stated that the execution of Mary Surratt was without justification. He was convinced she did not know the intention of Booth or the others. Johnson said he never saw an appeal on her behalf and only learned later of her daughter's plea, which was suppressed by Stanton (Associated Press, Tennessee State Library and Archives, micro # 1203, Box 1, item #13, p. 5 & McElwee, p. 7).

Chapter 8

CONGRESS BACK IN SESSION AND
ALL HELL 'BOUT TO BREAK LOOSE

Edward Beale, in the preface to his book *The Critical Year,* touched on a pertinent question.

> Why should a Northern people, not normally vindictive, have adopted toward the defeated South a policy which their grandchildren generally condemn as both harsh and unwise? War hatred was explicable; but post-war vindictiveness, following so closely the early magnanimity which the North... shared with its great generals and martyred president, was difficult to understand.[1]

The answer is Andrew Johnson and the dysfunctional relationship he built with Congress. By moving to restore the Southern states on his own, Johnson incurred the wrath of the Radical Republicans in Congress and agitated public opinion in the North as well.

When the 39th Congress came into session on December 4, 1865, many members were ready to cooperate with the Chief Executive, but Johnson was intent on doing things his own way.[2] Initially, moderate elements in Congress tried to work with the President but the relationship soon soured. For the first year of the Johnson Administration, Senator John Sherman of Ohio tried to be cooperative. "A widening breach," he reflected, "is taking place in the Union Party. Not only for my own sake but for the good of the country, I will keep quiet as possible on political questions in the hope to do good by conciliation." He wrote, "Johnson is suspicious of every one, and I fear will drift into his old party relations." Sherman became outraged at Johnson's base demeanor in a

---

[1] Beale, p. vii.
[2] Trefousse, p. 234.

presidential speech given on Washington's birthday and by March of 1866, the Senator was through.[3] From that time forward, he wholeheartedly supported the congressional effort to restore the Southern states.[4] Lyman Trumbull, senator from Illinois, also tried to work with the President. He introducing the Freedmen's Bureau and Civil Rights bills. Early in the process, he approached Johnson with drafts of these two pieces of legislation and expressed a willingness to compromise. He thought he had Johnson's approval, but he did not. Johnson's failure to support the Fourteenth Amendment (granting citizenship to blacks) pushed John A. Bingham, a moderate from Ohio, into the Radical camp. Many newspapers which initially backed Johnson, eventually abandoned him as well.[5]

Among the Radicals patience was short lived. Thaddeus Stevens, Representative from Pennsylvania, opposed Johnson's approach from the beginning. He saw the Southern States as conquered, foreign powers that should be dealt with severely.[6] Back in May of 1865, Stevens, concerned with Johnson's restoration policies, admonished that Congress alone had the power over Reconstruction and the President was usurping the power of the legislative branch. Stevens suggested that Johnson suspend further reconstruction and call a special session of Congress.[7] Other legislators made similar appeals. Senator Benjamin Wade called at the White House complaining that the Executive Branch was improperly appropriating control of the government.[8] Charles Sumner, senator from Massachusetts, visited Johnson in December of 1865 trying to influence him on how to handle black suffrage in the South. Sumner, arrogant and overbearing, threatened to make war on the White House. He left in a huff when Johnson used his hat as a spittoon.[9]

The period from December 1865 to July 1866 was marked by a break between the President and Congress. The schism proved to be critical for the reconstruction effort and extremely damaging to the President personally. The wedge was evident in Johnson's first address to Congress on December 4, 1865. Johnson asked the historian George Bancroft to craft his message. Affirming his authority through the Constitution, Johnson said the power to pardon was under the purview of the President, but the right to confer the vote upon blacks was in

---

[3]Beale, pp. 107-108.
[4]John Sherman, *Recollections of Forty Years in the House, Senate, and Cabinet.* Vol. I., (Chicago: The Werner Company 1895), p. 369.
[5]Beale, pp. 109 & 111.
[6]Milton, p. 263.
[7]Graf *et al.*, Vol. VIII., pp. 80 & 365.
[8]Welles, *Diary of Gideon Welles,* Vol. II., p. 325.
[9]Welles, *Diary of Gideon Welles*, Vol. II., p. 397. Trefousse, p. 237.

the hands of the states.[10] Johnson believed the Southern states had never left the Union, only experienced a temporary displacement at the hands of a hostile force.[11] With the hostile force defeated, the states should regain their status as soon as possible and without repercussion. Johnson did not want to impose a mandate upon any state, North or South, to provide suffrage to blacks. There was nothing in the Constitution to warrant such requirements.[12] This was a states' rights issue. Privately, Johnson's view that blacks were of a lower class and that the government of the United States should remain firmly in the control of whites likely shaped his public position.

SOUTHERNERS FAILED TO BE SEATED IN CONGRESS

When Congress reconvened, the Radical Republicans set out to stop the President's restoration efforts. The first order of business was to prevent the admission of Southern representatives and senators to their respective seats in the legislature. The challenge came on December 4, in the House of Representatives when Edward McPherson, clerk of the House, called the roll. As he read the list of members he bypassed each Southerner. In doing so he disallowed every newly-elected representative from the former Confederate states.

On December 18, Thaddeus Stevens made a speech in the House where he declared, that the Confederate states had to come back in as new states and only Congress, with the concurrence of the President, had the authority to act on the matter. Stevens was in no rush to see the Rebel states readmitted.

As there are no symptoms that the people of these provinces will be prepared to participate in constitutional government for some years, I know of no arrangement so proper for them as territorial governments. There they can learn the principles of freedom and eat the fruit of foul rebellion.[13]

Using biblical imagery, Stevens expressed his readiness to stop the Southern states from entry.

As these fallen rebels cannot at their option reënter the heaven which they have disturbed, the garden of Eden which they have deserted, and flaming swords are

---

[10]Graf *et al.*, Vol. IX., p. 471.
[11]Trefousse, p. 235.
[12]Graf *et al.*, Vol. IX., p. 473.
[13]*Congressional Globe*, 39th Congress, 1st session, p. 74. December 18, 1865.

set at the gates to secure their exclusion…. They ought never to be recognized as capable of acting in the Union, or of being counted as valid States, until the Constitution shall have been so amended as to make it what its framers intended; and so as to secure perpetual ascendency to the party of the Union; and so as to render our republican Government firm and stable forever.[14]

THE FREEDMEN'S BUREAU BILL OF 1866

The Bureau of Refugees, Freedmen and Abandoned Lands had been established back in March of 1865.[15] There was concern that the temporary aid it provided would go on too long making blacks dependent upon the government. Johnson was notified by Joseph Fullerton of the Bureau that as long as the federal government continued to supply assistance to ex-slaves they would never be prepared to take care of themselves.

Habitual dependence will prevent any class of people from making exertions for themselves. By the too generous action of some agents of the bureau in furnishing rations and clothing many able bodied freedmen have been lost from the fields.[16]

Dependency had already become an issue. When the assistant commissioner for the Bureau in North Carolina tried to discontinue aid to able-bodied blacks on Roanoke Island, they immediately became destitute and rations had to be provided. It would be a rough transition for the ex-slaves.

The Freedmen's Bureau Bill of 1866 extended civil rights to blacks. Senator Lyman Trumbull, the author, tried to work with President Johnson on this measure but Johnson proved uncooperative.[17] The Freedmen's Bureau Bill passed the Senate in January of 1866 and the House in February.

The bill was before the President when several black leaders, brought to Washington by Sumner, Stevens, and Wade, went to see him. Frederick Douglass led the delegation representing blacks from over 13 states plus the District of Columbia. Douglass pressed the President in behalf of voting rights for blacks, but Johnson quickly rebuffed the delegation stating his opposition to forcing black suffrage upon individual state governments.

---

[14]*Congressional Globe*, 39th Congress, 1st session, p. 74. December 18, 1865.
[15]Graf *et al.*, Vol. X., p. 127.
[16]Graf *et al.*, Vol. X., p. 66.
[17]Graf *et al.*, Vol. IX., p. xv.

While I say that I am a friend of the colored man, I do not want to adopt a policy that I believe will end in a contest between the races, which if persisted in will result in the extermination of one or the other.[18]

The President went on to say that each community should decide this issue, not Congress. "It is a fundamental tenet in my creed that the will of the people must be obeyed. Is there anything wrong or unfair in that?"[19] These remarks drew a smile from Douglass who respectfully disagreed.

In departing Douglass said, "You enfranchise your enemies and disfranchise your friends."[20] Suffrage for blacks, according to Douglass, would prevent the very conflict that Johnson had feared. The President countered that because the old masters controlled the blacks they would also control how the blacks voted. Douglass disagreed.

After the delegation left, Johnson was purported to have referred to the delegates as "those damned sons of bitches."[21] A reply came from Douglass and the delegation later that day which stated that the views of the President were unsound and prejudicial.

Men are whipped oftenest who are whipped easiest. Peace between the races is not to be secured by degrading one race and exalting another, by giving power to one race and withholding it from another, but by maintaining a state of equal justice between all classes.[22]

On February 19, Johnson vetoed the Freedmen's Bureau Bill which he said was inconsistent with the Constitution. He argued that the bill would establish a military rule over every part of the country where there were freedmen. Trials could take place without a jury of peers or rules of evidence. The bill proposed to remove land from owners without due process. Furthermore, positioning agents in every county would fashion a bureaucracy that would be of considerable expense. The government provided refugees and freedmen aid during the war and immediately thereafter but the Bureau was never intended to operate in perpetuity. The government could not feed and clothe ex-slaves for the rest of their lives. The idea of assistance was to help in the transition to freedom and self-sufficiency.[23]

---

[18]Graf *et al.*, Vol. X., p. 43.
[19]Graf *et al.*, Vol. X., p. 46.
[20]Graf *et al.*, Vol. X., p. 47.
[21]Graf *et al.*, Vol. X., p. 48.
[22]Graf *et al.*, Vol. X., p. 54.
[23]Graf *et al.*, Vol. X., pp. 120-122 & 124. Congress drafted another Freedmen's Bill in July similar to the first one defeated in February. Johnson vetoed it, but this time Congress overrode his veto (Graf *et al.*, Vol. X., pp. 697 & 700).

This was Johnson's first overt attempt to thwart Congressional reconstruction and letters of praise came to the White House affirming that he had taken the appropriate course of action.

> I am unwilling to be taxed for [the black's] support. We have soldiers, their widows and orphans and multitudes of the poor white population among us, who are legitimate subjects of Charity. Congress has presented no Bill for their relief. Nor has any been asked, for like the pure Anglo Saxon, they had rather starve than beg – or have their wants, & poverty paraded before the public.[24]

While the President's veto was sustained, opportunities to foster a healthy relationship with Congress were quickly slipping away. On Washington's birthday, three days after the veto, a crowd of supporters made their way to the White House to serenade the President in support of his stance on the Freedmen's Bill. Secretary McCulloch who had read in the newspapers that such a gathering was planned, suggested that Johnson avoid giving an impromptu speech.[25] Although the President promised to only make a brief acknowledgment, when the jubilant crowd called upon him to address them he got caught up in the moment and did not heed the warning. Restraint was not in his nature when it came to public speaking. Responding to voices from the crowd, the President attacked Radical Republicans and named three of his major opponents in Congress – Thaddeus Stevens, Charles Sumner, and Wendell Phillips.[26]

This address was truly an exercise in poor judgment on Johnson's part. His lack of tact was an embarrassment that hurt him. The response to the speech was unfavorable and viewed as undignified. Secretary Welles expressed his regret that Johnson allowed himself to get involved with answering insolent questions in the manner of a stump speaker.[27]

CIVIL RIGHTS BILL

On March 18, 1866, the Civil Rights Bill was on the President's desk. The legislation declared that all people born in the United States, with the exception of the American Indian, were citizens. Anyone denying a person of his equal rights would be guilty of a misdemeanor punishable by a fine of not more that $1,000,

---

[24]Graf *et al.*, Vol. X., p. 174.
[25]McCulloch, p. 393.
[26]Graf *et al.*, Vol. X., p. 151.
[27]Welles, *Diary of Gideon Welles,* Vol. II., p. 439.

incarceration of a year, or both. On March 26, Johnson asked his Cabinet for an opinion on this bill, which would give citizenship to 4,000,000 blacks who had just been freed from slavery. Johnson objected that the act gave citizenship to the Chinese and bestowed United States citizenship without conferring state citizenship. Although encouraged by many to approve the bill, Johnson vetoed it on March 27.[28] Johnson's opponents and some of his supporters were angered. This time his veto was overridden and the Civil Rights Bill passed. This was the first time a veto had been overturned on a major piece of legislation.[29]

After the Civil Rights Bill was passed, celebrations evolved into riots in many towns. In one city a black, in a state of intoxication, fired his gun. Suspecting that the shot came from a nearby house, a mob stormed the residence killing two or three members of the family.[30]

TRUMAN'S TRIP

Johnson sent several advisors on a tour of the Southern states to observe how restoration was proceeding. The President's aide, Benjamin Truman went on one of the fact-finding trips in April of 1866. He reported that Southerners longed for sustained peace, and former Confederate soldiers were willing to defend the Union.[31] A number of officers from both sides had gone into business together planting cotton.[32] Following the Christmas holiday of 1865, when the anticipation of free land failed to materialize, many blacks returned to their former plantations to work, not out of affection for the owners but because of familiarity with the environment.[33] Except for some remote areas, blacks were experiencing freedom.[34] Truman acknowledged that if the Freedmen's Bureau had not provided aid many blacks would have starved, but the Bureau, having served its purpose, should be disbanded and black soldiers should be discharged from the military.[35]

On April 2, President Johnson formally declared the war over in all states except Texas.[36] The action was a political move to thwart the Radicals. If the

---

[28]Graf *et al.*, Vol. X., pp. 312-315.
[29]Graf *et al.*, Vol. X., p. xi.
[30]Graf *et al.*, Vol. X., p. 449.
[31]Graf *et al.*, Vol. X., pp. 377-378.
[32]Graf *et al.*, Vol. X., p. 382.
[33]Graf *et al.*, Vol. X., pp. 384-385 & 390.
[34]Graf *et al.*, Vol. X., p. 384.
[35]Graf *et al.*, Vol. X., pp. 390-391.
[36]Graf *et al.*, Vol. X., p. 352.

Southern States were at peace then there would be no need for military control nor the Freedmen's Bureau.[37]

CABINET RESIGNATIONS

Secretary of the Treasury Hugh McCulloch said the cabinet was supportive of the President until he vetoed the Civil Rights bill. This marked a serious departure with many of his supporters including key members of Congress. Secretaries Dennison and Harlan, no longer able to support the President, resigned. Speed followed soon after. While Stanton could no longer sustain the President, he remained on the Cabinet. His presence was seen as critical to the Radical movement.[38]

Johnson had been repeatedly warned about Stanton's disloyalty. Even private citizens requested the Secretary of War's removal.[39] Why Johnson kept him in office for so long is unclear. When Johnson refused to remove Stanton, speculation mounted that something sinister was going on. The *Milwaukee Sentinel* asserted that Stanton had something on Johnson. Rumors circulated that Stanton was not removed because he could implicate Johnson in the assassination of Lincoln.[40]

FOURTEENTH AMENDMENT

As president, Johnson had no opportunity to veto an amendment, but he could wield his influence to keep an amendment from being approved. And that he did with the Fourteenth Amendment which bestowed citizenship upon blacks. Johnson tried to dissuade states from ratifying it, claiming that Congress had no right to propose an amendment with Southern states unrepresented in the legislature. It soon became understood among the leadership of Congress that no Southern state would be readmitted to the Union unless it passed the Fourteenth Amendment.[41]

---

[37]*London Times,* April 16, 1866, no Vol., #25473.
[38]McCulloch, pp. 390-391. Welles, *Diary of Gideon Welles,* Vol. II., p. 528, 553, & 581. Graf *et al.,* Vol. XIII., p. xii. Sumner sent Stanton a one-word telegram, "Stick" (Trefousse, p. 313).
[39]Graf *et al.,* Vol. VIII., p. 245, Vol. XI., pp. 237 & 241-242.
[40]Graf *et al.,* Vol. XI., p. 247.
[41]Graf *et al.,* Vol. X., pp. xii-xiii.

In July of 1866, Governor William G. Brownlow of Tennessee, by now a Johnson antagonist again, called a special session of the General Assembly in his state to ratify the Fourteenth Amendment. The Governor requested General George H. Thomas to provide troops to assemble the state legislature.[42] A year earlier, Johnson had sent Brownlow a telegram offering the services of General Thomas to support law and order in the state.

> Whenever it becomes necessary for the execution of the Law and the protection of the ballot box, you will call upon Genl. Thomas for sufficient military force to sustain the civil authority of the State.[43]

Now Brownlow was trying to take the President up on his offer. But even though federal troops would not be at his disposal, Brownlow pressed on with assembling his legislature. Lacking two members of the House to comprise a quorum, Brownlow had the Sergeant at Arms seize two legislators and hold them by force in a committee room in the Capitol. The two prisoners obtained a writ of *habeas corpus* from a judge who ordered their release, but the House ignored the order and declared a quorum present. The vote was taken and the Amendment was passed in Tennessee. Upon ratification, Brownlow wired the United States Senate notifying the clerk of the vote and conveying his compliments to the "dead dog" in the White House.[44]

Thomas had wired the President for directions on July 14. The telegram was received in the War Department, but it was not until three days later the President learned of the inquiry when Stanton delivered the message in a Cabinet meeting. According to Stanton's rendering of the telegram, Thomas stated that some of the members of the Tennessee legislature refused to attend sessions. He asked if he should have them arrested. The President, obviously not knowing the whole story, said, "If General Thomas had nothing else to do but to intermeddle in local controversies he had better be detached and ordered elsewhere."[45] As it turned out, the inquiry was of little consequence for Browlow got his quorum and the Fourteenth Amendment was approved by the Tennessee legislature.[46]

Tennessee was the first of the former Confederate states to approve the Fourteenth Amendment and the first of the Southern states brought back into the

---

[42]Milton, p. 316.
[43]"Telegraph: Johnson to Brownlow," Tennessee State Library and Archive, Microfilm #1203, Box 1, item 8.
[44]Welles, *Diary of Gideon Welles*, Vol. II., p. 557. Coulter, pp. 313-315.
[45]Welles, *Diary of Gideon Welles*, Vol. II., pp. 554 & 557.
[46]Milton, pp. 316-317.

fold by Congress. While the President was glad to see his adopted state back in the Union, the terms of readmission were repugnant to him.

THE MEMPHIS AND NEW ORLEANS RIOTS

Two riots in May and June of 1866 would sour the Reconstruction effort and hurt the President politically. About 6:00 p.m. on the evening of May 1, 1866, a riot occurred in the southern part of Memphis, Tennessee. While local newspapers gave differing accounts of the trouble, the *Memphis Daily Argus*, with a reporter on the scene, likely had the most accurate coverage.[47] The riot started in South Memphis when two police officers tried to arrest a tavern owner selling liquor. A number of black troops, who had been mustered out of service the day before, were frequent patrons of the saloon. These men attacked the policemen, killing one officer. The other ran for reinforcements bringing back about 15 fellow officers. It soon became evident that even more help was needed, so reinforcements were gathered from the police station. The additional officers were met at the South Street bridge by 100-150 black troops accompanied by whites from the area. Thus, began a running urban gun battle through the south end. The indiscriminate gunfire hit a fireman. After a while the police and posse charged the bridge about two blocks east of Main on South Street, forcing the blacks and their white allies back. But by this time the police were nearly out of ammunition and were being out flanked, so they retreated up Main Street. Here the reporter from the *Argus* was shot. The policemen continued to retreat as far as the Second Presbyterian Church on Beale and Main. They finally made a stand at Gayoso. Regular troops were called out at 10:45 to squelch the riot. Two policemen and 6 to 8 blacks were killed.[48]

In late July of 1866, a riot in New Orleans eclipsed that of Memphis with a bloodbath that took the lives of 38 people and left 146 wounded. Pardoned Confederates, in control of the state government in Louisiana, passed legislation discriminating against former slaves. Radicals, hoping to redress these wrongs, attempted to reconvene the constitutional convention that brought the state back

---

[47]The *Memphis Daily Avalanche* stated that the riot started when two youths, a black and a white, were fighting. Two policemen went to breakup the altercation. A crowd of about 15 to 20 armed adult blacks surrounded the police and assaulted them (*The Memphis Daily Avalanche*, May 2, 1866, Vol. 8, # 107).

[48]*The Memphis Daily Argus*, May 2, 1866, Vol. VIII, #44.

into existence in 1864. Efforts to impede the movement were made by the Mayor of New Orleans and his police force.[49]

On July 27 a large gathering of blacks marched to the steps of the city hall in New Orleans where they were addressed by Dr. A.P. Dostie, ex-governor Hahn, and others. Seditious remarks were made to the mob, inciting them to arm themselves for the purpose of overthrowing the state government.[50] Dostie's speech was exceptionally inflammatory in stirring up support for black suffrage. "If we are interfered with, the streets of New Orleans will run with blood," he prophesized.[51] Some of that blood would be his.

About 150 people assembled for the convention at noon on the 30th at the Mechanics Institute. Some participants were armed with pistols. At 1:00 p.m. a procession of 60 to 130 blacks marched up Burgundy Street and across Canal Street to the Mechanics Institute carrying an American flag. Some of the marchers were armed. Others carried clubs. As they crossed Canal Street a confrontation occurred with some spectators. A shot was fired. Most of those in the procession entered the Institute. There was a conflict with the police and another shot was fired. Soon there was indiscriminate gunfire into the building. A white flag was raised by those inside. The shooting stopped momentarily as the police rushed the building. Upon entering the Mechanics Institute, the police commenced shooting again. When they had emptied their weapons they retreated. A hastily erected barricade thrown up by the occupants inside was soon busted down as the police rushed the building a second time. Those who managed to escape the carnage inside were shot by the police as they fled through the doors. Those breaking through the police perimeter were shot by white citizens on the periphery. Those lying wounded on the ground were stabbed and had their heads bashed in with brickbats. Those who hid were routed out and shot. Some individuals were even shot blocks away from the scene. Some prisoners hauled away by the police were wounded and even killed after their capture.[52]

Dostie was knocked out with a brick-bat, shot, and pulled down the stairs by his hair. A crowd of policemen and bystanders gathering around him shot and stabbed him repeatedly. He was thrown into a dirt cart, and a policeman sat on his body. When Dostie tried to raise his head the officer would hit him in the face with his revolver. The prisoner was carried to the police station and dropped out

[49]Philip Henry Sheridan, Vol. II., *Personal Memoirs of P.H. Sheridan, general, United States army*, (New York: Charles L. Webster & Co., 1888), pp. 233-235.
[50]Graf *et al.*, Vol. XI., p. 25.
[51]Milton, p. 346.
[52]Sheridan, Vol. II., pp. 237-239.

on the pavement. His friends secured his release and he was carried to a hotel where he lived another six days.[53]

General Philip Sheridan wired Grant on August 1.

> You are doubtless aware of the serious riot which occurred in this city on the 30th. A political body, styling themselves the Convention of 1864, met on the 30th, for, as it is alleged, the purpose of remodeling the present constitution of the State. The leaders were political agitators and revolutionary men, and the action of the convention was liable to produce breaches of the public peace. *I had made up my mind to arrest the head men, if the proceedings of the convention were calculated to disturb the tranquility of the Department; but I had no cause for action until they committed the overt act. In the meantime official duty called me to Texas, and the mayor of the city, during my absence, suppressed the convention by the use of the police force, and in so doing attacked the members of the convention, and a party of two hundred negroes, with fire-arms, clubs, and knives, in a manner so unnecessary and atrocious as to compel me to say that it was murder.* About forty whites and blacks were thus killed, and about one hundred and sixty wounded. Everything is now quiet, but I deem it best to maintain a military supremacy in the city for a few days, until the affair is fully investigated. I believe the sentiment of the general community is great regret at this unnecessary cruelty, and that the police could have made any arrest they saw fit without sacrificing lives.[54]

As soon as Grant received the telegram he presented it to Johnson. When the President reported the events of the New Orleans riot to the press, he excluded the segment in Sheridan's report that referred to murder. [The italicized section above represents what was omitted by Johnson in the public report.] Sheridan objected to the omission and sent a more complete report on August 6. After the New Orleans episode, his relationship with the President disintegrated.[55]

The whole New Orleans incident could have been avoided had Stanton responded to a telegram sent by General Baird well before the riot. On August 28, Baird, standing in for General Sheridan who was in Texas, had written for orders on how to respond to the impending problem.

> A convention has been called, with the sanction of Governor Wells, to meet here on Monday. The lieutenant governor and city authorities think it unlawful, and

---

[53]Emily Hazen Reed, *Life of A.P. Dostie; or, the Conflict of New Orleans*, (New York: W.P. Tomlinson, 1868), pp. 313-316.

[54]Sheridan, Vol. II., pp. 235-236. Dr. Albert Hartsuff, army assistant surgeon, counted 38 dead and 146 wounded (Graf *et al.*, Vol. XI., p. 19).

[55]Sheridan, Vol. II., pp. 236-237. Graf *et al.*, Vol. XI., pp. 36-37.

propose to break it up by arresting the delegates. I have given no orders on the subject, but have warned the parties that I could not countenance or permit such action without instructions to that effect from the President. Please instruct me at once by telegraph.[56]

Stanton failed to respond, and the President never saw the message until after the riots were over.[57] The insurgences did great political damage to Johnson. Instead of the President displaying empathy for the victims, he blamed the Radicals.[58] In turn, the Radicals accused him of instigating the uprisings in Memphis and New Orleans – incidents that reinforced their stereotypical views of Southern intolerance and lack of regeneration.[59]

SWING AROUND THE CIRCLE

Johnson made another *Swing Around the Circle*. In the late summer of 1866, he took his message to the people to help influence the fall elections. The trip was built around a September speaking engagement he had in Chicago where he was invited to be the keynote speaker at a memorial for Stephen A. Douglas. While the President was admonished to avoid extemporaneous talks, he failed to heed the warning, and his tour became an unfortunate trip destined to do him great political damage.[60]

The presidential party left Washington, D.C. by train on August 28 with scheduled stops in Philadelphia, New York, Albany, Auburn, Niagara Falls, Cleveland, Detroit, Chicago, Springfield, St. Louis, Indianapolis, Louisville, Madison, Cincinnati, Columbus, Pittsburgh and Harrisburg to name a few. Johnson's entourage included Ulysses S. Grant, David Glasgow Farragut, William H. Seward, Gideon Welles, Alexander W. Randall, and George Armstrong Custer.

Johnson's speeches at various stops covered a variety of topics. He talked about his rise from a humble mechanic to the presidency and how Congress wanted to split the Union. He referred to the bitter struggle through which the country had just passed, and even though the rebellion was at an end much work was yet to be completed because Southern states were being denied representation

---

[56]*Trial of Andrew Johnson, president of the United States, before the Senate of the United States, on impeachment by the House of Representatives for high crimes and misdemeanors*, Vol. I. (Washington, D.C.: Government Printing Office, 1868), p. 152.

[57]Milton, p. 349. *Trial of Andrew Johnson*, Vol. I., pp. 152-153.

[58]Trefousse, p. 259.

[59]Milton, p. 370.

[60]Graf *et al.*, Vol. XI., pp. xiii-xiv.

in Congress. He condemned those who kept the Southern states out of the Union yet imposed taxes on them and denied their representation in Congress. He defended his authority to grant pardons and his right to remove individuals from office.[61] But after a while all of his speeches began to sound the same. With national newspaper coverage the readers undoubtedly tired of them. Some voters were likely repulsed.[62]

Furthermore, Johnson allowed himself to get entangled in a series of arguments with his audiences. Andrew Johnson was an extemporaneous speaker. "I have never made a prepared speech in my life, and only treat these topics as they occur to me," he said proudly.[63] His speeches encouraged a great deal of interaction with the crowd, which he obviously enjoyed when it was only bantering. But when hecklers egged him on, his impromptu remarks were often ill conceived and his behavior became fodder for newspaper reporters who shared the humiliating spectacle with the entire nation.[64] Welles warned Johnson about his speeches, but Johnson thought his secretary did not have an appreciation of his prowess as a speaker.[65]

At the first few stops, the President met a receptive audience. But by the time the party reached Cleveland, things began to turn sour. The crowd was disorderly and belligerent. Agitators started heckling him, and unfortunately Johnson came back with a rejoinder. The scene got ugly as hecklers tried to drown him with their jeering and commotion, but Johnson stood his ground committed to see the fight through to the end.[66]

Johnson's address in Chicago at the Douglas dedication went well but he ran into more difficulty in St. Louis. While he waited to enter a banquet hall, a crowd assembled in the street. At first Johnson declined to address them fearing that he would experience a repeat of Cleveland. Finally succumbing to the urging of local committee members, he walked out onto the balcony only to be goaded with the events of New Orleans. Similar problems awaited him in Indianapolis, where one man was killed in the unrest.[67] In Pittsburgh a huge crowd gathered to see Grant. When Johnson tried to address them they "hooted and hissed" and called for the General. The President was furious.[68] Johnson would not see another enthusiastic reception until his return to Washington.

---

[61]Graf *et al.*, Vol. XI., pp. 153-166 & 192-201.
[62]Beale, p. 368.
[63]Graf *et al.*, Vol. XI., p. 164.
[64]Trefousse, p. 266.
[65]Welles, *Diary of Gideon Welles*, Vol. II., p. 648.
[66]Milton, pp. 361-368.
[67]Welles, *Diary of Gideon Welles*, Vol. II., pp. 593-594. Graf *et al.*, Vol. XI., p. 215. Beale, p. 366.
[68]Temple, pp. 459-460.

The President became the subject of ridicule at the hands of David R. Locke, writing as Petroleum V. Nasby, and the cartoonist Thomas Nast. Their political satire and cartoons reached thousands of voters. Petroleum V. Nasby had great fun with Johnson's "Swingin Round the Cirkle." In analyzing the disastrous speaking tour he,

> Knowd wat wuz the matter. It come uv takin Grant and Farrygut along on the excursion. It distracted the attention uv the people. Hed there bin nobody but the President and the Cabinet along, there woodent hev bin nobody to hurrah for, and the sublime trooths, wich the President kin only jerk, wood hev impressed the people more than they did.[69]

The governors of Ohio, Indiana, Illinois, Michigan, Missouri, and Pennsylvania had all avoided the President on his tour.[70] About half way through the trip Grant, who had supported Johnson, abandoned the entourage. In Cincinnati the General left using the excuse that he wished to visit his father. Privately, he confided in a friend that he wished not "to accompany a man who was deliberately digging his own grave."[71] Seward had an attack of cholera after leaving Louisville and headed home. At one point it was doubtful that he would survive.[72]

The congressional election of 1866 was vitally important to the President who hoped to increase his support in Congress and limit the power of the Radicals. But the election produced a sweeping victory for Republicans who increased their majority in Congress and made impotent the President's power of veto. Following the election, there were 42 Republicans and 11 Democrats in the Senate. The House stood at 143 Republicans and 49 Democrats.[73]

SECOND ANNUAL MESSAGE TO CONGRESS

Johnson addressed a variety of issues in his second annual message to Congress on December 3, 1866. All state governments were functioning and federal government finances were better than anticipated the previous year. The

---

[69]Petroleum V. Nasby. *Swingin Round the Cirkle*. (Boston: Lee and Shepard, 1867), p. 263.
[70]Welles, *Diary of Gideon Welles*, Vol. II., p. 589.
[71]Welles, *Diary of Gideon Welles*, Vol. II., p. 592. Milton,
    p. 368.
[72]Welles, *Diary of Gideon Welles*, Vol. II., p. 594.
[73]Milton, p. 377.

economic outlook was so good that Johnson suggested the reduction of taxes and projected that the debt could be paid off within the next 25 years. Wounded soldiers were being cared for, treaties had been made with the Indians, and the Atlantic Telegraph had been established between Ireland and Newfoundland. Finally, Johnson warned of the danger of re-enslavement facing freedmen immigrating to other countries.[74] Missing from his message was anything substantive about Reconstruction.

DISTRICT OF COLUMBIA FRANCHISE BILL

The District of Columbia Franchise Bill, also known as the Black Suffrage Bill, passed Congress on December 14, 1866. It provided voting rights to black men in Washington, D.C. Johnson's objection was based largely on the fact that the voters of the District did not want the franchise extended to blacks. In a special referendum taken among residents just the previous year, 6,556 were against giving blacks the vote and only 35 in favor.[75] Furthermore, it seemed incongruent that representatives from a number of Northern states were forcing black suffrage upon the District when their own constituents refused to extend the privilege back home.[76] Johnson vetoed the Black Suffrage Bill on January 7, 1867 and that same day Congress overrode his veto.[77]

Johnson was quickly losing what little credibility he had. The vetoes of key legislation, cabinet resignations, and a failed speaking tour were putting him at odds with the majority in Congress and many supporters in the North. *Harper's*

---

[74]Graf *et al.*, Vol. XI., pp. 503, 508, 509, 512, 513, & 514.

[75]Graf *et al.*, Vol. XI., p. 577. Trefousse, p. 273.

[76]Several Northern states had laws making it difficult if not impossible for blacks to vote. In New York, blacks were required to meet conditions that whites did not have to fulfill. In Massachusetts, voters had to demonstrate a degree of literacy. In Pennsylvania and Indiana blacks had no voting rights at all. In 1865, referenda in Minnesota, Wisconsin, and Connecticut all rejected giving the vote to blacks (Graf *et al.*, Vol. XI., pp. 578-580).

[77]Graf *et al.*, Vol. X., p. 17.

Weekly lamented that when Johnson first became President he said treason must be made odious. Now it appeared that loyalty to the Union was being made odious.[78]

[78]*Harper's Weekly*, June 2, 1866, Vol. X., #492, p. 338.

Chapter 9

CONGRESSIONAL RECONSTRUCTION

In July of 1867, Henry L. Dawes, Republican Congressman from Massachusetts, stated "The President... *does* continue to do the most provoking things. If he isn't impeached it wont [sic] be his fault."[1] Truly Johnson did do the most provoking things. He seemed bent on antagonizing Congress and Congress, likewise, had lost patience with him. A case in point was his abundant use of pardoning power. Because of his liberal practices in dispensing absolution to Southerners, Congress tried to repeal his ability to pardon under the Second Confiscation Act of 1862. Johnson ignored the legislation allowing it to become law without his signature and continued to issue pardons as freely as before. So concerned that Johnson might do political damage between sessions, the 39th Congress voted to convene the 40th congressional session immediately following theirs.[2] The legislative branch was moving to take the matter of Reconstruction firmly under its own control.

TENURE OF OFFICE ACT

The Tenure of Office Act was an attempt to limit presidential power. The bill stated that anyone appointed to a civil office with the consent of the Senate was entitled to hold that position until a successor was appointed by the President and confirmed by the Senate. Furthermore, all of the members of the presidential

---

[1]Benedict, *A Compromise of Principle: Congressional Republicans and Reconstruction 1863-1869*, p. 253.
[2]Trefousse, p. 276. Normally the congressional session would not have begun until December of 1867 unless called into special session by the President (Browning, Vol. II., p. 134).

Cabinet would hold their positions for the duration of the term of the president who appointed them and for a month thereafter.[3]

On February 18, 1867, the Tenure of Office Bill went to the President for his signature.[4] The legislation was discussed in a Cabinet meeting and all members opposed it. Stanton, especially, expressed strong reservations against the bill, more so than any other Cabinet member.[5] Johnson argued that there were valid reasons, other than malfeasance, why someone should be removed from office. He vetoed the bill and Congress passed it over his veto.[6]

THE MILITARY RECONSTRUCTION ACTS

The First Military Reconstruction Bill established military control over the Southern States with the formation of five districts, each served by a commander. The legislation severely limited individual civil rights by setting aside *habeas corpus*, established military governance over civil authority, and doing away with trial by jury. Furthermore, it directed states to ratify the Fourteenth Amendment and construct new constitutions, which included provisions for black suffrage.

To Johnson, this bill placed too much power in the hands of the district commander who would be given dictatorial power over a military district.[7] A commander would not be accountable to any state law or civil body, could adjudicate criminal code to his own liking, would be held to no standard requiring evidence or even be compelled to keep records of proceedings, and could make arrests without warrants. This bill was a fundamental violation of the Constitution, which protected the welfare of individuals and their property.[8]

It was to punish the gross crime of defying the Constitution, and to vindicate its supreme authority, that we carried a bloody war of four years' duration. Shall we now acknowledge that we sacrificed a million... lives and expended billions of

---

[3]Graf *et al.*, Vol. XII., p. 95.

[4]Milton, p. 395.

[5]The bill was partially repealed in 1869 and 1887. It was finally declared unconstitutional in 1926 (Browning, Vol. II., pp. 132-133).

[6]Graf *et al.*, Vol. XII., p. 96. In August of 1867, Browning recorded in his diary concerning the Tenure of Office Bill. "The law is, manifestly unconstitutional, but an Executive officer cannot declare it so, and in my opinion it is not only the Presidents (sic) duty, but his best policy to conform to it till it can be brought before the Courts" (Browning, Vol. II., p. 155).

[7]Graf *et al.*, Vol. XII., p. 82.

[8]Graf *et al.*, Vol. XII., pp. 90 & 84.

treasure to enforce a Constitution which is not worthy of respect and preservation?[9]

On March 2, Johnson cast his veto and Congress overrode it. A Second Military Reconstruction Bill followed. Whereas the first act lacked provisions for implementation, the second provided for the registration of voters -- again a veto and again an override.[10]

ALASKAN PURCHASE

Secretary of State William H. Seward concluded the negotiations for the purchase of Alaska from the Russians on March 29, 1867, and the President sent the treaty to the Senate for ratification.[11] A special session was called and the acquisition approved.

One might think that with all the mutual antagonism brewing between Johnson and Congress it was surprising that this purchase came to fruition. Toward the end of Johnson's term, he reflected on the Alaskan purchase with Seward who shared some of the hidden obstacles that had to be overcome when the appropriation was hung up in the House of Representatives. Seward commented that during the negotiations for the purchase, the Russian minister paid John W. Forney, Secretary of the Senate, $30,000 in gold while R.J. Walker[12] and F.P. Stanton, former Representative from Tennessee, each received $20,000. Representative N.P. Banks of Massachusetts was paid $8,000 and Representative Thaddeus Stevens from Pennsylvania $10,000.[13]

---

[9]Graf *et al.*, Vol. XII., p. 92.

[10]Graf *et al.*, Vol. XII., p. xii. It is interesting to note that when serving as military governor of Tennessee, Johnson held manifest power not unlike what he was objecting to in this bill.

[11]Trefousse, p. 288. Seward was eager to acquire new territories for the United States. Welles said he had selfish motivations. "It [was] more the glory of Seward than the true interests of the county" (Welles, *Diary of Gideon Welles*, Vol. III., p. 96). That summer Seward would pursue the purchase of some islands owned by Denmark in the West Indies (Browning, Vol. II., p. 145).

[12]This possibly is Robert John Walker, former Senator from Mississippi.

[13]Graf *et al.*, Vol. XV., p. 26.

1867 HOUSE JUDICIARY COMMITTEE ON IMPEACHMENT

Frustration with Johnson was finding form in an effort to remove him from office. Representatives Benjamin Butler from Massachusetts and James M. Ashley of Ohio were the principal architects behind an impeachment effort brewing in the early months of 1867.[14] Other Radicals in the House shared their sentiments.[15] On January 7, Benjamin Loan, John R. Kelso, and James M. Ashley each on their own introduced resolutions to impeach the President. Ashley's charges included usurpation of power; corruption in administering appointments, pardons, and veto power; corruption in disposing of United States property; and interfering with an election.[16] Benjamin Loan, on the 14th, went as far as accusing Johnson of being involved in the assassination of Lincoln.[17]

In February of 1867, the House Judiciary Committee began secret inquiries into impeachment proceedings against Andrew Johnson. Allan Pinkerton had an attractive young woman flirt with the Committee's stenographer to obtain verbatim transcripts of the proceedings, and thus kept Johnson informed of the Committee's every move.[18]

John Surratt, the son of Mary Surratt, fled to Canada and then Europe after the assassination of Lincoln. In the spring of 1866, he was found among the Papal Zouaves in Rome. There he was captured but managed an escape to Egypt. He was recaptured in Alexandria in November of 1866 and brought to the United States the following February.[19] Upon Surratt's incarceration, a clerk from the House Judiciary Committee, acting for Congressmen Benjamin Butler and James M. Ashley, tried to get him to implicate President Johnson in the Lincoln assassination. But, John Surratt would not cooperate. He claimed he knew nothing of the case and would not "swear away his own soul" to condemn the President.[20] Undaunted, Ashley approached others to try to get them to implicate Johnson in the assassination of Lincoln.[21] All to no avail.

---

[14]A rumor circulated that James M. Ashley of Ohio had been bribed to introduce a resolution of impeachment in the House (Graf et al., Vol. XI., p. 593. Milton, pp. 416-417).
[15]Trefousse, p. 282.
[16]Trefousse, p. 283.
[17]Congressional Globe, 39th Congress, 2nd Session, January 14, 1867, pp. 443-446.
[18]Milton, p. 411 & 732.
[19]Graf et al., Vol. XII., p. 68.
[20]Graf et al., Vol. XII., p. 188.
[21]Graf et al., Vol. XII., p. 245.

Interest turned to the small diary John Wilkes Booth had in his possession at the time of his death. The diary contained two entries by Booth.[22] The pages from January through early June were missing as were 16 other pages removed from different sections of the book.[23]

Following Stanton's perusal at the time of Booth's death, the diary had been left in the possession of Judge Advocate General Joseph Holt. The material was considered of so little importance that it was not submitted as evidence in the trial of the Lincoln conspirators.[24] But by 1867, Radicals were trying to find any evidence upon which they could impeach Johnson, and interest in the diary was resurrected. Allegations were made that Johnson had removed incriminating pages to cover up his participation in the Lincoln assassination.[25]

Key to the investigation was the testimony of Lafayette C. Baker who led the group that captured Booth. Baker testified that when he gave the book to Stanton the pages were for the most part intact.[26] Others contradicted his testimony. Colonel Everton J. Conger and Luther B. Baker, cousin of Lafayette Baker, who were both present when Booth was taken, said the book appeared to be in the same condition it was when they first saw it. Stanton said the diary was as it was when he got it. His assistant, Thomas T. Eckert and Judge Advocate General Holt concurred.[27]

Baker's motives are questionable. Because of his earlier probe into the President's involvement with brokering pardons, he was forbidden access to the White House by Johnson and forced out of the military by Stanton. Had any incriminating evidence existed to link Johnson with the assassination of Lincoln, the House Committee would have been more than ready to accept it, for they were looking for anything to bring about Johnson's impeachment.[28]

Maybe Baker never read the diary in the first place. He did not complain of missing content, only missing pages. A ghostwriter wrote his memoirs and he admitted that after the publication he had not even read his own book.[29] Had he read the diary he would not have seized upon the apocryphal anecdote of Booth

---

[22]William Hanchett, *The Diary of John Wilkes Booth April, 1865*, (Springfield, IL: Illinois State Historical Society, 1979), pp. 39-40.

[23]It appears Booth used the book as a memo pad – tearing out pages as suited his needs (Hanchett, p. 50 & 52).

[24]Hanchett, p. 39.

[25]Milton, pp. 410-411.

[26]Hanchett, p. 42.

[27]Hanchett, p. 43.

[28]Graf *et al.*, Vol. XII., pp. 268-269.

[29]Hanchett, p. 43.

sleeping beside his dead horse to absorb the warmth of its body, which he included in his book, *History of the United States Secret Service*.[30]

Initially, Congressman Benjamin F. Butler was anxious to learn who had removed pages from the diary and for what motive. But when Baker could not substantiate his claims, the Congressman finally came to the conclusion that there was no reliable evidence against Johnson in the assassination of Lincoln. Two members of the committee commented on Baker's veracity saying, "It is doubtful whether he has in any one thing told the truth, even by accident."[31] After all the investigations, the Committee found nothing upon which to build a case.[32]

Instead of allowing the events to pass without public comment, Johnson disclosed in an interview with the *Cincinnati Commercial* in July of 1867, that he saw the impeachment effort as "a big joke."[33]

THIRD MILITARY RECONSTRUCTION ACT

When General Philip Sheridan, commander of the Fifth District, removed some officials from the civil government in Louisiana, a displeased Johnson had Attorney General Henry Stanbery issue a legal opinion on the action. Stanbery's rendering was that military commanders should not have control over civil laws or civil officers and should not be able to stop eligible people from voting. Congress reacted to the Attorney General's opinion by passing the Third Military Act, which gave commanders in the various districts full power to govern. A veto, issued on July 19, 1867, was overturned by Congress immediately.[34] There would be yet a Fourth Military Reconstruction Act which Johnson let become law without his signature.[35]

RETURN TO THE PLACE OF HIS NATIVITY

In June of 1867, Johnson made a trip to North Carolina to dedicate a monument to his father and speak at the University of North Carolina

---

[30]Lafayette C. Baker, *History of the United States Secret Service*, (Philadelphia: L.C. Baker, 1867), p. 508.
[31]Hanchett, p. 46.
[32]Trefousse, p. 284.
[33]Graf *et al.*, Vol. XII., p. 371.
[34]Graf *et al.*, Vol. XII., p. xiii.
[35]Graf *et al.*, Vol. XIII., p. xv.

commencement.[36] The self-proclaimed Moses title followed him even to his birthplace. A correspondent for *Harper's Weekly* accompanied Johnson on his trip to Raleigh. Along the way, the train was stopped by a herd of cattle. When the President went to the rear platform the cattle rushed to him. The reporter quipped, "It was feared that our 'Moses' Among the Bull Rushes would meet his end."[37]

Johnson's speech in Raleigh was quite lively with a great deal of interaction with the crowd. "Where are those I left behind.... Friends and companions of my childhood, where are you?" Johnson asked rhetorically. An old black nurse rushed from the crowd and throwing her arms around the President's neck, exclaimed, "Here's one of 'em." There was raucous laughter and shouts of "Go in Aunty!" The President, obviously taken by surprise continued, "Where are the gay roysterers, the Smiths and the Joneses?" A voice from the crowd shouted, "Gone into the distillery business, most of 'em." Johnson plodded on, "Where is the long list of men who lived at that day, and who commanded respect for constancy to principle?" A spectator retorted, "On the books of the pardon-broker." And there was great laughter.[38]

REMOVAL OF SECRETARY OF WAR STANTON

Stanton's power was vast. He controlled the regular army and the Freedmen's Bureau. Four of Johnson's secretaries, including Reeves and Moore came from the War Department. The only government telegraph in Washington was located in Stanton's offices and all messages coming and going could be viewed by the Secretary or delayed if he saw fit.[39] For example, when Governor Brownlow of Tennessee could not form a quorum he asked General Thomas to arrest legislators. Thomas wired the President for instructions. Three days later the wire was delivered to Johnson. Prior to the fateful New Orleans riots, General Baird telegraphed Johnson about the festering situation. The message was not delivered to the President until blood had been shed. Stanton later confessed to intentionally delaying the delivery of the message.[40]

The President finally came to the realization that Stanton was his greatest impediment. By August of 1867, he was ready to remove him from office. Johnson shared his intention with General Grant and offered him the acting

---

[36]Graf *et al.*, Vol. XII., p. xvi.
[37]*Harper's Weekly*, June 29, 1867, Vol. XI., #548, p. 410.
[38]*Harper's Weekly*, June 29, 1867, Vol. XI., #548, p. 410.
[39]Beale, p. 103.
[40]Beale, pp. 104-105.

position as Secretary of War. Although Grant said he thought the removal unwise, he would not shrink from performing his duty and he accepted the post.[41] But Grant, still harboring misgivings, wrote to Johnson that day concerning the removal of Stanton.

> His removal can not [sic] be effected against his will without the consent of the Senate. It is but a short time since the United States Senate was in session and why not then have asked for his removal if it was desired? It certainly was the intention of the Legislative branch of the Govt. to place Cabinet Ministers beyond the power of Executive removal and it is pretty well understood that, so far as Cabinet ministers are effected by the "Tenure of office Bill" it was intended specially to protect the Sec. of War who the country felt great confidence in.[42]

On August 5, 1867, Johnson notified Stanton that his resignation as Secretary of War would be accepted.[43] The notice was succinct. "Public considerations of a high character constrain me to Say, that your resignation as Secretary of War will be accepted."[44] The next day, Stanton replied that he would not resign the office before the next session of Congress. "Public considerations of a high character... constrain me not to resign."[45] Johnson remarked privately that he would leave Stanton hanging on the hooks of uncertainty for a few days before suspending him.[46]

The President had another meeting with Grant on the 11th and again asked if the General would take the job *ad interim*. He also inquired if there were any discord between them for he had heard rumors. Grant replied that he had nothing against the President. Welles asserted in his diary that Johnson knew before the appointment of Grant that the General had gone over to the Radicals.[47]

On August 12, Johnson appointed Ulysses S. Grant Secretary of War *ad interim*.[48] That same day he sent another message to Stanton notifying him of his suspension as Secretary of War. This time the President's communiqué was more

[41]Moore, pp. 107-108. Welles thought the removal of Stanton ill timed. If Johnson had removed Stanton the previous year, Grant might not have been won over by the Radicals and the country would have been with the President (Welles, *Diary of Gideon Welles*, Vol. III., p. 158). As early as June 15, 1866, Welles noted in his diary that Grant had agreed to accept the position of Secretary of War, *ad interim* (Welles, *Diary of Gideon Welles*, Vol. II., p. 529).
[42]Graf *et al.*, Vol. XII., p. 447.
[43]Graf *et al.*, Vol. XII., p. 461. Moore, p. 108.
[44]Gaf *et al.*, Vol. XII., p. 461.
[45]Graf *et al.*, Vol. XII., p. 461.
[46]Moore, p. 108.
[47]Welles, *Diary of Gideon Welles*, Vol. III., pp. 155 & 167.
[48]Graf *et al.*, Vol. XII., p. 475.

direct. Stanton was ordered to cease performing any functions pertaining to the office and transfer all records to Ulysses S. Grant.[49] Stanton replied that he was compelled to deny Johnson's authority to remove him without the consent of the Senate.[50] At this point the President confided in his secretary, W.G. Moore, that Stanton had been working to have him removed from office.[51] Grant took possession of the War Department.

There is an element of irony in the fact that Stanton, who had been the Cabinet member most adamantly opposed to the Tenure of Office Act was now adamantly clinging to it. The Secretary had stated, "No person of proper sense of honor would remain in the Cabinet when asked to resign."[52]

REMOVAL OF GENERALS PHILIP H. SHERIDAN AND DANIEL E. SICKLES

On August 26, Johnson removed General Philip Sheridan and General Daniel Sickles from the Fifth and Second Districts respectively.[53] Sheridan believed Johnson turned against him because he objected to the editing of his New Orleans report.[54] When Johnson ordered the removal of Sheridan, he extended Grant the courtesy of providing critique of the proposed removal.

> Before you issue instructions to carry into effect the enclosed order, I would be pleased to hear any suggestions you may deem necessary respecting the assignment to which the order refers.[55]

But when Johnson received a letter from Grant the next day protesting the removal of Sheridan from the Fifth Military District, Johnson labeled it insubordinate.[56] In a subsequent meeting with Johnson, the General retracted his objections. Holding steadfast to his removal of Sheridan, Johnson stated,

> If Congress can bring themselves to impeach me, because in my judgment a turbulent and unfit man should be removed and because I, in the honest discharge

---

[49]Graf *et al.*, Vol. XII., pp. 476-477.
[50]Graf *et al.*, Vol. XII., p. 477.
[51]Moore, p. 109.
[52]Moore, p. 110.
[53]Browning, Vol. II., p. 159. Moore, p. 111.
[54]Sheridan, Vol. II., pp. 236-237.
[55]Moore, p. 110.
[56]Graf *et al.*, Vol. XII., p. 489. Moore, pp. 111-112.

of my duty to my county and the Constitution, exercise my judgment and remove him, let them do it.[57]

In an interview with the *Boston Post*, Johnson was asked why Sheridan was removed. He stated that the General exercised authority he did not possess and in using the powers legitimately assigned to him, did so in a capricious manner.[58]

SECOND AMNESTY PROCLAMATION

On September 7, 1867, Johnson issued his Second Amnesty Proclamation whereby he pardoned all except the executive officers (including department heads, agents to foreign powers, and governors) of the Confederacy, those with military rank above brigadier general or naval captain, those who mistreated Union prisoners of war, those still confined in civil or military custody, and all those involved in the assassination of Lincoln.[59]

JENNIE A. PERRY[60]

Jennie A. Perry's relationship with the President is somewhat of an enigma. Perry was the widow of naval engineer William C. Perry. She contacted Johnson on numerous occasions threatening to reveal what remained an undisclosed issue unless she received remuneration. Henry A. Smythe, collector for the port of New York, was involved in arranging to make payments to her. She avowed in her letters that Johnson made inappropriate advances to her. On June 24, 1867, Perry sent a letter to Johnson asking him to pardon a friend lest she expose the claims she had on him and Henry Smythe.[61] On October 11, a notorious woman, believed to be Perry, had signed a damaging affidavit that Johnson got her inside the White House and behind locked doors forced himself upon her.[62] Later in the month, using the pseudonym Ann Judson, Perry wrote a letter admonishing Johnson to do

---

[57]Welles, *Diary of Gideon Welles*, Vol. III., p. 154.
[58]Graf *et al.*, Vol. XII., p. 505.
[59]Graf *et al.*, Vol. XIII., p. 42.
[60]Jennie Perry had been in the pardon-brokerage business and had been involved in the New York Customhouse investigation (Graf *et al.*, Vol. XIII., p. 96). On March 22, 1867, there was a movement in the House to impeach Henry A. Smythe and remove him from office (*Congressional Globe*, 40th Congress, 1st Session, (March 22, 1867) p. 282).
[61]Graf *et al.*, Vol. XII., pp. 352-353.
[62]Graf *et al.*, Vol. XIII., p. 157.

right by Jennie Perry for fear that she would reveal her secret.[63] Ten days later Perry wrote to Johnson. "My Blood is on your *Soul*," she said imploring him for favors he had given other ladies.[64] She alleged that Andrew Johnson had an illegitimate son in Philadelphia. "Do not let me Expose you and Smythe. The intamacy [sic] that I have had with you must be told."[65] On March 4, 1868, an anonymous letter to Johnson claimed that Mrs. Perry had information that would come out in the newspaper soon and encouraged the President to settle her claim.[66] There is no evidence he ever did.

THIRD ANNUAL MESSAGE TO CONGRESS

On December 3, 1867, Johnson presented his Third Annual Message to Congress. He reported on the progress of the Pacific Railway, the disposition of public lands, and a proposed treaty with Denmark for the acquisition of the islands of St. Thomas and St. John in the Virgin Islands.[67] He said commerce in the South was inhibited due to the insecurity caused by the threat of confiscation and the dread of Negro supremacy.[68] He complained of the military reconstruction acts and rejected the idea of black suffrage and rule.[69]

THE SENATE DEALS WITH STANTON'S REMOVAL

Johnson had suspended Stanton while Congress was in recess. This was not in violation of the Tenure of Office Act, which allowed for such actions during congressional recess. But when Congress came back into session legislators wanted a reckoning. On December 12, 1867, when the Senate was back in session, Johnson notified them as to his reasons for removing Stanton. The Senate delayed taking action for a month, which gave the President's opponents time to muster resources to reject the removal. Congress and the President would soon be at loggerheads.

---

[63]Graf *et al.*, Vol. XIII., pp. 181-182.
[64]Graf *et al.*, Vol. XIII., p. 197.
[65]Graf *et al.*, Vol. XIII., p. 197.
[66]Graf *et al.*, Vol. XIII., p. 608.
[67]Graf *et al.*, Vol. XIII., pp. 280, 300-301, & 305.
[68]Graf *et al.*, Vol. XIII., p. 290.
[69]Graf *et al.*, Vol. XIII., pp. 285 & 289.

On January 7, Colonel Moore showed the President journals in which Grant said that if the Senate reinstated Stanton, he would restore the department to Stanton immediately. Grant obviously had a change of mind on the Tenure of Office Act and concluded that he would be subject to fine or imprisonment if he broke the law. But even if Grant surrendered the office to Stanton, Johnson told Secretary Moore, that might be good. If the Senate reinstated Stanton and terminated Grant they would have deposed the General who, in the words of the President, "had served the purpose for which he had been selected."[70]

Johnson had an opportunity to avoid the showdown with Congress. On January 12 and 13 respectively, both Reverdy Johnson and Sherman had advised him to nominate Governor Jacob D. Cox of Ohio as the Secretary of War prior to the Senate acting upon Stanton's removal. Even Grant urged the President to nominate Cox. It was understood that the Governor's nomination would quickly gain bipartisan confirmation, General Grant could relinquish the office easily, and most importantly there would be no confrontation with Congress on the Stanton issue. Thomas Ewing, former Senator from Ohio, concurred with the Cox appointment and urged Johnson to put the Governor's name in nomination and he would be confirmed, but time was of the essence. Cox's name had to be submitted immediately, Ewing said. Johnson showed no inclination to act upon the recommendation.[71]

On the 13th the reinstatement resolution was brought to a vote in the Senate and adopted. That evening the Senate notified Grant and Johnson that the suspension of Stanton was invalid. Early on the 14th, Grant, considering himself relieved of his duties as the Secretary of War, went to the War Department to surrender his keys. He locked up the office and turned the keys over to an Adjutant-General who carried them upstairs to Stanton.[72] Grant's resignation gave Stanton the opportunity to physically occupy the War Office again. The next time Stanton would not be removed as easily.

EXCHANGE WITH GRANT

On the morning of January 14, Johnson was notified that Grant had vacated the War Department. Johnson was disturbed by the General's actions which he labeled duplicitous. Grant was called to the Cabinet meeting that day where the

---

[70]Moore, p. 115.
[71]Graf *et al.*, Vol. XIII., pp. 500 & 523. Milton, pp. 481-482.
[72]Milton, p. 482.

President asked him why he took the actions he did. Grant said he had further examined the penalties and decided that he did not want to face five years of imprisonment or a fine of $10,000.[73] The General told Johnson that according to Section 2 of the Tenure of Office Act, his function as Secretary of War, *ad interim* ceased from the moment of notification by the Senate.[74] But had the General not stated that he would either remain as the head of the department or vacate it in time for Johnson to appoint another? Just the previous Saturday Grant had told him that if ever he found he could not fulfill the appointment he would relinquish the office to Johnson. Furthermore, Grant had attended the President's levee on the 13th and had ample opportunity to inform Johnson of his intentions then. Johnson accused Grant of meeting with Stanton at Stanton's residence before attending the President's function and agreeing upon a course of action. They had laughed at the fact that the Radicals had legislated Grant, their choice for president, out of the War Department.[75] The General stammered through an apology and asked to be excused.

The President's accusation infers that he had Grant followed or had a spy within Stanton's household. How else would he have known such detail? Regardless, why the charade when he clearly knew of Grant's intentions *a priori*? Grant's actions should not have been a surprise. If Johnson truly had been concerned, he should have had a frank discussion with the General on the 13th at the levee.

On the 28th, Grant wrote a letter to the President recalling the events of the Cabinet meeting, painting a different picture from Johnson's recollections.[76] Grant said that after reading the Tenure of Office Bill, he determined that he had to vacate the office of Secretary of War as soon as Stanton was reinstated by the Senate even though the "President should order me to retain it, which he never did."[77] The General stated that he believed Johnson understood his position that if the Senate reinstated Stanton, Grant's powers as Secretary of War *ad interim* would cease immediately.[78] In a meeting with Johnson on January 11, Grant said he informed the President that because he did not wish to be fined or imprisoned, he would relinquish the office to Stanton upon notification from the Senate.[79]

Johnson responded that while they exchanged ideas on what course to take in the event of non-concurrence by the Senate, the conversation ended with the

---

[73]Welles, *Diary of Gideon Welles*, Vol. III., pp. 259-260.
[74]Graf *et al.*, Vol. XIII., p. 468.
[75]Moore, pp. 115-116.
[76]Graf *et al.*, Vol. XIII., pp. 498-500.
[77]Graf *et al.*, Vol. XIII., p. 498.
[78]Graf *et al.*, Vol. XIII., p. 499.
[79]Graf *et al.*, Vol. XIII., p. 500.

understanding that should Grant prefer to disassociate himself from the controversy, he would return the office to the President before a decision was made so that Johnson would find someone else to take the job.[80]

> After a protracted interview, during which the provisions of the "tenure of office bill" were freely discussed, you said that, as had been agreed upon in our first conference, you would either return the office to my possession in time to enable me to appoint a successor before final action by the Senate upon Mr. Stanton's suspension, or would remain as its Head, awaiting a decision of the question by judicial proceedings. It was then understood that there would be a further conference on Monday, by which time I supposed you would be prepared to inform me of your final decision. You failed, however, to fulfil [sic] the engagement, and on Tuesday notified me, in writing, of the receipt by you of official notification of the action of the Senate in the case of Mr. Stanton, and at the same time informed me that, according to the act regulating the tenure of certain civil offices, your "functions as Secretary of War ad interim ceased from the moment of the receipt of the notice." You thus, in disregard of the understanding between us, vacated the office without having given me notice of your intention to do so.[81]

Grant responded on February 3, affirming his position that the two parted on the 11th without any commitment on Grant's part that he would continue to occupy the office of Secretary of War *ad interim* against the wishes of the Senate.[82]

> And now, Mr. President, where my honor as a soldier and integrity as a man have been so violently assailed, pardon me for saying that I can but regard this whole matter, from the beginning to the end, as an attempt to involve me in the resistance of law, for which you hesitated to assume the responsibility in order, and thus to destroy my character before the country.[83]

In an effort to reconstruct the facts, Johnson turned to his Cabinet members asking for their recollections of the meeting of January 14th.[84] Gideon Welles' memory of the conversation was the same as the President's, as was Hugh McCulloch's.[85] Hugh McCulloch said that "Grant was so drunk at the Cabinet

[80]Graf *et al.*, Vol. XIII., pp. 508-509.
[81]Graf *et al.*, Vol. XIII., p. 509.
[82]Graf *et al.*, Vol. XIII., pp. 522-523.
[83]Graf *et al.*, Vol. XIII., p. 524.
[84]Graf *et al.*, Vol. XIII., p. 526.
[85]Graf *et al.*, Vol. XIII., pp. 526 & 529.

meeting that it would be hardly surprising if he did not recollect what he said."[86] Orville Browning, Secretary of the Interior, stated that on January 14, Grant took his seat at the table. Referencing a note he had sent to the President that morning, the General said his duties as Secretary of War, *ad interim* had terminated with the Senate's action. Speaking of Grant, Browning recalled,

> That the resolution reached him last night, and that this morning he had gone to the War Department; entered the Secretary's room; bolted one door on the inside; locked the other on the outside; delivered the key to the Adjt Genl. and proceeded to the Headquarters of the Army.[87]

Postmaster General Alexander Randall recalled that at the cabinet meeting, the President asked Grant if he had not agreed to remain as Secretary of War and be willing to abide by any judicial actions that might result from the Senate's disagreement with the appointment or return the appointment to Johnson in time for him to assign another before any further senatorial action.[88]

William Seward recalled that before the President entered the room, Grant arrived at the Cabinet meeting and said to him that he was not there as a member of the Cabinet, but there at the request of the President. Johnson arrived and in the course of business, Grant reiterated his reason for being present. He was no longer a member of the Cabinet because had resigned the position of Secretary of War, *ad interim*. The President expressed that his desire had been to constitutionality test the Tenure of Office Act in the courts – specifically his right to suspend members of the Cabinet and that Grant had agreed to the strategy. He had expected Grant to occupy the position even if the Senate had disapproved Stanton's suspension, and should the General change his mind, Johnson would be given adequate notice. Grant said that he had agreed to that tactic until as recently as the previous Saturday. In a conversation with the President on that day, he shared that he did not want to subject himself to fine or imprisonment.[89]

On February 10, Johnson sent Grant a copy of the cabinet members' recollections.[90] Grant replied the next day that this was his first intimation that Johnson held a different view of the events.[91]

In typical fashion, Johnson played out his battle with Grant in the public forum. He told a reporter from the *Cincinnati Commercial* that he lamented

[86]Milton, p. 495.
[87]Graf *et al.*, Vol. XIII., p. 527.
[88]Graf *et al.*, Vol. XIII., p. 530.
[89]Graf *et al.*, Vol. XIII., p. 532-534.
[90]Graf *et al.*, Vol. XIII., p. 547.
[91]Graf *et al.*, Vol. XIII., p. 554.

Grant's abandonment of the post stating that if given timely notification the law could have been tested with another person in the position. The executive branch was never intended to serve the legislature in blind obedience.[92]

WILLIAM T. SHERMAN IS CONSIDERED

By now, Johnson was very anxious to remove Stanton from the War Department as evidenced by his frantic effort to find a replacement. No doubt he knew the danger of attempting to replace the Secretary at this time, yet he was insistent. Welles recorded in his diary, "These acts of the President will excite the Radicals, and the violent ones will undoubtedly improve the opportunity to press on impeachment."[93]

A potential scenario had been considered by the Radicals for some time – the arrest of the President. What would Johnson do if Congress attempted to seize the executive branch of the government?[94] As a precautionary measure, the President attempted to position General William T. Sherman in Washington. Even as far back as October of 1867, he had discussed the possibly with the General.[95] Johnson trusted Sherman and the General was empathetic with the President.[96]

After Grant vacated the post of Secretary of War, the President asked Sherman if he wanted the job *ad interim*. While Sherman did consider the offer, he had doubts as to whether he should be the instrument of Stanton's removal. His father-in-law, Thomas Ewing, advised him to avoid the entanglement, as did his brother Senator John Sherman.[97] W.T. politely tried to decline, but Johnson kept up the pressure.

In late January, Johnson tried to create a new military district for Maryland, Delaware, Virginia, and West Virginia in which he intended to place Sherman in command and then make him Secretary of War, *ad interim*.[98] On February 6, Johnson issued the order creating the district and moving Sherman to

---

[92]Graf *et al.*, Vol. XIII., p. 541.
[93]Welles, *Diary of Gideon Welles*, Vol. III., p. 285.
[94]Welles, *Diary of Gideon Welles*, Vol. III., p. 272.
[95]John Sherman, Vol. I., p. 414.
[96]Welles, *Diary of Gideon Welles*, Vol. III., p. 272. John Sherman, Vol. I., p. 415. Welles in his diary noted on January 3, 1868, "The President is desirous of making close friendship with Sherman" (Welles, *Diary of Gideon Welles*, Vol. III., p. 254).
[97]Graf *et al.*, Vol. XIII., p. 497. John Sherman, Vol. I., p. 416. Ewing would not heed his own advice. He later let Johnson put his name in for Secretary of War (Moore, pp. 121-122).
[98]Moore, p. 116.

Washington.[99] The next day he rescinded his order, and on the 12th he re-issued it leaving out the directive to relocate the General. On the following day, he nominated Sherman as brevet general.[100] Such indecisiveness reflects Johnson's panic.

On the 14th, Sherman telegraphed his brother that if forced to go to Washington he might have to resign. He also told his brother to oppose his confirmation as brevet general.[101] On that same day he wrote to Johnson, via Grant, expressing the hope that the idea of creating a new command for him and nominating him for brevet would be abandoned. Sherman had only recently learned of his appointment through Grant and had read about the brevet general nomination in the newspaper.[102] Even though Johnson would not receive Sherman's communication for five days, he was busy exploring other possibilities for a replacement.

On February 15, John Potts, the Chief Clerk at the War Department was approached with the offer of replacing Stanton. Potts begged off. Three days later, Johnson was considering General Lorenzo Thomas for the job. On the 19th Johnson receive Sherman's letter of the 14th through army headquarters and finally forsook the notion of appointing Sherman. He told the General he could keep his present command.[103]

THE APPOINTMENT OF GENERAL LORENZO THOMAS

Johnson was not going to stop until Stanton was removed from office. "Self-respect demanded it," he told Moore.[104] Even the threat of impeachment would not deter him, albeit that threat seemed diminished. Sensing weakening support for Radicalism, the failed impeachment attempt in December, and the general fear among legislators of Johnson's successor, the President felt confident that he could successfully have Stanton replaced and escape impeachment.

On February 21, 1868, Johnson called General Lorenzo Thomas to the White House and appointed him Secretary of War, *ad interim*. Thomas was given his letter of appointment and an order for Stanton to vacate, which the General delivered to the Secretary. At 11:00 am Stanton was notified that he had been

---

[99]Moore, p. 118.
[100]Moore, p. 119.
[101]John Sherman, Vol. I., p. 420.
[102]Graf *et al.*, Vol. XIII., pp. 559-560.
[103]Moore, p. 119. Graf *et al.*, Vol. XIII., p. 568.
[104]Moore, p. 120.

removed. At first the Secretary appeared compliant and asked for a copy of the orders, but when Thomas returned with copies Stanton, having consulted with Grant in the meantime, had changed his mind.[105]

At a masked ball that night at the Willard Hotel, Thomas boasted that he would be in charge of the War Department the following day.[106] But instead, the next morning Stanton had Thomas arrested. The General went to the White House accompanied by a marshal. He subsequently posted bail and called upon the Attorney General before going back to the White House.[107] After talking with the President, he returned to the War Department.[108]

The Cabinet did not learn of the removal of Stanton or appointment of Thomas until the morning of February 21 when it was presented as an afterthought at the close of the Cabinet meeting.[109] Welles commented,

> It is an error with [the President] that he does not more freely communicate with his Cabinet and friends. This whole movement of changing his Secretary of War has been incautiously and loosely preformed without preparation. The Cabinet was not consulted. His friends in the Senate and House were taken by surprise, and were wholly unaware of the movement.[110]

Johnson admitted he had tarried in removing Stanton.[111] The irony of the situation, as reported by Welles, was that the Radicals were tiring of Stanton and "a little skillful management would have made a permanent break in that party. But the President had no tact himself to effect it."[112] The result of the removal strengthened Stanton and united the Radicals.[113]

On February 22, President Johnson reported to the Senate on his actions in removing Stanton and appointing Thomas. He cited a practice that had been in place for every chief executive since the founding of the government – the power of the president to remove all officers except the judiciary.[114] Then he questioned the authority of the Tenure of Office Act itself and cited the passage that referred to who actually made the initial appointment. Obviously, Johnson had not

---

[105]Moore, pp. 120-121. Graf et al., Vol. XIII., p. 575.

[106]Welles, Diary of Gideon Welles, Vol. III., p. 290.

[107]Welles, Diary of Gideon Welles, Vol. III., p. 285. Moore, p. 121.

[108]When his case came up on February 26th, Thomas was discharged because Stanton declined to prosecute (Moore, p. 122).

[109]Welles, Diary of Gideon Welles, Vol. III., pp. 284 & 289.

[110]Welles, Diary of Gideon Welles, Vol. III., p. 289.

[111]Welles, Diary of Gideon Welles, Vol. III., p. 284.

[112]Welles, Diary of Gideon Welles, Vol. III., p. 315.

[113]Welles, Diary of Gideon Welles, Vol. III., p. 315.

[114]Graf et al., Vol. XIII., p. 580.

appointed Stanton. His predecessor had appointed him. Stanton too notified Congress of the President's action. This time he ordered a guard placed at the Department building, and prepared to hole up in his office for the duration.

Lorenzo Thomas, merely a pawn in Johnson's dispute with Congress, was never really taken seriously by the President nor the Cabinet members. It is unclear if he was ever invited to Cabinet meetings. Upon occasion, he would appear at the meetings, but members were not inclined to freely transact business in his presence. He was viewed as unfit -- a weak, indiscreet, old man.[115] On February 24, only three days after the Thomas appointment, the President submitted to Congress the name of Thomas Ewing for Secretary of War.[116] The Senate took no action on the recommendation.[117]

As the specter of impeachment became more and more menacing, Johnson's allies feared his nonchalant attitude would be a disservice to him in preparing his defense.[118]

[115]Browning, Vol. II., pp. 189, 194, & 200. Welles, *Diary of Gideon Welles*, Vol. III., pp. 289 & 303.

[116]Moore, pp. 121-122.

[117]William H. Rehnquist, *Grand Inquests: The Historic Impeachments of Justice Samuel Chase and President Andrew Johnson*, (New York: Morrow, 1992), p. 217.

[118]Trefousse, p. 270.

Chapter 10

IMPEACHMENT

Congress was growing exasperated with Andrew Johnson. His obstructionism with their attempts at Reconstruction and his exertion of presidential power were onerous. An early attempt at impeachment initiated in January of 1867 had stalled for lack of support.[1] The proposal had lingered for almost a year without sufficient cause to warrant action and was ultimately voted down in the Republican-dominated House in December of 1867 by a vote of 57 to 108.[2] But the President's removal of Stanton on February 21, 1868 and the appointment of General Lorenzo Thomas as Secretary of War, *ad interim* caused Congress to immediately resurrect ideas of impeachment. The President's violation of the Tenure of Office Act, expressly created to limit his power, gave new life to the effort.[3]

The nation was struggling with fundamental questions of separation of powers. If the duty of the executive branch was to carry out the laws, is it ever appropriate for the President to disobey a law in order to test it in the courts? Every citizen has such a right. "Is the President of the United States not to be allowed the same privilege?"[4] But, would not chaos result if the President challenged every law he was to enact. "If Andrew Johnson should be allowed to set aside laws because he professed to have scruples as to their constitutionality, the country would deserve the anarchy into which it would inevitability fall."[5] What if Congress, however, passed laws to usurp the power of the President?

---

[1]Edmund G. Ross, *History of the Impeachment of Andrew Johnson, President of the United States, by the House of Representatives, and His Trial by the Senate for High Crimes and Misdemeanors in Office, 1868,* (New York: B. Franklin, 1965), p. 46.
[2]Ross, p. 52.
[3]Ross, pp. 57 & 68.
[4]Graf *et al.*, Vol. XIII., p. 634.
[5]*Harper's Weekly,* April 25, 1868, Vol. XII., #591, p. 258.

How is that ever corrected in the courts unless the Chief Executive can put forth a challenge?

THE HOUSE VOTES FOR IMPEACHMENT

Thaddeus Stevens offered a resolution in the House calling for the impeachment of the President and on February 24 a vote was taken. The result, by party affiliation, was 126 for and 47 against impeachment.[6] The next day the House Committee went to the Senate to make the announcement. Thaddeus Stevens entered the chamber, threw his hat on the floor, and read a paper taken from his pocket. He announced that the people of the United States had impeached the President.[7]

On February 29, the House came up with ten articles. Most dealt with the removal of Stanton, the installation of Thomas, and the control of departmental funds.[8] On March 3, two articles were combined into one and two more added -- one authored by Benjamin Butler and another drafted by James Wilson and redacted by Thaddeus Stevens. The new Article X accused the President of disgracing Congress and Article XI was a précis of the first ten articles.[9]

The next day the House impeachment managers were before the Senate bar with eleven Articles of Impeachment, and on March 7, the President was served.[10] The articles seemed incredibly weak. In Welles' estimation they contained "a mountain of words, but not even a mouse of impeachment material."[11]

Johnson's opponents were not above concocting evidence in support of their charges. The previous year the wife of a clerk on the House Judiciary Committee considering impeachment had informed Johnson that it was commonly accepted

---

[6]Welles, *Diary of Gideon Welles*, Vol. III., p. 292. Moore, p. 122. *Congressional Globe,* 40th Congress, 2nd Session, February 24, 1868, p. 1400.

[7]Milton, p. 513.

[8]*Congressional Globe,* 40th Congress, 2nd Session, February 29, 1868, pp. 1542-1543.

[9]Trefousse, p. 316. As the printer delivered the articles of impeachment to the House, fifteen to twenty newspaper correspondents mobbed him. The reporters rushed the printer pushing him and his bundles into a committee room where a meeting was in session. After they took the packages from him and cut them open, they raced to the telegraph in the reporters' gallery of the House to transmit the news to their papers (*Harper's Weekly*, March 21, 1868, Vol. XII., #586, p. 179).

[10]Welles, *Diary of Gideon Welles*, Vol. III., p. 303. *Congressional Globe,* 40th Congress, 2nd Session, March 4, 1868, pp. 1647-1649.

[11]Welles, *Diary of Gideon Welles*, Vol. III., p. 299.

among the Radicals that if the Committee could not find sufficient evidence, they would fabricate it.[12]

IN JOHNSON'S DEFENSE

When news of Johnson's impeachment became known, offers came from outraged citizens who were willing to sustain him in office by use of force. The grassroots outpouring was considerable. An offer came from Nebraska for a hundred-man bodyguard ready to "give their lives in the cause of liberty and protection of the respected chief Magistrate of the Nation."[13] A man in Kirkwood, Missouri pledged his property and life in defense of his country's honor.[14] An invitation came from Columbus, Ohio to raise 20,000 men in support of Johnson's Constitutional rights.[15] Pledged support of a hundred-thousand loyal black men came from South Carolina.[16] Citizens from Indiana sent Johnson money for his legal fund.[17] How much of this was hyperbole and how much would have materialized had Johnson been removed of course is unknown, but there were real concerns among those in Congress of armed resistance. When a large quantity of nitroglycerine disappeared in New York City, it was feared that it would find its way to Washington to be used for nefarious ends.[18] Even though additional policemen were placed around the Capitol. Congress adjourned anyway thinking it unsafe. Stanton doubled the guard at the War Department.

On March 12, Henry Stanbery resigned from his position as Attorney General to take the lead as the President's Counsel.[19] Stanbery would become ill during the proceedings and be absent for several weeks, but recover in time to submit a closing argument.[20] The rest of Johnson's highly regarded defense team included Jeremiah S. Black, Benjamin R. Curtis, William S. Groesbeck, William M. Evarts, and Thomas A.R. Nelson.[21]

Jeremiah Black resigned early in the proceedings because of his involvement with a client for whom he was trying to regain guano rights on the Island of Alta

---

[12]Moore, p. 107.
[13]Graf *et al.*, Vol. XIII., pp. 592-593.
[14]Graf *et al.*, Vol. XIV., p. 68.
[15]Graf *et al.*, Vol. XI., p. 648.
[16]Graf *et al.*, Vol. XIV., p. 38.
[17]Graf *et al.*, Vol. XIV., p. 39.
[18]Welles, *Diary of Gideon Welles*, Vol. III., p. 297.
[19]Graf *et al.*, Vol. XIII., pp. 647-648. Welles, *Diary of Gideon Welles*, Vol. III., p. 311.
[20]Graf *et al.*, Vol. XIV., p. 50.
[21]Welles, *Diary of Gideon Welles*, Vol. III., p. 308.

Vela.[22] Black solicited the President's support of an armed naval vessel to oust his client's opponents.[23] An aggravated Johnson said he would rather die than yield to such dishonor, and he refused the demands.[24] In turn, Black notified the President of his resignation on March 19.

> Your determination to determine nothing for the relief of the owners of Alta Vela makes it impossible for me to serve you longer as counsel in the impeachment case. They cannot allow their rights to be trifled with and I cannot advise them to submit in silence to the outrage perpetuated upon them. They must seek elsewhere for the justice which you deny them.[25]

Welles thought Black's Alta Vela case was merely a pretext for bailing out on the Defense, for Black was being considered as a Democratic candidate for the presidency.[26]

On more than one occasion, Johnson threatened that if his defense was not conducted according to his wishes, he would appear before the Senate in person. His counselors were adamant that he not testify before the tribunal, but they could not keep him from giving interviews to the press during the trial.[27]

INTERVIEWS DURING THE IMPEACHMENT TRIAL

In the midst of all of this turmoil Johnson, against the advice of Counsel, gave numerous newspaper interviews. His insatiable desire to speak his piece brought him nothing but trouble. The President never grasped the power of the press or the public relations debacles that could result from his unguarded remarks.

On March 8 and 9, Johnson had interviews with the *New York World* in which he revealed the fact that John Adams had dismissed his Secretary of State in a manner that paralleled the Stanton removal. In 1800, President Adams told Timothy Pickering of the need to change the administration of the Office of State

---

[22]Graf *et al.*, Vol. XIII., p. 657. From the very beginning, Johnson had been warned against using Black as his Counsel (Graf *et al.*, Vol. XIII., pp. 600 & 658). "The President seems to think that the Judge (Black) attempted to take advantage of the present condition of affairs to press a favorable consideration of the (Alta Vela case)" (Moore, p. 127). There was concern that Black was working in collusion with Stanton (Welles, *Diary of Gideon Welles*, Vol. III., p. 319).
[23]Graf *et al.*, Vol. XIV., p. 49. Ross, p. 103. Moore, p. 128.
[24]Moore, p. 128.
[25]Graf *et al.*, Vol. XIII., p. 657.
[26]Welles, *Diary of Gideon Welles*, Vol. III., p. 319.
[27]Trefousse, p. 318. Keeping Johnson from appearing before the Senate was a continuous battle (Moore, pp. 123, 127, & 130).

and gave the Secretary the opportunity to resign. Pickering refused and Adams sent him a notice discharging him from further service.[28]

Johnson's Counsel and Cabinet were furious that this carefully guarded secret had been revealed. Stanbery admonished the President.

> You are now… in the hands of your lawyers, who will speak and act for you, and I must begin by requesting that no further disclosures be made to newspaper correspondents…. This is all wrong, and I have to request that these talks, or conversations, be stopped. They injure your case and embarrass your counsel.[29]

Other Cabinet members also denounced the disclosure. The President was taken aback and apologized saying that the removal of Pickering was public knowledge. He got no sympathy.[30]

But even a strong rebuke from his closest advisors did not stop the interviews. Johnson's combative nature would not allow him to remain silent and the newspaper article was the primary vehicle for him to get the word out to his constituents. In an April 3 interview with the *Cincinnati Commercial*, while the trial was underway, Johnson responded to specific inquires about individual congressmen opposing him. He was also asked about Lorenzo Thomas who had just testified in the Senate. He replied,

> I warned him to be very careful how he proceeded, as I wanted every thing done quietly and peacefully, for no other purpose than to test the validity of the Tenure-of-office Law…. Well, Thomas felt very big when he got to be the Secretary of War. Stanton had treated him pretty sharply on some occasions, and here, he thought, was a good chance for him to show himself a bigger man than Stanton…. He went over to the War Office and talked to Stanton, and came back to me in a few minutes very much rejoiced. He said he had seen Stanton, that it was all right, and that he would get possession of the War Office just as soon as Stanton could pack up his papers…. I never saw a man more elated over a position in my life. But the first thing he knew, Stanton had reconsidered his determination to pack up and leave, and the next time he called at the War Office the trouble began.[31]

The President went on to share his regret of the Thomas appointment. He said Thomas got so puffed up with self-importance he could not contain himself.[32]

---

[28] Graf *et al.*, Vol. XIII., p. 636.
[29] Welles, *Diary of Gideon Welles*, Vol. III., p. 311.
[30] Welles, *Diary of Gideon Welles*, Vol. III., p. 311.
[31] Graf *et al.*, Vol. XIV., pp. 9-10.
[32] Graf *et al.*, Vol. XIV., p. 10.

Johnson gave two interviews with the *New York World* which found their way into print on May 15, the day before the first critical vote of the impeachment trial. In this encounter, the President discussed with the reporter a list of the senators' names who were for acquittal and those who were in doubt.[33]

PRELIMINARIES IN THE SENATE

At one o'clock on March 5, 1868, the Chief Justice of the Supreme Court entered the Senate chamber to take the oath. After a Senior Associate Justice swore him in, he in turn administered the oath to the senators as their names were called alphabetically. When Benjamin Wade, the Senate *pro tempore*, rose from his seat, Senator Thomas A. Hendricks of Indiana raised the issue of Wade's eligibility to sit in judgment over a trial in which he could be the direct beneficiary.[34] According to the Presidential Succession Act of 1792, the Senate *pro tempore* would become the president if the sitting president were to be removed and there was no vice president. In the discussion that followed, John Milton Thayer of Nebraska made a pertinent point.

> The question of interest is made against the taking of the oath by the honorable Senator from Ohio, [Mr. Wade,] upon a rule of law in the courts that a person having an interest in the verdict which may be rendered is excluded from sitting upon that jury. If that rule is to prevail here I am surprised that the honorable Senator from Indiana did not raise the question at an earlier stage in the progress of these proceedings today. There is another rule of law or the same rule applicable with equal force which excludes from the jury a person related by blood or marriage to the accused. If the objection is good in one case is it not equally good in the other? If it should exclude the honorable Senator from Ohio why should it not exclude the honorable Senator from Tennessee, [Mr. Patterson?][35]

The debate continued the next day until Hendricks withdrew his objection and Wade was sworn.[36]

The Radicals were so assured of having the votes to convict they missed an opportunity to whittle away at the opposition and change *a priori* the composition of those sitting in judgment. Impeachment rule XXII stated that impeachment

---

[33]Graf *et al.*, Vol. XIV., pp. 65 & 67.
[34]*Congressional Globe,* 40th Congress, 2nd Session, March 5, 1868, pp. 1671-1672.
[35]*Congressional Globe,* 40th Congress, 2nd Session, March 5, 1868, p. 1678.
[36]*Congressional Globe,* 40th Congress, 2nd Session, March 6, 1868, p. 1700.

would be sustained by two-thirds of the members present.[37] Because Patterson was Johnson's son-in-law, the argument for his removal was strong. Replacing the Senator with a Radical would have set the stage for impeachment. Numerically, the key was replacement not removal.

The Radicals made a tactical error the previous year that would prove detrimental to their cause. In March of 1867, Senator Lafayette Foster retired leaving a vacancy in the largely honorary position of Senate President *pro tempore*. With Andrew Johnson in the White House and no vice president, this position, which stood in line of succession at the time, became very important. Two men sought the position, Ben Wade of Ohio, a Radical Republican, and William Pitt Fessenden of Maine, a conservative Republican. The Republican caucus chose Wade. Wade would prove to be a poor choice for the Republicans.[38]

The Chief Justice stated that during the impeachment proceedings, the Senate would be considered a separate body from when it was convened in a legislative capacity. Members would be under a different oath. The presiding officer was the Chief Justice not the President *pro tempore*. The Chief Justice put his motion to a voice vote and the Senate concurred.[39]

On March 7, the President's attorneys were before the Senate bar asking for 40 days to prepare a defense. Benjamin Butler reflected that God took 40 days to destroy the whole world. The Defense had to settle for ten.[40] Johnson's Counsel responded to all of the Articles of Impeachment on March 23. The salient points were three. Stanton had been appointed by Lincoln not Johnson, and the appointment was for the duration of Lincoln's term only. The President was merely exercising free speech in commenting on the actions of Congress, a right afforded to every citizen. And finally, Johnson did not make a public speech declaring that the 39th Congress was an unauthorized congress.[41]

POLITICAL MANEUVERING AND DEAL MAKING

On the morning of March 17, R.W. Latham, president of the Washington, Georgetown, and Alexander Railroad, called upon Johnson in behalf of Senator Pomeroy. The President was occupied with his lawyers, so his secretary W.G.

---

[37] *Trial of Andrew Johnson,* Vol. I., p. 14.
[38] Rehnquist, p. 211.
[39] *Trial of Andrew Johnson,* Vol. I., p. 12.
[40] David Miller DeWitt, *The Impeachment and Trial of Andrew Johnson, Seventeenth President of the United States,* (New York: Russell & Russell, 1967), pp. 396-397.
[41] Graf *et al.,* Vol. XIII., pp. 664-689.

Moore met with Latham. Latham said that an impeachment conviction would be a certainty unless there was an immediate change in the membership of the presidential Cabinet. Latham had a full replacement roster to recommend.[42]

Pomeroy called upon the President the next day. While he made no recommendation in regard to the Cabinet other than to express disdain for Seward, he said he would entertain any suggestions from the President. He was obviously waiting for a response to Latham's demands. He did not get one.[43]

But concessions were made for critical votes. There were key votes that Johnson needed for acquittal and he made allowances to them. As a concession to Grimes and Fessenden, Johnson nominated General Schofield for Secretary of War on April 25. The nomination was made without consulting the Cabinet.[44] Concessions were also made to Senator Ross. On May 4, Major Perry Fuller called upon Browning at the behest of Senator Ross to suggest that if the President would send the constitutions of South Carolina and Arkansas to Congress without delay, it would "extend a salutary influence" over the trial and that Ross and others would vote against impeachment.[45] Johnson complied.

THE TESTIMONY

The trial commenced on March 30. The senate chamber was packed with House members in attendance, impeachment managers sitting to the left of the Chief Justice, and attorneys for the Defense to the right. The galleries were filled to capacity.[46] Representative Benjamin Butler, one of the House managers, made the opening argument for the Prosecution. He read for three hours from a written manuscript.[47] Butler made a special point in defining an impeachable high crime or misdemeanor as,

---

[42]Moore, pp. 125-126.
[43]Moore, p. 126. It had been alleged that at one time Senator Samuel C. Pomeroy of Kansas wanted to sell his vote for patronage (Trefousse, p. 324).
[44]Welles, *Diary of Gideon Welles*, Vol. III. pp. 338 & 409-410.
[45]Browning, Vol. II., p. 195.
[46]Benjamin F. Butler, *Autobiography and Personal Reminiscences of Major-General Benj. F. Butler; Butler's book,* (Boston: A.M. Thayer, 1892), p. 929.
[47]*Trial of Andrew Johnson,* Vol. I., 147. Butler had only three days to prepare his opening remarks. And with only nine hours sleep over those three days he mounted the opening arguments. Newspaper reporters were trying anxiously to get copies of his speech in advance. The speech was being typeset in the government printing office in disparate parts requiring a code to put the pages in proper consecutive order (Butler, pp. 928-929).

One in its nature or consequences subversive of some fundamental or essential principle of government, or highly prejudicial to the public interest, and this may consist of a violation of the Constitution, of law, of an official oath, or of duty, by an act committed or omitted, or, without violating a positive law, by the abuse of discretionary powers from improper motives, or, for any improper purpose.[48]

Such a definition widened the scope of an impeachable offense so that any malversation could be considered a high crime.[49] The next day, the Prosecution began presenting evidence and calling witnesses.

On April 9, the Prosecution closed and Benjamin R. Curtis opened for the Defense.[50] The most compelling argument offered by the Defense was that the case did not come under the Tenure of Office Act because Stanton had been appointed by Lincoln and not by Johnson.[51] Stanton was merely serving at the pleasure of Johnson. His tenure expired with Lincoln's assassination and he could have been removed at any time. Furthermore, the law had not been violated because Stanton was still in office. In fact, he was currently occupying the position day and night. The tenth article said that Johnson's *Swing-Around-the-Circle* speeches were impeachable. Curtis challenged the senators to show how this was an offense under the Constitution.

Following Curtis' remarks, one of the House managers, George A. Boutwell of Massachusetts expressed a desire to cast Johnson into a great black hole in the farthest recesses of the universe.[52] William M. Evarts, a member of the President's Defense team, followed this brief astronomical odyssey by stating if the Congressman could overcome the laws of nature, the Constitution would not stand in his way.[53]

The first witness for the President was General Lorenzo Thomas. Thomas was sworn and examined by Mr. Stanbery. The General related the particulars of his appointment and described how he notified Stanton of his removal on February 21. Thomas described how he was arrested the next day, released on bail, and went to the War Department to meet with Stanton again.

Q. When did you next go to the War Department that day?

---

[48]*Trial of Andrew Johnson,* Vol. I., p. 88.
[49]*Trial of Andrew Johnson,* Vol. I., pp. 88-89.
[50]Welles, *Diary of Gideon Welles,* Vol. III., p. 330.
[51]*Trial of Andrew Johnson,* Vol. I., p. 382.
[52]Ross, p. 98.
[53]Ross, p. 99.

A. I went immediately from there, first stopping at the President's on my way, and stating to him that I had given bail. He made the same answer, "Very well; we want it in the courts." I then went over to the War Office, and found the east door locked. This was on the 22d the office was closed. I asked the messenger for my key. He told me that he had not got it; the keys had all been taken away, and my door was locked. I then went up to Mr. Stanton's room, the one that he occupies as an office, where he receives. I found him there with some six or eight gentlemen, some of whom I recognized, and I understood afterward that they were all members of Congress. They were all sitting in a semi-ellipsis, the Secretary of War at the apex. I came in the door. I stated that I came in to demand the office. He refused to give it to me, and ordered me to my room as Adjutant General. I refused to obey. I made the demand a second and a third time. He as often refused, and as often ordered me to my room. He then said, "You may stand there; stand as long as you please." I saw nothing further was to be done, and I left the room and went into General Schriver's office, sat down and had a chat with him, he being an old friend. Mr. Stanton followed me in there, and Governor Moorhead, member of Congress from Pittsburgh. He told Governor Moorhead to note the conversation, and I think he took notes at a side table. He asked me pretty much the same questions as before.

Q. State what he did ask.

A. Whether I insisted upon acting as Secretary of War, and should claim the office. I gave a direct answer, "Yes;" and I think it was at that time I said I should also require the mails. I said that on one occasion, and I think then. I do not know whether it is on the memorandum or not. Then there was some little chat with the Secretary himself....

Mr. Stanton turned to me and got talking in a familiar manner....

I said, "The next time you have me arrested, please do not do it before I get something to eat." I said I had had nothing to eat or drink that day. He put his hand around my neck, as he sometimes does, and ran his hand through my hair, and turned to General Schriver and said, "Schriver, you have got a bottle here; bring it out." [Laughter.]....

Q. What then took place?

A. Schriver unlocked his case and brought out a small vial, containing I suppose about a spoonful of whiskey, and stated at the same time that he occasionally took a little for dyspepsia. [Laughter.] Mr. Stanton took that and poured it into a tumbler and divided it equally and we drank it together.

Q. A fair division?

A. A fair division, because he held up the glasses to the light and saw that they each had about the same, and we each drank. [Laughter.] Presently a messenger came in with a bottle of whiskey, a full bottle; the cork was drawn, and he and I took a drink together. "Now," said he, "this at least is neutral ground." [Laughter.][54]

Other witnesses would follow, including Lieutenant General William T. Sherman, but none were as entertaining as Thomas.

On April 22, the impeachment managers made their formal appeal for conviction. Representative John A. Logan, one of the impeachment managers, expressed the pain that animated the Northern opposition.

When we saw the carnage amid the slain, the unutterable woe of the wounded – when we remembered the shriek of the widow, and the sob of the orphan – when we reflected on the devastation of our land, and the burdens now on our people – when we turned us about and saw in every direction the miseries and the mischiefs which follow every war, no matter how just, and when we reminded ourselves that all this would not have been, had treason been executed for its overt acts before yet its hands were red; and when we felt, as we do all feel, that to delay might bring all this and more again upon us, we could not and did not pause. We urged this trail at "railroad speed."… If he is guilty, then there is no speed too great for his deserts. If he is innocent, there is none too great for his deliverance.[55]

Six days later, William M. Evarts proceeded in behalf of the President concluding on May 2.[56] And on May 4, John A. Bingham, Representative from Ohio, delivered the final argument for impeachment on behalf of the impeachment managers.

But yesterday the supremacy of the Constitution and laws was challenged by armed rebellion; to-day the supremacy of the Constitution and laws is challenged by executive usurpation.[57]

---

[54] *Trial of Andrew Johnson*, Vol. I., pp. 428-429.
[55] *Trial of Andrew Johnson*, Vol. II., p. 17. In his opening remarks, Stanberry had objected to the haste at which the trial was proceeding. He complained that it was going at "railroad speed" (*Trial of Andrew Johnson*, Vol. I., pp. 21 & 22).
[56] *Trial of Andrew Johnson*, Vol. II., pp. 268 & 389.
[57] *Trial of Andrew Johnson*, Vol. II., p. 390.

Bingham's fundamental point and possibly his strongest legal argument was that the President was responsible for enforcing the laws of the land and if he were free to choose which laws to ignore and which ones to enforce there would be no rule of law at all.[58] "If the President may dispense with one act of Congress upon his own discretion, may he not in like manner dispense with every act of Congress?"[59] Upon completion of the speech the galleries burst forth in applause. The Chief Justice called for order and threatened to remove the spectators.[60]

POLITICAL PRESSURE

There were 54 senators eligible to vote. Forty-two were Republicans, nine Democrats, and three Johnson Conservatives. Doolittle of Wisconsin, Dixon of Connecticut, and Norton of Minnesota were known as Johnson Conservatives; although elected Republicans, they were supporters of the President. Two-thirds of the Senate was needed to convict. Only 36 votes were needed on any single article to oust the President from office. Nineteen votes in Johnson's favor would acquit him.

Between the deliberations on Monday and the voting on Saturday, the pressure was brought to bear on Republican senators who were considering acquittal. The Republican pressure to convict was blatant from the outset. Spies infiltrated social gatherings in hopes of influencing those who were undecided. Detectives watched their homes. Every opportunity was used to entice and persuade them to vote against the President. Threats of political ostracism were made by their constituents. Any Republican who failed to convict knew he was committing political suicide.[61]

THE SIDESHOW

Professional gamblers came to Washington to wager on the outcome of the trial. The odds favored acquittal.[62] Spiritualists took up Johnson's cause and mediums relocated to the capital to invoke the occult in the President's defense.

---

[58]Emily Field Van Tassel & Paul Finkelman, *Impeachable Offenses: A Documentary History from 1787 to the Present*, (Washington, D.C.: Congressional Quarterly, 1999), p. 227.
[59]*Trial of Andrew Johnson*, Vol. II., p. 407.
[60]*Trial of Andrew Johnson*, Vol. II., p. 469.
[61]DeWitt, pp. 517-518.
[62]DeWitt, p. 518.

Office seekers were deluging Ben Wade with requests for positions in the new administration.[63] Radicals talked a janitor into bringing them the contents of trashcans in the White House.[64] Toward the close of the trial, Butler commented to Evarts that he wished he were with the Defense.[65]

THE CLOSED-DOOR DELIBERATION

The impeachment managers had been growing uneasy over the strength of the various articles and the outcome of the trial. A closed-door conference was called to give the senators the chance to state their positions. On May 11, the senate galleries were emptied as deliberations began in secret. Every senator was given an opportunity to express his opinion on each of the articles.[66] There would be no written transcript of these proceedings.

It soon became clear that certain articles were in doubt. By the end of the session, impeachment hopes rested on Articles II, III, and XI; the strongest being XI.[67]   Senators Fessenden, Fowler, Grimes, Henderson, Trumbull, and van Winkle declared they would not support any of the Articles and all twelve Democrats pledged to vote for acquittal.[68] Only one more vote was necessary to squelch the whole impeachment effort.[69] Initially, the managers had been very confident of conviction, but by now consternation swelled their ranks.[70] The Radicals never really entertained the possibility they might lose until sentiments were brought out in this closed-door meeting.[71]

Word leaked out to the public quickly. The next day the *Cincinnati Daily Gazette* announced that following the session on the 11th it was obvious that the President would be acquitted.[72]

---

[63]Milton, p. 585. McCulloch, p. 401.
[64]Milton, pp. 537 & 552.
[65]Trefousse, p. 322.
[66]DeWitt, p. 519.
[67]Ross, p. 133.
[68]McCulloch, p. 404.
[69]Ross, pp. 131-133.
[70]Ross, p. 129.
[71]Welles, *Diary of Gideon Welles*, Vol. III., p. 351.
[72]*Cincinnati Daily Gazette*, May 12, 1868, vol. 79, #269.

CAUCUSES

Following the closed-door deliberation, a number of caucuses were convened during the week leading up to the vote on the 16th. Two meetings were held on May 15 at the residence of Senator Pomeroy where strategizing Radicals placed their hopes on Article XI. It was decided that the vote on XI must be positioned first on the agenda when the Senate reconvened.[73]

The pressure was intense on Edmund G. Ross who remained uncommitted throughout the whole trial. Ross roomed at a boarding house where Vinnie Ream lived. Ream was the young woman consigned to sculpt the Lincoln statue. Radicals tired to persuade her to influence Ross, but she refused. On Friday May 14th, a telegram from Ross' home state of Kansas demanded that the Senator vote for conviction. General Sickles called upon the Senator at his residence late one evening and remained until 4 o'clock in the morning trying to persuade him. Even minutes before the vote on the 16th, Ross was approached by Pomeroy who said a vote for acquittal would be political annihilation.[74]

Had such overt tampering been found with jurors in any other court setting there would have been an investigation and the verdict would have been suspect, but here in this highly visible setting, Republicans were shameless in exuding pressure.

THE VOTE ON ARTICLE XI

On Saturday May 16, the court was called into session. All senators were present with the exception of Grimes. From the earlier closed session it was obvious that Article XI had the best chance of passing. Senator George H. Williams of Oregon, the senatorial voice for the House Managers, called for the vote on Article XI. Fessenden asked for an adjournment of 30 minutes so that Grimes could be brought in on his sick bed.[75] Three days earlier, Grimes had suffered a seizure resulting in paralysis. Senator Grimes arrived shortly thereafter looking quite pale and had to be lifted into his seat.[76]

The Chief Justice had the secretary read Article XI and call the roll. Fessenden voted "Not Guilty." Fowler responded when his name was called in an

[73]Welles, *Diary of Gideon Welles*, Vol. III., p. 357.
[74]DeWitt, pp. 539-540, 543, & 544.
[75]Milton, p. 608.
[76]Welles, *Diary of Gideon Welles*, Vol. III., p. 353.

undistinguishable tone. Some thought he had voted "Guilty." When the question was repeated, he yelled "Not Guilty." Grimes struggled to his feet to vote not guilty. Ross had been sitting quietly tearing up paper and dumping the pieces into his lap. When his name was called he stood and the litter fell to the floor. Not guilty was his vote. Ross' vote had been pivotal. Even though the clerk continued to call the roll, everyone knew it was over. Johnson stood acquitted on Article XI.

All the Democrats had voted not guilty. Most of the Republicans voted guilty with the exception of seven; William P. Fessenden, Joseph S. Fowler, James W. Grimes, Johns B. Henderson, Edmund G. Ross, Lyman Trumbull, and Peter G. van Winkle. The final vote was 35 to 19; one vote short of the necessary two-thirds needed for conviction.[77]

When the Chief Justice called for the reading of Article I, Senator Williams immediately moved for a postponement of further voting. A delay of 10 days was granted, but not until the Chief Justice announced the results of the day's vote.[78]

Thaddeus Stevens waved his arms in the air as he was carried from the chamber yelling, "The country is going to the devil."[79] The impeachment managers were certain that members of Congress had been bribed.[80] A messenger from the Willard Hotel reached Johnson at 12:30 with a telegram announcing that the President had been acquitted on the eleventh article.[81]

THE RECALCITRANT REPUBLICANS

The brief recess coincided with the Republican convention in Chicago where Grant was nominated to run for the presidency.[82] The recess gave the Radicals time to pressure the seven recalcitrant Republicans who failed to support the impeachment conviction on Article XI.

The seven obstinate senators were the subjects of intense deliberation among the more radical Republicans. The pressure continued to the last possible moment. The wrath of the Radicals seemed to focus on Ross.[83] Stanton sent General Sickles to Ross' room for a final appeal, but Sickles got sidetracked by a woman and never saw Ross.

---

[77]Graf *et al.*, Vol. XIV., p. 568.
[78]Welles, *Diary of Gideon Welles*, Vol. III., pp. 358-359.
[79]Trefousse, p. 327.
[80]Graf *et al.*, Vol. XIV., p. 82.
[81]Welles, *Diary of Gideon Welles*, Vol. III., p. 358.
[82]Welles, *Diary of Gideon Welles*, Vol. III., pp. 361-362.
[83]Welles, *Diary of Gideon Welles*, Vol. III., p. 359.

THE VOTE ON ARTICLE II AND III

On the morning of May 26, the Radicals held what would be their last caucus to garner support to delay the vote. Finding they lacked the support needed to delay any further, it was decided this would be the day of reckoning.[84]

The Radicals still thought they had a chance to convert some of the wayward Senators who had voted for the President on Article XI. Although Fessenden, Trumbull, Henderson, and Grimes were lost, Van Winkle, Fowler, and Ross possibly could be influenced. Ross, who had not committed against any of the remaining articles, was the primary target.

On the morning of the 26th, a motion was made and passed to rescind the order of voting on the articles. Ross voted with the Radicals on preliminary motions. The Johnson supporters feared that he might have swung over.

The Chief Justice had the clerk read the second article and call the roll alphabetically. All seven of the non-compliant Republicans held firm to "Not guilty." Article III was entered and the roll was called with the same result. The impeachment attempt was dead. The Radicals voted for adjournment, but the Chief Justice made the point of announcing the result of the balloting and that the President had been acquitted.

The President's Cabinet was meeting as scheduled on the day of the voting.[85] An early telegram informed the White House that Ross was voting with the Radicals. The next communiqué brought the news that the voting on Articles II and III had gone the way of the previous vote on the Article XI. Johnson was acquitted.[86]

OUTPOURING OF EFFUSION

As soon as it was evident that the Senate had failed to convict on May 26, there was an outpouring of effusion from well wishers. Messages of congratulations were intercepted at the telegraph office by impeachment managers searching for evidence that certain senators had been bribed.[87]

---

[84]Welles, *Diary of Gideon Welles*, Vol. III., pp. 367-368.
[85]Browning, Vol. II., p. 199.
[86]Michael L. Benedict, *The Impeachment and Trial of Andrew Johnson,* (New York: Norton, 1973) p. 124.
[87]Graf *et al.*, Vol. XIV., p. 82.

Immediately following the Senate's adjournment, Stanton notified Johnson that he had relinquished charge of the War Department leaving everything in the care of Brevet Major General Townsend. Johnson had no intention of returning General Thomas to head the Department. Instead, General John Schofield would become the new Secretary of War on June 2, 1868.[88] Stanton continued to live in the District of Columbia. In December of 1869, his name was presented to the Senate as a Supreme Court Justice. He was confirmed but died before he could be installed.[89]

The President nominated Stanbery to his old post as Attorney General, but the Senate quickly rejected him.[90] On June 22, Johnson sent William M. Evarts' name to the Senate for the Attorney General position. He was approved.[91]

Tennessee did not return Fowler to the Senate. He remained in Washington until his death. Van Winkle was through. Trumbull finished his term and was out. Grimes never recovered from his stroke. Fessenden died in September of 1869. Ross was threatened, burned in effigy, and warned not to return to Kansas. Yet, he did. When Grover Cleveland became President, he asked Ross to become the governor of the New Mexico territory. Henderson and his fiancée were burned in effigy. He returned to St. Louis to practice law. In 1884, he was elected to the chairmanship of the Republican National Convention in Chicago. Sumner later told Henderson that he had been wrong about the impeachment, but he added, "I would rather you would say nothing about it until I am dead."[92] Thaddeus Stevens would introduce five more articles of impeachment that July but they would generate little interest.[93] By August he was dead.

The entire impeachment trial consumed twenty-three days. The Prosecution had called 25 witnesses and the Defense 16.[94] Most of the time was expended arguing over the admissibility of evidence.[95] James Garfield, member of the House of Representative who would one day become the President of the United States, commented on how unwieldy members of Congress were because of their love of public speaking. "We have been wading knee deep in words, words, words… and are but little more than half across the turbid stream." It was not

---

[88]Browning, Vol. II., p. 200. Graf *et al.*, Vol. XIV., p. 117.

[89]Graf *et al.*, Vol. XVI., p. 154. DeWitt, p. 596.

[90]Browning, Vol. II., p. 200. Welles, *Diary of Gideon Welles*, Vol. III., p. 375.

[91]Browning, Vol. II., p. 203. Welles, *Diary of Gideon Welles*, Vol. III., p. 390. Stanbery requested the appointment of his nephew to West Point. It appears the President ignored the request (Graf *et al.*, Vol. XIV., p. xvi).

[92]Milton, p. 632.

[93]Welles, *Diary of Gideon Welles*, Vol. III., p. 391. DeWitt, p. 597.

[94]*Congressional Globe,* 40th Congress, 2nd Session, supplement.

[95]Milton, p. 549.

difficult for Garfield to imagine impeachers who, given the alternative between the President's conviction coupled with their silence and his acquittal coupled with their unlimited opportunity to talk, would instantly speak.[96]

Johnson managed to escape conviction by the narrowest of margins primarily because the charges against him were incredibly weak. Could not the impeachment managers have created stronger articles to deal with presidential malfeasance, obstruction of Congress, and unauthorized use of power?[97] What about the President's involvement in the pardon-brokerage business?[98] It is likely the Radicals were so assured of success at the time that the specific charges were of little consequence.

While some senators may have honestly believed the President had not violated the Tenure of Office Act, others thought an inept Johnson was better than Benjamin Wade who would have succeeded him. Wade was a Radical who not only offended many moderates and Conservatives but even some Radicals. Fear of his occupation of the White House likely turned impeachment votes in Johnson's favor. Furthermore, Republicans who wanted Grant elected to the presidency thought Wade would interfere with the General's campaign.[99] Then there is Edmund G. Ross, who is credited with the critical vote that saved Johnson. Ross was a freemason as was the President. Could it be Ross helped the widow's son?[100]

The impeachment process took a toll on the President and the presidency.

---

[96]Benedict, *The Impeachment and Trial of Andrew Johnson,* p. 124.

[97]Van Tassel & Finkelman, p. 225.

[98]*Chicago Tribune* March 31, 1866, Vol. 19, #300.

[99]Rehnquist, p. 211. Van Tassel & Finkelman, pp. 226-227.

[100]http://en.wikipedia.org/wiki/List_of_Freemasons/citation

Chapter 11

FINAL DAYS IN THE WHITE HOUSE

With the impeachment issue at closure, attention turned to the next presidential election. The Republicans nominated Ulysses S. Grant in late May during the impeachment trial.

On July 4, 1868, the Democrats gathered in New York City to develop their platform and select candidates. While the President denied any ambition for further public service, he actively sought the Democratic slot with considerable hopes of being nominated.[1] Johnson permitted his name to be presented at the Democratic Convention. He did well on the first round of balloting, but his support soon waned and he failed to get the nomination.[2] The Convention chose Horatio Seymour instead. Johnson took the news without emotion.[3]

Seymour's chances of winning the election were slim. When an October 13 poll of selected Northern states revealed Grant leading Seymour, the *New York World* strongly suggested that the Democrats abandon the Seymour-Blair ticket for someone else who could make a better showing. In the election, Seymour would only carry eight states, and Grant would become the 18th President of the United States.[4]

Following the trial, Johnson continued his presidential duties of declaring amnesty and vetoing legislation. He issued his Third Amnesty Proclamation on July 4, 1868. This time he pardoned everyone except individuals under indictment for treason or other felonies.[5] This amnesty, in effect, exonerated everyone except

---

[1]Welles, *Diary of Gideon Welles*, Vol. III., p. 394. Graf *et al.*, Vol. XIV., p. 303.
[2]Welles, *Diary of Gideon Welles*, Vol. III., pp. 396-397.
[3]Welles, *Diary of Gideon Welles*, Vol. III., p. 398.
[4]Milton, p. 644.
[5]Graf *et al.*, Vol. XIV., p. 318.

Jefferson Davis and John Surratt.[6] Johnson's Fourth Amnesty Proclamation, issued on Christmas Day 1868, provided amnesty to all Rebels.[7]

On June 20, 1868, Johnson was presented with the Arkansas Statehood Bill that he vetoed.[8] The veto was quickly overridden. A few days later, he vetoed the admission of North and South Carolina, Louisiana, Georgia, Alabama, and Florida as well. The same argument as used with Arkansas applied. The veto was overturned.[9] Congress pushed on and passed a resolution that excluded Virginia, Texas, and Mississippi residents from participation in the next presidential election.[10] Johnson vetoed that legislation and Congress overrode his veto.[11]

On July 18, 1868, Johnson proposed Constitutional Amendments for the Senate's consideration. Of concern was the line of succession in the event of a vacancy in the executive office. The Presidential Succession Act of 1792 designated the Senate *pro tempore* as the next in line behind the vice president. Johnson proposed that following the vice president the job should go to an officer in the executive department because the President *pro tempore* of the Senate had vested interests in the outcome of an impeachment trial.[12] Johnson's other two proposals were for the direct election of state senators and a limit on the terms of the judiciary. With the exception of changes to the line of succession, there was nothing new in the President's proposals. Johnson had pushed for similar changes as early as 1845.[13] His suggestions were ignored.

Gideon Welles was under the impression that Johnson was advocating these amendments to re-start his political career. Welles confided in his diary, "Mistaken man, if such are his thoughts! This is no time to bring forward and encourage constitutional changes."[14]

As the congressional session was winding down, Congressman William Mungen of Ohio warned Johnson that it was important to move promptly on a tax bill before him. The fear was that Stevens would try to marshal his forces and start the impeachment process all over again. The Congressman suggested Johnson act expeditiously whether he intended to sign the bill or veto it. "If their tax bill is

---

[6]Browning, Vol. II., p. 204.
[7]Graf *et al.*, Vol. XV., p. 332.
[8]Graf *et al.*, Vol. XIV., p. 240.
[9]Graf *et al.*, Vol. XIV., p. 270.
[10]Graf *et al.*, Vol. XIV., p. xvii.
[11]Graf *et al.*, Vol. XIV., p. xviii.
[12]Graf *et al.*, Vol. XIV., p. 378.
[13]Graf *et al.*, Vol. XIV., p. 379.
[14]Welles, *Diary of Gideon Welles*, Vol. III., p. 407.

passed and becomes a law, Stevens can not [sic] hold Congress together a day longer."[15]

By mid-summer, 29 of the 37 states had ratified the Fourteenth Amendment including Tennessee, Arkansas, Florida, North Carolina, Alabama, South Carolina, and Louisiana. Seward declared ratification on July 20. The next day Georgia voted to ratify the Amendment.[16]

POCKETS OF LAWLESSNESS

Pockets of lawlessness still remained throughout the South. Although various atrocities were brought to the President's attention, he did little if anything to render aid.

A committee appointed by the legislature of Tennessee called upon Johnson to ask him to send in troops to protect the people of the state against the Klu Klux Klan. In some areas the Klan paid visits twice a week to the homes of Union men. "Murders are common, particularly among the colored people against whom the 'Klan' seems to have a peculiar and mortal hatred."[17] In Wayne County, Tennessee in August of 1868, there was a conflict between the Sheriff and the Klu Klux Klan at an iron works east of Waynesboro. A group of 56 Klan members were lured into an ambush by the local sheriff and his posse.[18] In Giles County, Tennessee, 25 to 30 armed Klan members entered two houses with the intention of robbing former Union officers living there. Help was requested.[19]

Three hundred black militiamen terrorized Marion, Arkansas robbing stores, burglarizing houses, stealing horses, and insulting ladies. An appeal was made for federal troops.[20] Armed blacks were occupying a district near Savannah, Georgia.[21]

There was no protection for citizens in many of the parishes in Louisiana. People were being shot down in the roads and in their homes. The judge of the 12th Distinct refused to enter his parish unless under guard. The Sheriff of Franklin resigned because he was powerless to issue arrests. People in Caddo Parish said thugs had beset their homes. Women and children in the St. Landry

---

[15]Graf *et al.*, Vol. XIV., p. 380.
[16]Graf *et al.*, Vol. XIV., p. 358.
[17]Graf *et al.*, Vol. XV., p. 47.
[18]Graf *et al.*, Vol. XIV., p. 512.
[19]Graf *et al.*, Vol. XV., p. 278.
[20]Graf *et al.*, Vol. XV., p. 348.
[21]Graf *et al.*, Vol. XV., p. 351.

Parish had been murdered. In all total, 150 people had been murdered in a period of 45 days. Blacks and Union men were the primary targets. A secret organization, known as the Knights of the White Camellia, had threatened to assassinate the Lieutenant Governor and the Speaker of the House. Appeals were made for help, but they fell on deaf ears.[22]

FOURTH ANNUAL MESSAGE

Johnson's Fourth Annual Message to Congress in December of 1868 called attention to the disorganized state of the Union. The states of Virginia, Mississippi, and Texas were still being excluded from Congress and their citizens prohibited from voting in presidential elections.[23] Johnson called for the direct election of the president and vice president by popular vote instead of through electors and the limitation of their tenure to only one term. He also advocated the direct election of senators by the people instead of giving that authority to the state legislatures, and finally he proposed limiting terms of federal judicial appointments.[24] His proposals were ignored. By now no one was listening.

FINAL EXTRAVAGANZAS

Johnson turned 60 in December of 1868 and he celebrated with a children's party at the White House. On the evening of December 29, the United States Marine Band played for three hundred young people in attendance. The President's grandchildren and son Frank were there. The evening included dinner and dancing until 11:00. Grant did not permit his children to attend.[25]

Johnson hosted the annual New Years Day reception at the White House for Washington dignitaries. General Butler attended to the displeasure of some Johnson supporters. Welles was especially perturbed, "Butler undertakes to discriminate between the man and the President; says he has no controversy... with Andrew Johnson."[26] Welles was also aggravated with the President Elect.

[22]Graf et al., Vol. XIV., pp. 472-474. Richard Nelson Current, *Those Terrible Carpetbaggers*, (New York: Oxford University Press, 1988), p. 125.
[23]Graf et al., Vol. XV., pp. 281-282.
[24]Graf et al., Vol. XV., p. 303.
[25]Welles, *Diary of Gideon Welles*, Vol. III., p. 494. *The Evening Star*, December 29, 1868, Vol. 32, #4931. *The Evening Star*, December 30, 1868, Vol. 32, #4932.
[26]Welles, *Diary of Gideon Welles*, Vol. III., p. 497.

According to Welles, Grant and his family left Washington for Philadelphia to avoid paying the customary New Years Day visit.[27]

FINAL BUSINESS

Before he left office, Johnson pardoned three Lincoln assassin conspirators -- Samuel A. Mudd, Edward Spangler, and Samuel B. Arnold.[28] He also allowed the families of the other Lincoln conspirators to move the bodies of dead relatives from their place of internment to family plots. Anna Surratt exhumed the body of her mother[29] and Edwin Booth removed the body of his brother.[30]

With the exception of a crazy woman found wandering the halls of the White House intent upon killing the President, things were uneventful in the final weeks of the Johnson Administration.[31]

"The robe of office, by constitutional limitation, this day falls from my shoulders," begins Johnson's farewell address.[32] But this elegant beginning soon turned to a less dignified parting shot at those in Congress who had acted in complete disregard of the Constitution in robbing the presidency of power and authority.

> When the rebellion was being suppressed by the volunteered services of patriot soldiers amid the dangers of the battle-field [sic], these men crept, without question, into place and power in the national councils. After all danger had passed, when no armed foe remained, when a punished and repentant people bowed their heads to the flag and renewed their allegiance to the Government of the United States, then it was that pretended patriots appeared before the nation, and began to prate about the thousands of lives and millions of treasure sacrificed in the suppression of the rebellion.[33]

On March 4, the day of Grant's inaugural, Johnson stayed in the White House signing last-minute bills and did not attend the celebration. Grant had snubbed Johnson's last two social functions and now the outgoing president was going to reciprocate. Johnson would have nothing to do with the inauguration of his

---

[27]Welles, *Diary of Gideon Welles*, Vol. III., p. 491.
[28]Graf *et al.*, Vol. XV., p. 369.
[29]Graf *et al.*, Vol. XV., p. 420.
[30]Graf *et al.*, Vol. XV., pp. 431-432.
[31]Trefousse, p. 351.
[32]Graf *et al.*, Vol. XV., p. 505.
[33]Graf *et al.*, Vol. XV., pp. 510-511.

successor.[34] It was probably just as well for he would not have been welcome if he had been present. Grant had informed the Committee on Ceremonies that he would not ride in the same carriage as Johnson nor address him during the inauguration. While Browning and McCulloch advised participation, Welles suggested the President not attend.[35]

Greeting Welles that final day, the President said, "I think we will finish our work here without going to the Capitol."[36] Evarts, anxious to process a pardon, left the White House before the others.[37] At a little past twelve noon the President shook hands with each remaining cabinet member and they descended the stairs to the portico of the main entrance and departed in their respective carriages. Within a few minutes, Grant arrived.

---

[34]Trefousse, pp. 350-351.
[35]Welles, *Diary of Gideon Welles*, Vol. III., pp. 536-537.
[36]Welles, *Diary of Gideon Welles*, Vol. III., p. 540.
[37]Browning, Vol. II., p. 243.

Chapter 12

ONE LAST HURRAH

After leaving the White House, Andrew Johnson temporarily moved into the home of Gideon Welles, his Secretary of the Navy, until March 18, 1869 when he returned to Greeneville, Tennessee.[1] The trip home was amid admiring supporters who poured out their geniality at every stop along the way. His route included Lynchburg, Virginia where he was met by an enthusiastic throng. Eight years before they were ready to lynch him in Lynchburg, but now they gave him a jubilant welcome. Johnson arrived at his home in Greeneville on March 20.[2]

But when the celebration faded -- when the adulation ceased, Johnson found Greeneville a very dull place. "A lifeless village," he wrote to his son Andrew.[3] A quiet retirement in Eastern Tennessee was not in Johnson's plans. There would be time for one last hurrah.

Johnson had hardly settled into his home in Greeneville when he gave an interview with the *Cincinnati Commercial*. Sitting in his parlor beneath portraits of Lincoln, Jackson, Washington, and one of himself, ex-President Johnson reflected on his experience in the White House and his efforts to restore the post-war South.[4] Johnson claimed that had his restoration policies been adopted, the nation would be a united people.[5] He chided Grant for his inexperience in public

---

[1]*The Evening Star*, March 4, 1869, Vol. XXXIII., #4987. His daughter Mrs. Martha Patterson and her children had moved to the Welles house earlier on the day of March 4. Welles, *Diary of Gideon Welles*, Vol. III., pp. 542 & 556. Truman claimed Johnson stayed with John F. Coyle, editor of Washington's *National Intelligencer* (Truman, p. 440).

[2]Welles, *Diary of Gideon Welles*, Vol. III., p. 560.

[3]Graf *et al.*, Vol. XVI., p. 6.

[4]Graf *et al.*, Vol. XV., p. 539.

[5]Graf *et al.*, Vol. XV., p. 538.

life and lack of direction. "It can not [sic] be said that he will lose his course, for he has no course to go by, but drifts about at the mercy of wind and wave."[6]

POLITICAL AMBITIONS BACK IN TENNESSEE

The ex-president pursued his political agenda as soon as he returned to Tennessee soil. While politics was his *raison d'être* there was now a stronger motivation at work for a return to the national arena -- vindication. Vindication above all else was the driving force that would cause him to seek public office one last time. Having experienced the humiliation of impeachment, Johnson desired most of all to demonstrate his importance, and he needed a national venue to do so.

Johnson's first attempt to justify himself came in 1869 when he sought an appointment to the U.S. Senate. Senator Joseph S. Fowler, Republican from Tennessee, declined to run for re-election. Fowler, it must be remembered, supported Johnson's acquittal during the impeachment trial. In anticipation of the Tennessee legislature meeting in October to choose the next U.S. Senator, Johnson stumped the state giving speeches and conducting interviews with the press.

Most of Johnson's speeches were eclectic ramblings – a string of his favorite clichés knotted together without a clear focus. On April 3, he spoke to a large crowd in Knoxville, where he blasted Congress for making it difficult for the Southern states to re-enter the Union.[7] He reminded his audience that he was the one who had set blacks free in Tennessee.[8] Addressing the cost of the War he said, "I would to God that the Government had not the credit to borrow a dollar to carry on a war. If the people had had before hand to pay the cost of the war, we should never have had one."[9] From Knoxville he campaigned through Chattanooga, Murfreesboro, and Nashville.[10] Speaking in Memphis on April 15, Johnson reminded his fellow citizens that while serving as military governor of Tennessee, he assessed the population to raise money to help the destitute women and children of Confederate soldiers.[11] In a three and a half hour speech at Clarksville on June 1, Johnson objected to the powerless position of the

---

[6]Graf *et al.*, Vol. XV., p. 538.
[7]Graf *et al.*, Vol. XV., p. 570.
[8]Graf *et al.*, Vol. XV., pp. 570-571.
[9]Graf *et al.*, Vol. XV., p. 573.
[10]Trefousse, p. 356.
[11]Graf *et al.*, Vol. XV., p. 608.

presidency and declared that Congress was now in the seat of authority.[12] "In an hour of madness, we lost hold of our moorings, and bad men have mutinied, thrown away the compass whose needle ever pointed our course in the path of liberty and justice, assumed the helm, and have driven us far on toward the breakers of despotism."[13]

In the midst of this canvas Andrew Johnson's son Robert committed suicide. Robert like his older brother Charles, who died in April of 1863, had been an alcoholic for a number of years with a life that tragically fell short of its potential.[14] Johnson returned to Greeneville to bury his son. Young Andrew, Jr. promised his mother that he would never use intoxicants; a promise that Robert had made years before and which he himself would not be able to keep.[15]

Andrew Johnson never relinquished his underlying bitterness of Ulysses S. Grant. On June 27, he agreed to an interview with the *New York Herald*. When asked about the current administration in Washington, Johnson unleashed on the President. He called Grant a mean, spiteful man full of jealousies and lies.[16]

[Grant is] the greatest farce that was ever thrust upon a people.... The little fellow has nothing in him.... He is mendacious, cunning and treacherous.... He [is] a little upstart, a coward, physically and intellectually.... His soul is so small that you could put it within the periphery of a hazel nutshell and it might float about for a thousand years without knocking against the walls of the shell.[17]

When the Tennessee legislature began balloting on October 19, Johnson's chances looked dubious. Both the *Nashville Republican Banner* and *Memphis Avalanche* had opposed him.[18] At one point he was two votes short of victory. When he learned that the former president of the Nashville and Chattanooga Railroad had made arrangements to purchase the votes for him for $1,000 a piece, he had the deal called off.[19] When days of balloting produced no winner, Johnson's opponents threw their support behind Henry Cooper, the brother of

---

[12]Graf *et al.*, Vol. XVI., pp. 15-16 & 26.
[13]Graf *et al.*, Vol. XVI., p. 18.
[14]In March of 1866, President Johnson had talked of sending Robert on a sea voyage to dry him out, but Robert objected and backed out at the last moment to continue his major vocation as a drunk (Trefousse, p. 240. Welles, *Diary of Gideon Welles*, Vol. II., p. 468).
[15]Trefousse, pp. 356 & 442.
[16]Graf *et al.*, Vol. XVI., p. 44.
[17]Graf *et al.*, Vol. XVI., pp. 40-41.
[18]Trefousse, p. 357.
[19]Reeves, E.C. Tennessee State Library and Archives, microfilm #1203, Box 1, item 10, p. 3.

Johnson's former aide Edmund Cooper.[20] Johnson lost by four votes.[21] A bitterly disappointed Johnson returned to Greeneville.

With his eye still fixed on a return to Washington, Johnson continued to deliver speeches and give interviews to a hungry press that kept his name before the citizenry of the state. On May 27, 1871, he delivered a speech at an industrial exposition in Knoxville -- a natural venue for this former tailor. Johnson offered a solution to the criminal-justice system saying, "I would divide all offenders into two classes; the first class I would hang, and the second class I would deprive of the power of propagating their species."[22] This drew a loud applause. Johnson went on to say, "You have no right to create debts and impose their payment upon your children. You have no right to create a debt that shall exist longer than an average lifetime – say thirty-three years."[23] His position on these topics resonated with the crowd.

Addicted to the adjuration of public appearances Johnson would never return to the sedentary life of Greeneville. In December of 1871, he wrote to his daughter, "I long to see the return of Spring when I will be set free from this place for ever I hope."[24]

Johnson declined to run for the vacant congressional seat in his old First District but when Tennessee gained an additional congressional seat, he sought the Democratic nomination. On May 22, 1872, he was notified of the opening by a friend in Nashville who asked for permission to put his name in for the nomination. Presumably Johnson gave his approval, for his name was announced.[25]

Two days earlier the *Indianapolis Journal* published an article accusing Johnson of having an affair with a neighbor in Greeneville -- Mrs. Emily Harrold, wife of the postmaster in the village. It was alleged that Mrs. Harrold had been seduced by the ex-President. Upon discovery, she committed suicide by shooting herself in the head with a revolver.[26] The Nashville *Republican Banner* said that Mrs. Harrold was a close friend of Eliza Johnson.[27] Such troubles never seemed to jar Johnson from his focus.

---

[20]Graf *et al.*, Vol. XVI., p. xii.
[21]Temple, p. 439.
[22]Graf *et al.*, Vol. XVI., p. 245.
[23]Graf *et al.*, Vol. XVI., p. 248.
[24]Graf *et al.*, Vol. XVI., p. 282.
[25]Graf *et al.*, Vol. XVI., p. 303.
[26]*The Indianapolis Journal*, May 20, 1872, no Vol. #9,471.
[27]*Republican Banner*, Vol. 59, #127, May 28, 1872. The 1870 federal census for Greeneville, Tennessee (#1531) lists 49-year old Emily Herold, wife of James Herold occupation tailor.

In a speech at Knoxville on August 10, Johnson denied even being a candidate for office.

> I came to your city on private business, and was induced by some of your citizens to remain and make a few remarks upon the political questions of the present day.[28]

Many of Johnson's speeches at the time expressed his favor for the one-term principle and the election of the president directly by the people.[29] He used these forums to boast about levying a tax on rich Confederate men to support the wives and children of the men who were fighting for them.[30] His speeches and interviews were also laced with amusing anecdotes and political twaddle.

The *Cincinnati Commercial* conducted an interview with him on August 20. When discussing a death threat whereby a thousand men had been awaiting the opportunity to assassinate him since his days as military governor, Johnson said, "If my crime dates away back to the Military governorship, these one thousand men are rather tardy."[31] On August 24, he delivered a speech in Nashville where he asked no greater favor than to be wrapped in the Constitution and the Stars and Stripes and to be buried among the hills and valleys of Tennessee.[32] On this point both he and his political opponents held mutual goals.

At a speech in Memphis on September 11, he drew a laugh with a brief anecdote.

> Why I fell in company with a man the other day who told me he had just seen an old friend of mine and he said to him: "Well, are you going to vote for Johnson?" "Yes." "Well, if Johnson had caught you at the time of the war he would have hung you." "Yes, and by G__ if I had caught him then I would have hung him."[33]

Johnson modified his story of how he entered the race. "This candidacy has not been of my seeking. I came down to Nashville on private business, and there was a convention being held."[34]

At an October speech in Brownsville he gave his old familiar We-had-all-the-power-in-Congress speech referring to the time when Lincoln came into office.[35]

---

[28]Graf *et al.*, Vol. XVI., pp. 331-332.
[29]Graf *et al.*, Vol. XVI., p. 369.
[30]Graf *et al.*, Vol. XVI., p. 365.
[31]Graf *et al.*, Vol. XVI., p. 341.
[32]Graf *et al.*, Vol. XVI., p. 348.
[33]Graf *et al.*, Vol. XVI., p. 367.
[34]Graf *et al.*, Vol. XVI., p. 371.
[35]Graf *et al.*, Vol. XVI., pp. 386-387.

Johnson believed that he was impeached because he stood as an obstacle to Congress carrying out its plans.[36]

> When I shall be brought to the dying couch, and my pulse shall be growing still in death, and the warm current that now animates my existence shall be growing cold and motionless, the most pleasing reflection that can pass though my mind when I shall be about to close my eyes forever, and sleep the sleep of peace – the most pleasing reflection will be that I occupied a place in the confidence and respect of those whom I served so long, and for whom I would have been proud to perish.[37]

It was all political speak, but the people loved it.

After his defeat in the senatorial race in 1869, Johnson had developed a friendship with a young lawyer in Greeneville by the name of E.C. Reeves. Reeves became his secretary.[38] The night before the Democratic Convention in Nashville, Johnson called Reeves to his room at the Maxwell House and asked that his name be withdrawn from consideration. "Gen. Cheatham and his brother have always been my friends. It will interfere with my future plans, and I cannot afford to antagonize the General, nor will I. I do not want the office, will not accept it if it is offered to me." Johnson told Reeves that he had his eye on the United States senatorial seat that would be vacant in 1875, and that Reeves should withdraw his name if it was put forth in nomination for Congress. Johnson said he would rather have the vindication of being re-elected to his old Senate seat than anything else. "For that I live, and will never die content without that vindication. Now, I have revealed to you my plans.... 'No one else knows them, and if I hear ought of them, I'll know you are a damned traitor.'"[39]

Johnson's desires were carried out and the convention nominated Confederate Major General Benjamin F. Cheatham by acclamation. But Reeves, on his return trip home to Greeneville, learned that later Johnson had made a speech to an immense gathering in Nashville and announced his candidacy as an independent.[40] Reeves was astonished. He believed that Johnson's actions had been the result of intoxication.[41] With Johnson in the race, the Democratic vote was split and the Republican candidate was elected. Johnson never gave Reeves an explanation for his actions.

---

[36]Graf *et al.*, Vol. XVI., p. 390.
[37]Graf *et al.*, Vol. XVI., p. 398.
[38]Trefousse, p. 358.
[39]Reeves, p. 2.
[40]Reeves, p. 2.
[41]Milton, p. 753.

LIFE HANGING BY A YELLOW RIBBON

The year 1873 was difficult for Andrew Johnson. During a cholera epidemic in Eastern Tennessee in which he contracted the disease he almost died. Thinking his days were over, he committed to writing his views on death and dying.[42] But death was cheated at the hands of his daughter Martha. By early July he was improving.[43]

That same year, the ex-President also suffered a financial crisis which occurred when Jay Cooke's enterprise collapsed.[44] When Johnson left the presidency he converted thousands of dollars in bonds into cash which he deposited in the First National Bank of Washington. A financial crisis forced the bank to close its doors, and Johnson stood to lose a total of $73,000.[45]

Renewed accusations of Johnson's involvement in the Mary Surratt case were probably the biggest blow to the ex-President. On August 26, Judge Advocate General Joseph Holt wrote an article for the Washington *Daily Morning Chronicle* in which he tried to vindicate himself in the Surratt dealings by asserting that Johnson had seen and ignored the Surratt appeal for clemency.[46] Over the years as questions were raised about the appeal and its denial, Holt became the fall guy. Tired of the accusations, he was now trying to exonerate himself.

According to Johnson, on July 5, 1865, Holt brought papers to the White House library where he and the President met to discuss the Lincoln-conspirators case. No recommendation for commutation was mentioned for Surratt. The issue of gender was discussed with the Judge arguing that Surratt being a woman should have no bearing on the sentence. Holt wrote the order approving the death sentences and Johnson signed it. The Judge rolled up the papers and departed.[47]

Judge Holt, on the other hand, stated that the military commission trying the case was reluctant to sentence Mary Surratt to death because of her gender and age. Stanton, arguing that the death sentence would draw her son from hiding, persuaded the commission to convict and then make a request to the President for

---

[42]"I have nothing to fear. Approaching death is to me the mere shadow of God's protecting wing. Beneath it I almost feel sacred. Here, I know, can no evil come. Here I will rest in quiet and peace." (*Bristol News*, August 10, 1875, Vol. 10, #50).

[43]Graf *et al.*, Vol. XVI., p. 431.

[44]Jay Cooke was a financier who worked closely with the Secretary of the Treasury to secure loans to finance the War.

[45]Trefousse, pp. 364-365. Graf *et al.*, Vol. XVI., p. 454. *The Evening Star*, October 13, 1873, Vol. 42, #6416.

[46]*Daily Morning Chronicle*, August 26, 1873, Vol. XI., #86.

[47]*Daily Morning Chronicle*, November 12, 1873, Vol. XI., #162.

clemency. Holt asserted that he presented the petition to Johnson who read it in his presence.

In his August 26th article, the Judge contended that for him to conceal the commissioners' recommendations would have brought immediate exposure and censure from the President. None of which happened. Johnson ordered no investigation and made no condemnation. Holt presented letters from Judge John A. Bingham, Attorney General James Speed, James Harland Secretary of the Interior, Rev. Dr. Butler, and others supporting his innocence and recalling conversations with the President in regard to the executions.[48]

Judge John A. Bingham prepared the petition for Surratt's clemency, which recommended commutation of the death sentence to imprisonment. The Judge specifically asked Stanton and Seward if the petition had been seen by the President and his advisors.

> I called upon Secretaries Stanton and Seward, and asked if this petition had been presented to the President before the death-sentence was by him approved, and was answered by each of those gentlemen that the petition was presented to the President, and was duly considered by him and his advisers before the death–sentence upon Mrs. Surratt was approved, and that the President and the Cabinet, upon such consideration, were a unit in denying the prayer of the petition.[49]

Bingham wanted to make that fact known to the public, but Stanton advised against any disclosure. James Speed affirmed that before the execution he saw Surratt's records in the President's office and the attached recommendation signed by commission members recommending leniency. James Harlan, a Secretary of Interior under Johnson, recalled a discussion between the President and Cabinet members over the issue of commutation. While he could not remember whether this occurrence took place at a regular Cabinet meeting or at an informal gathering of several members, he knew there were three to four other members present -- likely Seward, Stanton, and Speed. As he entered the room one of the cabinet members "was addressing the President in an earnest conversation on the question whether the sentence ought to be modified on account of the sex of the condemned."[50] Upon inquiring, Harland was told that the entire case had been reviewed by the Attorney General. Rev. Dr. J. George Butler of St. Paul's Church recalled a conversation with Andrew Johnson during a social call he made at the White House on the evening of the executions. The President said that requests

---

[48]*Daily Morning Chronicle*, August 26, 1873, Vol. XI., #86.
[49]*Daily Morning Chronicle*, August 26, 1873, Vol. XI., #86.
[50]*Daily Morning Chronicle*, August 26, 1873, Vol. XI., #86.

had been made for executive clemency, but he would not be moved for the appeals held little merit.[51]

Gideon Welles, referring to his diary, noted that the petition for clemency had never been seen by the Cabinet. He did find mention that the President was indisposed due to illness during the later part of June.[52]

Johnson responded to Holt's charges in a letter to the editor of the *Washington Chronicle* on November 12. He accused Holt of withholding the petition signed by the five members of the court who recommended commutation of the death sentence for Surratt. He questioned why Holt had remained silent over the eight years since the Lincoln assassination waiting until memories were faded by time.[53] Johnson refuted Bingham's statement saying that the Cabinet had not even met during the time between the sentencing and the execution.[54]

The recommendation of the five judges was part of a bundle of papers loosely held together by a yellow ribbon.[55] Although Judge Holt claimed he brought the complete findings of the Court to the White House, Johnson did not recall seeing a recommendation for clemency.[56]

Johnson thought Holt was making his attack in the article to better himself politically. "The Surratt case afforded him the opportunity – he used it. You know a boy can't fly his kite in a dead calm – he must have wind."[57]

A CANDIDATE FOR THE U.S. SENATE IN 1875

Johnson's desire for vindication was still fervent in 1874 when the opportunity to return to Washington presented itself again for a third time. He wrote to a supporter, "If I could be returned to the United States Senate in accordance with popular sentiment reflected by the Legislature, it would be appreciated by me as the greatest compliment of my life, and a deserved rebuke to treachery and ingratitude."[58] Not all were impressed with Johnson's pursuit of

---

[51]*Daily Morning Chronicle*, August 26, 1873, Vol. XI., #86.
[52]Graf *et al.*, Vol. XVI., p. 472. Welles, *Diary of Gideon Welles*, Vol. II., p. 327.
[53]Graf *et al.*, Vol. XVI., pp. 475 & 485.
[54]The next Cabinet meeting was held on the day of execution. There was no mention of the conspirators' trial or executions in Welles diary for that gathering (Welles, *Diary of Gideon Welles*, Vol. II., pp. 327-328.)
[55]Graf *et al.*, Vol. XVI., p. 482.
[56]Graf *et al.*, Vol. XVI., p. 485.
[57]*The Evening Star*, October 13, 1873, Vol. 42, #6416.
[58]Trefousse, p. 369.

public office. The *New York Times* expressed the shame of a former president running about pursuing a job that he likely would not get.[59]

Johnson completed another *Swing Around the Circle* – this time a small circle within the state of Tennessee. Months before the statewide election in November, he traveled throughout the state giving speeches and drawing large crowds, all in support of getting his party elected to the legislature.[60]

Johnson wrote to his son Andrew, Jr., "I do not expect to be at home until the Senatorial election is over unless your mother gets worse."[61] Mrs. Johnson was suffering from consumption.[62]

In a speech at Shelbyville on October 6, 1874, Johnson warned against electing a president to a third-term. He said it would be the last free election the country would ever have. The Democracy would be replaced with a monarchy.[63] In a speech in Chattanooga later that month, Johnson blamed the failure of his restoration plan on Congress and reiterated that the Surratt trial had been fair.[64]

In December, Johnson moved to Nashville so he could support his candidacy for the January appointment.[65] In order to garner the necessary support, he promised Republicans that if elected he would remain independent and would not attack Grant.[66]

On January 26, 1875, Andrew Johnson was chosen on the 53rd ballot to fill a seat in the United States Senate.[67] A supporter ran to Johnson's room to tell him the news of his election and passed out from exhaustion. While Johnson was splashing some water on the messenger, Reeves entered followed by another supporter who grabbed the Senator-elect and turning him upside down danced around in celebration.[68]

The new senator remarked, "Thank God for the vindication."[69] His son Andrew shared his sentiment, "Thank God, you are elected and your past course vindicated."[70] Johnson's daughter Martha called it the greatest victory of his life.[71]

---

[59]Trefousse, p. 370.
[60]Graf *et al.*, Vol. XVI., p. xiv.
[61]Graf *et al.*, Vol. XVI., p. 637.
[62]Graf *et al.*, Vol. XVI., p. 638.
[63]Graf *et al.*, Vol. XVI., p. 595.
[64]Graf *et al.*, Vol. XVI., p. 605.
[65]Graf *et al.*, Vol. XVI., p. xv.
[66]Temple, p. 442.
[67]Reeves, p. 2.
[68]Stryker, p. 834.
[69]Trefousse, p. 372.
[70]Graf *et al.*, Vol. XVI., p. 684.
[71]Graf *et al.*, Vol. XVI., p. xvi.

The next session of Congress would have normally started in December of 1875, had President Grant not called a special session in March to consider a treaty with Hawaii. Senator Johnson was soon on his way to Washington.[72] On March 5, 1875, Andrew Johnson walked onto the floor of the United States Senate to applause. Flowers covered his desk. A few of his old nemeses were there, and he shook hands with all who approached. Vice President Henry Wilson, who had voted to impeach Johnson, now swore him in right after Hannibal Hamlin who was also newly elected.[73]

In a *New York Tribune* interview, Johnson was fervent about his independence in the Senate. He pledged to never be in a position where he would be forced to support a party measure or vote for something that in his judgment was wrong. He was only accountable to the people whom he represented.[74]

In a *New York Herald* interview Johnson said he had no private grievances or complaints to be redressed. He insisted, "My election settled all personal injuries ever inflicted."[75] But his claim was far from truthful for he had let it be known elsewhere that he had two purposes in taking the senate position – to punish the Southern brigadiers and to make a speech against Grant.[76]

On March 22, Johnson made that speech and in doing so broke his pledge by assailing President Grant.[77] It would be his last on the floor of the Senate. Senator Frelinghuysen from New Jersey presented a resolution sustaining Grant's support of the Kellogg administration in Louisiana.[78] Johnson objected to the proposed resolution given the fact that the special session had been called to deal with an unrelated issue. But the topic having been raised, Johnson took some time to render his opinion. He asserted that Kellogg was a usurper and Grant was supporting him. The Senator said the United States was now nothing more than a military despotism, which had been run "well-nigh to destruction."[79] He warned against electing Grant to a third term. "And when that is done, farewell to the liberties of the county."[80] The galleries erupted in applause. After blasting away for what must have been an hour or more, Johnson concluded by asking that all

---

[72]Graf *et al.*, Vol. XVI., p. xvi.

[73]Trefousse, p. 373.

[74]Graf *et al.*, Vol. XVI., p. 707.

[75]Graf *et al.*, Vol. XVI., p. 712.

[76]Trefousse, p. 373.

[77]Temple, pp. 442-443.

[78]In the Louisiana gubernatorial election of 1872, both William Pitt Kellogg and his Democratic opponent claimed victory. President Grant affirmed Kellogg as the legitimate governor. The Democratic Party was indignant and engaged in a heated fight with the New Orleans Police requiring federal troops. Kellogg was eventually impeached.

[79]Graf *et al.*, Vol. XVI., p. 737.

[80]Graf *et al.*, Vol. XVI., p. 723.

lay aside party differences and embrace the Constitution.[81] The Tennessee Tailor had drawn the last stitch in mending his political career.

JOHNSON DEAD

Johnson returned to Greeneville in the spring of 1875. On July 28, he took a train to Carters Station to see his daughter Mary Stover Brown. Mrs. Johnson had been staying with the Browns for some time.[82] From there he had plans to travel on to Ohio to set the record straight in regard to some speeches made by Governor Morton of Indiana.[83]

Johnson arrived at his daughter's farm about 11:00 am. After lunch he went to his room and while talking to his granddaughter had a stroke and fell from his chair. He complained that his right side was paralyzed. Family members wanted to send for a doctor immediately but Johnson objected. Medical aid was eventually summoned.[84] When help did arrive, Johnson recovered briefly and engaged in conversation.[85] The next day, however, he had another stroke and fell into unconsciousness. He died on the morning of July 31, 1875.

Andrew Johnson's body lay in state in the Greeneville courtroom while thousands of mourners passed by the closed casket ornamented in wreaths and flowers. A gilded frame containing a photo of the ex-President lay upon the closed casket.

At noon on August 3, the casket was placed in a hearse hitched to four bay horses. All family members, except his wife who was ill and his daughter Mary Stover Brown who was caring for her mother, followed the hearse to the place of interment.[86] The funeral procession was more than a quarter mile long. A cross made of evergreen boughs and flowers was laid upon the grave with a sign that said, "The People's Friend – He Sleepth."[87] Johnson was buried with the flag of his country as his winding sheet and the Constitution for his pillow.[88]

---

[81]Graf *et al.*, Vol. XVI., p. 745.

[82]*Bristol News*, August 3, 1875, Vol. 10, #49.

[83]McElwee, p. 2.

[84]Dr. Cameron arrived at the Brown farm the night of Johnson's stroke (McElwee, p. 7).

[85]*Bristol News*, August 3, 1875, Vol. 10, #49.

[86]Johnson joined the Greeneville Masonic Lodge on May 5, 1851 (Graf *et al.*, Vol. XI., p. 620). On June 20, 1867, Masonic officers moved him from a fourth degree to 33rd degree Mason (Trefousse, p. 286).

[87]*Bristol News*, August 3, 1875, Vol. X., #49.

[88]Reeves, p. 3.

A FINAL WORD

Andrew Johnson's dramatic rise from the tailor shop to the White House was impressive. Without any formal education, he achieved positions of great influence and accrued a sizable estate of which most would have been proud. During the course of his political career he held elective offices ranging from an alderman in Greeneville, Tennessee to the President of the United States.

But even with these accomplishments it is easy to dismiss Johnson's life as one without distinction. His was not an especially attractive personality. What Johnson lacked in humor, he made up for in seriousness.[89] He is largely remembered for escaping impeachment conviction by a single vote and for his obstructionist stance using the presidential veto – 21 in all total.[90] With these exceptions there is little to garner our attention. Johnson left few memorable speeches and his tenure as a chief executive provided little to emulate. We are hard pressed to note many social, economic, or political contributions. His beloved homestead provision was not original – it had been tried before. His Constitutional amendments limiting terms and providing for the direct election of officials had been advocated earlier by others. He failed as a statesman and was not an exceptionally astute politician.

Johnson seemed to have been unable to overcome his prejudices against the upper social class which he distained and blacks whom he saw as inferior. He had a proclivity to scrap with white aristocrats, and he appeared to enjoy seeing them bristle under his attack.

Johnson's relationship with senators from the South, according to Jefferson Davis, had never been pleasant due to an almost morbid sense of pride. While many of his Southern associates pretended to aristocracy, Johnson rejoiced in his own plebeian origin. Davis said he had "the pride of having no pride."[91]

While Johnson demonstrated a compassion for blacks, they remained beneath him. A case in point is when he received P.B. Randolph, a black man, at the White House in July of 1866. Randolph was there to obtain funding for black schools in New Orleans. While Johnson did invite him to stay for dinner, it was not at the Presidential table. Randolph ate in a room presumably by himself.[92]

---

[89]Winston, p. 62.

[90]Van Tassel & Finkelman, p. 223.

[91]John J. Craven, *Prison Life of Jefferson Davis. Embracing Details and Incidents in His Captivity, Particulars Concerning His Health and Habits, Together with Many Conversations on Topics of Great Public Interest,* (New York: Carleton, 1866), p. 299.

[92]Trefousse, p. 268.

The war left deep bitterness on both sides, which Johnson could not fully grasp. While his stance for the Union during the War was admirable, he could not empathize with the personal loss Northerners felt or their need to see justice. He failed to impose any real consequences on secessionists and let Rebel states back into the Union without penalty or sanction. Had Johnson imposed some restrictions on the South immediately after the war, Northerners might have been appeased. But he stood by as a desire for justice turned into a vengeful thirst for revenge that only time could quench. Nor did Johnson have an appreciation for the devastating effect the conflict had upon Southerners. By and large he turned a deaf ear to their troubles.

Johnson had little appreciation for the power of the press. Frequently, he revealed information that should not have found its way into print. He shared defense strategy during his impeachment trial and unnecessarily raised the ire of the public with his undignified attacks against his opponents in Congress. He was a stump speaker, as Welles called him, with an elevated opinion of his ability to handle himself amid verbal attacks. Against hecklers, he would lose his dignity. Such encounters trapped him into making inappropriate statements that were recorded in newspapers all across the country, frequently creating a public-relations mess.

During his impeachment trial Johnson revealed to a reporter for the *Cincinnati Commercial* how he became aggravated into saying things during his *Circle Speeches*. As soon as he appeared to speak in Cleveland, people in the crowd started hooting at him, and he was goaded into a response.[93]

> I have been in political life a long time and am naturally combative. I don't propose to be hooted down by any body.... So they went for me, and I went for them, and we had it hot and heavy for awhile.... If I used any rough expressions they were put into my mouth by my enemies. I said a good deal then that I might not have said if they had not provoked me to it.[94]

Johnson often lacked tact and political acumen. His blundering frequently created needless obstacles that could have been avoided. Again from the *Cincinnati Commercial* interview, he responded to a question about imbibing while on his speaking tour. When asked if he had been intoxicated on the trip he countered, "I didn't drink half as much as one or two others, about whose

---

[93]Graf *et al.*, Vol. XIV., p. 12.
[94]Graf *et al.*, Vol. XIV., p. 12.

condition nobody dares to say a word."[95] His comments were needless and unguarded.

Johnson's decision–making process was often flawed. He frequently missed opportunities to act, habitually delaying decisions until the opportune time had passed. For example, Johnson had ample occasion to remove Stanton but waited until the consequences of his actions were severe. He had an opportunity to submit Governor Jacob D. Cox's name for the position of Secretary of War, which would likely have avoided the entire impeachment process. He did not act. Johnson failed to consult with his Cabinet members on numerous crucial issues and take advantage of their expertise, possibly because if an idea did not originate with him, he viewed it with suspicion.

His critics said that he was never overburdened with any sense of personal debt of gratitude if it stood in the way of his success.[96] Oliver Temple asserted that Johnson's only deity was ambition.[97] "He was at all times for himself. Personal ambition controlled his life."[98] When faced with a new problem, Johnson would deliberate over the probable outcome and its effect upon him personally. When decisions were finally made he was tenacious, never reconsidering the results.

> I have always tried to be guided by a conscientious conviction of right; and I have laid down for myself, as a rule of action, in all doubtful questions, to pursue principle; and in the pursuit of a great principle I can never reach a wrong conclusion.[99]

Johnson fashioned himself as a rugged, uncompromising individual who knew what was right and had the tenacity to hold to his principles regardless of the consequences -- a persona that proved to be a major impediment in his decision-making process. He was never one who liked compromise. "Compromise... I almost wish the term was stricken out of the English language," he said.[100]

While there were numerous insinuations of sexual impropriety, allegations of infidelity remain supposition. Regardless of the truth behind the assertions, it is obvious that Johnson was vulnerable to attractive women and was easily

---

[95]Graf *et al.*, Vol. XIV., p. 13.
[96]Temple, pp. 452 & 456.
[97]Temple, pp. 465-466.
[98]Temple, p. 463.
[99]Graf *et al.*, Vol. IV., p. 632.
[100]Winston, pp. 110-111.

enamored by flattery. Whether or not he used his position to exploit sexual favors is a matter of conjecture.

While military governor of Tennessee, Johnson was very generous to charming females seeking passes through the lines. One very attractive rich widow named Carter habitually traveled back and forth between Nashville and Franklin, Tennessee every week. One day she asked Johnson's Secretary, Benjamin Truman, for a pass to carry six barrels of salt to Franklin. Salt was a precious community to the Confederacy. While it was surmised this commodity was destined for Rebel hands, Johnson said to give her the pass for, "Mrs. Carter was a lovely woman." But women he deemed unattractive did not fare as well – the case in point of the wife of a Rebel sitting in a northern prison. The woman, described by Truman as "the biggest woman I had ever seen outside [of] a museum," called upon Johnson for authorization to go through the lines.[101] Johnson turned from her rudely and directed his Secretary to make out a pass. The woman interjected, "And return." Johnson turned back to her and said, "We don't want you to return." The woman became furious and threatened to take the Governor over her knee for a spanking. Johnson said, "Madam, it would take the whole Union army to spank you." After she received her desired pass, the Governor turned to Truman and commented that her husband ought to be grateful he was in prison.[102]

Johnson had some questionable relationships with women. He pardoned Mary Blake, the proprietor of a bordello in Washington.[103] Mrs. Cobb, a Washington pardon broker, enjoyed free access to the Presidential mansion, coming and going through the private entrance as she pleased. There were accusations that Johnson kept a mistress in the White House.[104] Jenny Perry's accusations implied improper conduct and the assertions of an affair with a neighbor in Greeneville comprise an unflattering picture.

Johnson's drinking habits caused him much trouble. Being drunk at his inaugural was a sign of poor judgment to say the least. But even having suffered this monumental embarrassment, liquor continued to be a large part of his life. An assistant to Senator Trumbull of Illinois wrote, "There is too much whiskey in the White House."[105] Others leveled similar complaints.[106] Johnson's secretary, E.C. Reeves, believed Johnson's actions in his run for Congress in 1872 had been the

[101]Truman, p. 436.
[102]Truman, p. 437.
[103]Graf *et al.*, Vol. X., p. 609.
[104]Welles, *Diary of Gideon Welles*, Vol. II., pp. 453-454.
[105]Beale, p. 17.
[106]Welles, *Diary of Gideon Welles*, Vol. II., pp. 453-454 & 461.

result of intoxication.[107] But such behavior can be viewed as relative. Benjamin Truman acknowledged that Johnson "did take two or three or four glasses of Robertson County whisky some days; some days less, and some days and weeks no liquor at all. So, as drinking went in Tennessee, Johnson would have been termed a strictly temperate man."[108]

Johnson's close friends were few. In 1850, he wrote to his daughter Mary while she was a student at Rogersville Female Academy, admonishing her to exercise care in making friends. "To day [sic] persons are friendly to morrow [sic] they burst into as many pieces as a touchmenot [sic].... Be friendly with all and too friendly with none."[109] E.C. Reeves, Johnson's secretary after his presidency, said that Johnson always preserved an air of distance with his associates. Even after six years, Johnson still referred to his secretary as Mr. Reeves.[110]

Johnson's concern for the common man as exemplified in his relentless pursuit of a homestead bill is laudable as is his stance for the Union during the war. He risked his life trying to dissuade Tennesseans from joining the secessionist movement and worked tirelessly to rebuild the state as military governor. These hallmarks of his career show Johnson at his best. While serving as President, he sought to resort the former Confederate states on his own, much in line with Lincoln's plan. This alienated him from the Radical elements in Congress. Likely Lincoln would have faced the same challenges, but Johnson's conciliatory approach to the South and the wholesale issuance of pardons did not set well with many Northerners who had suffered great loss during the war. When he opposed the Freedmen's Bureau and Civil Rights bills in 1866, he succeeded in alienating many moderates as well and spelled his downfall.

It must be acknowledged that Andrew Johnson was president during a very difficult period in the history of the United States. The country had just gone through a brutal civil conflict that left many dead on the battlefield and multitudes disabled. The war forced many more into abject poverty. It would have been a tough watch for any chief executive. The challenge of trying to bring the South back into the Union to the satisfaction of some vindictive elements in the North was a difficult task. Wisdom, statesmanship, cooperation, compassion, and a

---

[107]Milton, p. 753.
[108]Truman, p. 438.
[109]Graf *et al.*, Vol. I., pp. 592-593.
[110]Milton, p. 753.

sense of justice were needed to bring the country out of the shadow of the Great Rebellion. These traits were not to be found in Andrew Johnson.

BIBLIOGRAPHY

Books and Articles

Acts of the State of Tennessee, Passed at the First Session of the Thirteenth General Assembly for the Years 1853-4. Nashville: M'Kennie and Brown, 1854.

American Speaker; A Selection of Popular Parliamentary and Forensic Eloquence, Particularly Calculated for the Seminaries in the United States. Philadelphia: Birch and Small, 1811.

Associated Press, Tennessee State Library and Archives, micro # 1203, Box 1, item #13.

Baker, La Fayette C. *History of the United States Secret Service*. Philadelphia: L.C. Baker, 1867.

Ball, William Watts. *The State That Forgot*. Indianapolis: Bobbs-Merrill Company, 1932.

Bassett, John S. (ed.), *Correspondence of Andrew Jackson,* 7 Vol., 1931.

Beale, Howard K. *The Critical Year; A Study of Andrew Johnson and Reconstruction*. New York: F. Ungar Pub. Co., 1958.

Benedict, Michael L. *A Compromise of Principle: Congressional Republicans and Reconstruction 1863-1869*. New York: W.W. Norton, 1974.

Benedict, Michael L. *The Impeachment and Trial of Andrew Johnson*. New York: Norton, 1973.

Browning, Orville Hickman, *The Diary of Orville Hickman Browning*, 2 Vol., Springfield, IL: Trustees of the Illinois State Historical Library, 1925.

Brownlow, William G. Stephen V. Ash (ed.) *Secessionists and Other Scoundrels: Selections from Parson Brownlow's Book*. Baton Rouge: Louisiana State University Press, 1999.

Butler, Benjamin F. *Autobiography and Personal Reminiscences of Major-General Benj. F. Butler; Butler's book.* Boston: A.M. Thayer, 1892.

Chase, Edward. *The Memorial Life of General William Techumseh Sherman.* Chicago: R.S. Peale, 1891.

Coulter, E. Merton. *William G. Brownlow, Fighting Parson of the Southern Highlands.* Chapel Hill: University of North Carolina Press, 1937.

Crabtree, Beth G. and James Welch Patton. (eds.) *Journal of a Secesh Lady: The Diary of Catherine Ann Devereux Edmondston, 1860-1866.* Raleigh: North Carolina Department of Cultural Resources, Division of Archives and History.

Craven, John J. *Prison Life of Jefferson Davis. Embracing Details and Incidents in His Captivity, Particulars Concerning His Health and Habits, Together with Many Conversations on Topics of Great Public Interest.* New York: Carleton, 1866.

The Confederacy: Selections from the Four-volume Macmillan Encyclopedia of the Confederacy. New York: Macmillan Library Reference USA, 1998.

Current, Richard Nelson. *Those Terrible Carpetbaggers.* New York: Oxford University Press, 1988.

DeBow, J.D.B. *Statistical View of the United States: Embracing Its Territory, Population--White, Free Colored, and Slave--Moral and Social Condition, Industry, Property, and Revenue, the Detailed Statistics of Cities, Towns and Counties: Being a Compendium of the Seventh Census to Which are Added the Results of Every Previous Census, Beginning with 1790, in Comparative Tables, With Explanatory and Illustrative Notes, Based Upon the Schedules and Other Official Sources of Information.* Washington: Beverley Tucker, Senate Printer, 1854.

DeWitt, David Miller. *The Impeachment and Trial of Andrew Johnson, Seventeenth President of the United States.* New York: Russell and Russell, 1967.

Graf, LeRoy P., Ralph W Haskins, and Paul H Bergeron, *The Papers of Andrew Johnson.* 16 Vol., Knoxville: University of Tennessee Press, 1972.

Hanchett, William. *The Diary of John Wilkes Booth, April, 1865*, Springfield, IL: Illinois State Historical Society, 1979.

Journal of the Senate of Tennessee at the Twenty-fourth General Assembly, Held at Nashville. Knoxville: James Williams, 1841.

Julian, George W., "George W. Julian's Journal – The Assassination of Lincoln," *Indiana Magazine*, Vol. XI., #4, December 1915.

Kunhardt, Philip B., Jr., Philip B. Kunhardt III, and Peter W. Kunhardt. *Lincoln: An Illustrated Biography.* New York: Knopf, 1992.

McCulloch, Hugh. *Men and Measures of Half a Century; Sketches and Comments*. New York: C. Scribner's Sons, 1888.

McElwee, William Eblin. *Johnson Papers*, Tennessee State Library Archives, microfilm #1203, Box 1, item #13.

McKitrick, Eric L. *Andrew Johnson; A Profile*. New York: Hill and Wang, 1969.

Milton, George Fort. *The Age of Hate; Andrew Johnson and the Radicals*. New York: Coward-McCann, Inc., 1930.

Moore, W.G. "The Notes of Colonel W.G. Moore, Private Secretary to President Johnson, 1866-1868," *The American Historical Review*, Vol. XIX, 1914, 98-132.

Nasby, Petroleum V. *Andy's Trip to the West, Together with a Life of Its Hero*. New York: J.C. Haney and Co., 1866.

Nasby, Petroleum V. *Swingin Round the Cirkle*. Boston: Lee and Shepard, 1867.

Pitts, Clyde. (ed) *Thomas Bragg Diary 1861-1862*, Southern Historical Collection, University of North Carolina Library.

Plum, William R. *The Military Telegraph During the Civil War in the United States: With an Exposition of Ancient and Modern Means of Communication, and of the Federal and Confederate Cipher Systems; Also a Running Account of the War Between the States*. 2 Vol., Chicago: Jansen, McClurg and Company, 1882.

Quaife, Milo Milton. *The Diary of James K. Polk*, 4 Vol., Chicago: A.C. McClurg and Co., 1910.

Reed, Emily Hazen. *Life of A.P. Dostie; or, The Conflict of New Orleans*. New York: W.P. Tomlinson, 1868.

Reeves, E.C., *Johnson Papers*, Tennessee State Library Archives, microfilm #1203, Box 1, item #10.

Rehnquist, William H. *Grand Inquests: The Historic Impeachments of Justice Samuel Chase and President Andrew Johnson*. New York: Morrow, 1992.

Reid, Whitelaw. *After the War: A Tour of the Southern States, 1865-1866*. New York: Harper and Row, 1965.

Richardson, James D. *A Compilation of the Messages and Papers of the Presidents, 1789-1897,* 10 Vol., Washington: Government Printing Office, 1896-1899.

Riddleberger, Patrick W. *1866 The Critical Year Revisited*. Lanham, MD: University Press of America, 1984.

Ross, Edmund G. *History of the Impeachment of Andrew Johnson, President of the United States, by the House of Representatives, and His Trial by the Senate for High Crimes and Misdemeanors in Office, 1868*. New York: B. Franklin, 1965.

Savage, John. *The Life and Public Services of Andrew Johnson; Including his State Papers, Speeches and Addresses*. New York: Derby and Miller, 1866.

Sheridan, Philip H. *Personal Memoirs of P.H. Sheridan*, 2 Vol., New York: Charles L. Webster, 1888.

Sherman, John. *Recollections of Forty Years in the House, Senate, and Cabinet*. 2 Vol., Chicago: The Werner Company, 1895.

Stryker, Lloyd Paul. *Andrew Johnson; A Study in Courage*. New York: Macmillan Co., 1929.

"Telegram: Johnson to Brownlow," Tennessee State Library and Archive, Microfilm #1203, Box 1 item 8.

Temple, Oliver Perry and Mary B. Temple. *Notable Men of Tennessee, from 1833 to 1875, Their Times and Their Contemporaries*. New York: The Cosmopolitan press, 1912.

Trefousse, Hans L. *Andrew Johnson, A Biography*. New York: W.W. Norton and Company, 1989.

Trial of Andrew Johnson, President of the United States, Before the Senate of the United States, on Impeachment by the House of Representatives for High Crimes and Misdemeanors, 3 Vol., Washington: Government Printing Office, 1868.

Trowbridge, J.T. *The South: A Tour of its Battlefields and Ruined Cities, A Journey Through the Desolated States, and Talks with the People*. Hartford: L. Stebbins, 1866.

Truman, Benjamin C. "Anecdotes of Andrew Johnson," *The Century Magazine*, Vol. 81, # 1, January 1913, 435-440.

Van Tassel, Emily Field and Paul Finkelman, *Impeachable Offenses: A Documentary History from 1787 to the Present*. Washington: Congressional Quarterly, 1999.

Welles, Gideon. "Lincoln and Johnson," *The Galaxy*, Vol. XIII, April 1872.

Welles, Gideon. *Diary of Gideon Welles, Secretary of the Navy under Lincoln and Johnson*, 3 Vol., Boston: Houghton Mifflin, 1909.

Welsh, Michael E. "Legislating a Homestead Bill: Thomas Hart Benton and the Second Seminole War," *The Florida Historical Quarterly* Vol. LVII, # 2, (October 1978): 157-172.

Wheeler, John H. *Historical Sketches of North Carolina from 1584 to 1851*, 2 Vol., Philadelphia: Lippincott, Grambo and Co., 1851.

Winston, Robert W. *Andrew Johnson, Plebeian and Patriot*. New York: H. Holt and Company, 1928.

Internet

http://www.northernfern.com/Genealogy/f_56.htm
http://en.wikipedia.org/wiki/List_of_Freemasons/citation

Newspapers

Bristol News
Cincinnati Daily Enquirer
Cincinnati Daily Gazette
Congressional Globe
The Daily American
Daily Morning Chronicle
The Evening Star
Harper's Weekly
The Indianapolis Journal
Jonesborough Whig
London Times
The Memphis Daily Argus
The Memphis Daily Avalanche
Nashville Daily Times and True Union
Nashville Union and American
New York Herald
New York Times
New York Tribune
Republican Banner
The Star and North Carolina Gazettee

ABOUT THE AUTHOR

Gary Donhardt holds a Ph.D. from Ohio University, and has served as a fellow at Vanderbilt University's Peabody College and at the Candler School of Theology, Emory University. He has received awards from the American Association of University Administrators and the American Association for State and Local History. He is currently at the University of Memphis.

ACKNOWLEDGEMENTS

I would like to thank Janann Sherman and Darla M. Keel for their critique of this work.

INDEX

E

F

T